The Scripted Self: Textual Identities in Contemporary Spanish Narrative

Preface   v

Introduction   1

Part One — The Self Remembered   13

1   Nostalgia for a prescribed identity in *Todas las almas*
by Javier Marías.
RUTH CHRISTIE   15

2.   Memory and oblivion: personal and rural identities in the
narrative writings of Julio Llamazares.
JOHN MACKLIN   31

3.   Place, memory and death in José María Merino,
El caldero de oro and *Cuentos del Barrio del Refugio*.
JUDITH DRINKWATER   49

Part Two — Re-siting the Self   63

4.   Autobiography as fiction in *Todas las almas* by
Javier Marías.
RUTH CHRISTIE   65

5.   Double identity: Memory, duplicity and dissimulation
in Antonio Muñoz Molina's *Beltenebros*.
JOHN MACKLIN   83

6. 'La soledad de las islas': towards a topography of identity
    in Belén Gopegui, *La escala de los mapas*, and
    Juan José Millás, *La soledad era esto*.
    JUDITH DRINKWATER   99

Part Three — Postmodern Personae   115

7. Modernity and postmodernity: Personal and
    textual identities in Juan Goytisolo's *Makbara*.
    JOHN MACKLIN   117

8. Self-writing and 'lo que pudo ser' in *Corazón tan blanco*
    by Javier Marías.
    RUTH CHRISTIE   135

9. Postmodern identities: writing by women and
    Rosa Montero's *Amado amo*.
    JUDITH DRINKWATER   153

Conclusion   169

Bibliography   175

Preface

This study forms part of a project on contemporary Spanish writing being undertaken by the authors in the University of Leeds. Two symposia have been held in the University in 1994 and 1995 attended by academic critics from the United Kingdom and Spain and with the participation of the writers Eduardo Mendoza, José María Merino, Juan José Millás, Rosa Montero and Manuel Vicent. These symposia have been sponsored by the Instituto Cervantes, Leeds, which also supported this publication. In addition, the project has benefited from a generous grant from the Academic Development Fund of the University of Leeds to develop a bibliographical database on contemporary Spanish narrative, and Professor John Macklin was awarded a personal research grant from the Dirección General de Relaciones Culturales y Científicas of the Ministerio de Asuntos Exteriores to consult primary material in Spain. All of this support is gratefully acknowledged.

Leeds, September 1995   Ruth Christie
                                         Judith Drinkwater
                                         John Macklin

Introduction

This is not a history of the *nueva narrativa española*, but an exploration of one aspect of it. It has developed from a recognition that underlying many contemporary novels written in Spain is a concern with questions of identity, self, and the relationship of these to narrative writing. Such preoccupations are not, of course, anything new. Realist fiction is inseparable from the rise of the bourgeoisie and the triumph of individualism, and never entertains any doubt that the characters it depicts are autonomous individuals, best understood in terms of their physical and psychological attributes and through their social interactions. Modernism locates the self in the workings of consciousness and abandons the public perspective of realism in favour of the portrayal of heightened states of subjectivity. Postmodernist narrative fiction is concerned with the extent to which all of these — character, society, subjectivity — are not represented by, but constructed through, language, and other systems of signs which are essentially textual. Within Spain, moreover, there has been a long tradition of writing about the self, especially in the twentieth century, from the Heideggerian concept of *dasein* explored in the writings of Ortega y Gasset, with his celebrated formulation, 'yo soy yo y mi circunstancia', to the work of Miguel de Unamuno with its obsessive preoccupation with the self, identity and the 'querer ser'. For some critics, such as Germán Gullón,[1] these journeys into interior space, which are such a pronounced feature of contemporary Spanish writing, are a return to such early twentieth-century preoccupations, and mark a belated espousal of modernity in Spanish literature after the supposed aberrations of social realism in the 1960s and 1970s. It can even be argued that literary modernism reaches its full potential in Spain in the late twentieth century in the work of writers such as Juan Goytisolo and Luis Martín-Santos.

The novels considered in this book, however, are read in the context of a much larger discourse which, whilst still concerned with questions of self and identity, challenges realist and modernist notions of individuality. It is a discourse in which the insights of literary criticism overlap with, and complement, insights from other disciplines and fields of thought, notably philosophy and linguistics. Within this discourse, which is, broadly speaking, an ongoing discussion of what constitutes postmodernism, a central preoccupation has been the so-called 'death of the subject'. This preoccupation is so obsessive that Frederic Jameson has spoken of it as a 'fashionable theme', and claims that nearly all writing seems to be about the

---

1   Germán Gullón, 'La perezosa modernidad', *Insula*, 464-5 (1985), 8.

'end of the autonomous bourgeois or monad or individual'.[2] Significantly, the influence of postmodernist thought, in its poststructuralist guise, has involved the most radical questioning of identity, even to the extent of querying whether 'identity' is a meaningful category at all. Some writers appear to embrace, in Gerald Graff's words, 'a refusal of the entire bourgeois view of reality, epitomised by the subject-object paradigm of rationalist epistemology'.[3] In contemporary Spanish narrative, then, the question of identity has been posed in new and varied forms and formulations; in quasi-Unamunian terms of *intrahistoria* and collective memory, for example, or in response to the emergence of regional and feminist movements. Broadly, there are three interdependent sets of issues which are brought into relief in analysing contemporary narratives of the self. The first relates to the literary-historical questions about the contemporary novel's relation to realism and modernism, and its openness to writing from abroad with its concomitant theories of self and discourse.   The second focuses on socio-political concerns, from changed political circumstances (the ending of the dictatorship, the recovery of old freedoms and the discovery of new ones) to socio-economic developments (increased affluence, Europeanisation, changed regional perceptions, sexual liberation). The third deals with poststructuralist concepts which are broadly concerned with the philosophy of language.

We have not referred to *nueva narrativa española* in the title of this book because no real consensus has yet emerged as to whether any such thing exists or what its membership might be, and even if *nueva narrativa* does exist, not all the writing included here conforms to such a designation. Nonetheless, the last two decades have produced new circumstances in Spain — the end of censorship, technological changes which have affected book production and its relationship to other media, new forms of book market, more prizes, new literary reviews, a public which buys and reads its own authors, new relationships with Europe and the world, and increased foreign interest in Spanish writing. It is clear that over the past twenty years there has been an unparalleled upsurge in the writing of novels, mainly by authors who have only come to prominence in the past twenty years. The choice of 1975 as the starting point for this new burgeoning of narrative can appear to be merely a convenient date for the literary historian, but it is the existence since this date of a plurality of styles and modes in literary output in Spain which justifies speaking in terms of post-Franco, post-1975, post-

---

2   Frederic Jameson, 'Postmodernism, or the Cultural Logic of Late Capitalism', *New Left Review,* 146 (1984), 63.

3   Gerald Graff, 'Babbitt at the Abyss: The Social Context of Postmodern American Fiction', *TriQuarterly,* 33 (1975), 321.

Transition narrative writing. This writing is characterised by an unprecedented diversity, and for many commentators it is this which is the defining characteristic of the period. For some, such as Manuel Vázquez Montalbán, it is the reader who creates diversity in literary production through the exercise of free choice: 'Eso es lo que se produce con posterioridad al franquismo: el propio lector cualificado es el que impone la diversidad del gusto y consagra así lo que podríamos llamar eclecticismo vinculado a la idea de la postmodernidad'.[4] This is a new 'hora del lector' in which the readers take their place alongside academics and critics in influencing what is written and valued. Critics have tried to make sense of what can appear a confusing and eclectic panorama by dividing it into specific generic categories, such as the *novela histórica, novela negra, novela erótica*, or *novela intimista*. There is, however, considerable disagreement about the value of much contemporary writing. For some, the huge increase in output can be interpreted as a sign of vitality and as providing the necessary mass of production which will engender a few masterpieces, whereas others see signs of excess, indulgence and lack of quality. The divorce between writing and the socio-political world is a persistent anxiety. Santos Sanz Villanueva, one of the foremost critics in the field, writes of the gap between the novel and contemporary Spanish reality.[5] Others have taken up this theme: Luis Alfredo Béjar complains of the 'ocultación de la realidad', of 'fantasía carente de imaginación', and of 'fabulación sin verdad'.[6] Julio Llamazares, writing in *El País* in June 1991, refers to 'un panorama tan desalentador como desconcertante'.[7] He is of the opinion that the Spanish, having tried for so long to discover 'la verdad' that was hidden from them, once again feel the attraction of 'la mentira' in literature.[8] At the same time, many see the principal change in prose fiction since 1975 as being a return to the realist mode after a period of intense experimentalism born of the assimilation of literary theory and novels from abroad, especially from Latin America. This return is to certain realist forms, in contrast to the experimentalism of the early 1970s, but not to the beliefs underlying conventional realist practice.

---

4   Manuel Vázquez Montalbán, 'La novela española entre el postfranquismo y el postmodernismo', *La Renovation du Roman Espagnol depuis 1975,* ed. by Yvan Lissorgues (Toulouse: Presses Universitaires du Mirail, 1991), p.21.

5   Santos Sanz Villanueva, 'El realismo en la nueva novela española', *Insula,* 464-5 (1985) 7-8

6   Luis Alfredo Béjar, in *Narrativa española actual* (Cuenca: Ediciones de la Universidad Castilla-La Mancha), 1990, p.42.

7   Julio Llamazares, 'La nueva novela española', in *En Babia* (Barcelona: Seix Barral, 1991), p.119

8   *En Babia*, p.118

Even in writers apparently as unproblematical as Julio Llamazares, the stability and confidence of the realist perspective gives way to a probing of the self in a world which appears increasingly fictional. The return to realism is distanced, parodic, humorous, and non-didactic, and the notions of the self which permeate the work of several of the writers considered in this volume clearly diverge considerably from the ideas of person and character which informed classical realism. There seems to be a consensus among critics that the emblematic novel of this return is Eduardo Mendoza's *La verdad sobre el caso Savolta*.[9]

It can be argued that the late seventies constituted a first phase in post-Franco writing, in which political concerns were pre-eminent and narrative engagement with the world meant dealing with the legacy of the Civil War and Francoism, and led to memorialist writing, or to what became known as the 'nuevo periodismo'. After the cultural 'movida' of the early eighties came a 'desencanto' with the new democracy and a decline in interest in the political in favour of a return to 'narratividad' and the 'placer de contar'. This is also the decade when 'nuevo' becomes a buzz word. In 1981 Alfaguara launched the 'Nueva Ficción' series; in 1983, Ediciones Libertarias brought out its 'Nueva narrativa española', and Plaza y Janés followed in 1988 with 'Bajo el signo de lo nuevo'. A considerable amount of the adverse criticism of contemporary fiction is due to this obvious commercialisation, and to the fact that novelty is a major key to commercial success. Prizes, manipulation of public taste through management of literary supplements, advertising (with Planeta being one of the top thirty advertisers in Spain), and government cultural policies, have all helped to promote 'lo nuevo' and configure the contemporary scene. We might argue that it is precisely this scenario, and its wider socio-political ramifications, that gives rise in contemporary narrative to what amongst some novelists we might call a return to the subject, to the extent that Constantino Bértolo has commented on 'el gusto por el intimismo, por el estudio de una soledad que no se vive como problema, sino como atmósfera grata y adecuada para la lucidez',[10] a further reminder that concern with the self does not necessarily entail anguish and alienation.

Since 1975 is perceived by many to be a key date in the development of the Spanish novel, it is worth pointing out that the death of Franco did not usher in the expected clutch of brilliant novels which it was assumed had been written during the dictatorship but had remained unpublished due to

---

9   See, for example, Santos Sanz Villanueva, *Insula*, 464-5, or Santos Alonso, 'Una realidad en la última novela española', *Insula*, 512-3 (1989), 11-12.

10   *Historia crítica de la literatura española*, General Ed. Francisco Rico, vol.ix, *Los nuevos nombres 1975-1990*, ed. by Darío Villanueva [et al] (Barcelona: Editorial Crítica, 1992), p.297.

censorship and the adverse political climate. It has become clear that the relationship between political authoritarianism and novel-writing is not simply one of repression-subversion, despite the fact that many critics would adhere to the idea that the contemporary novel seeks ways to defend personal liberty now that collective liberty has been achieved. The prevailing tendency of the new novel is seen as one of internalisation, of a looking inward, and a turning away from the preoccupation with external social or political themes. The commonly held view, mentioned above, which takes into account both realist and modernist approaches to literature, sees the new novel in terms of subjectivity (or even egocentricity), in opposition to the apparent objectivity of the tradition of the 'novela social'. But the hope that an 'authentic' self, which could at last be expressed in writing, would emerge when political and social rights were attained has not been fulfilled.

There has been no surge of repressed individuality in contemporary Spanish fiction, but rather a series of variations on the theme of self and identity which range from ontological crisis to a detached and unemotional exploration of the issue. For Julio Llamazares, for example, 'cada novela es una reflexión sobre sí mismo', novels are fairly straightforward tales told of, and to, oneself.[11] But the concept of the 'death of the subject' haunts other novels, and results in the writing of an elusive, postmodern, and occasionally anguished, self. The period focus is valuable here as a means of understanding the complexity of the phenomena of 'internalisation', where the relationship of writing to its socio-political context, however problematical, can be fruitfully explored. It can be argued that repression conferred on the writer a clear identity, as dissident, and conversely that, as social and political freedom increases, so also do problems of locating identity. This has led, so it is argued, to strains of nostalgic writing, the novel of memory which seeks to retrieve what was lost in the educational and family atmosphere of the Franco regime. For Santos Alonso, many contemporary novels are peopled with 'seres disorientados en busca de su libertad, su clarificación ideológica y su identidad [...] buscando recuperar los rasgos peculiares de su identidad', and true identity is seen as something lost or denied and the real self as something which could be recovered.[12] The contemporary Spanish novel has not, however, produced any confident affirmation of selfhood, and instead, notions such as authenticity and self-expression have taken on a problematical character. The loss of certitude brought about by new political conditions has tended to find its expression in the discourses of postmodernity with their emphasis on the fragility of the divide between reality

---

11   *Historia crítica de la literatura española*, p.303.
12   Santos Alonso, 'Un renovado compromiso con el realismo y con el hombre', *Insula*, 464-5 (1985), 9-11.

and fiction and on the rhetorical and constitutive power of language. Rather than explain the contemporary novel's 'ensimismamiento'[13] or 'privatización'[14] as a desire to avoid falsification, a new solipsism which represents an escape from the 'verdad única, mercado único y ejército único' of the 'totalitarismo democrático', as Manuel Vázquez Montalbán argues,[15] the authors of this book prefer to link it to a much wider concern with identity as inevitably illusory, and, in exploring the variations on aspects of identity and the self as they arise in contemporary narrative, they attempt to expand the notion that there has been a simple change from an external to an internal focus in Spanish writing. The repressed self as subject, seat and source of the individual's perspective is no longer taken for granted, and furthermore, the very idea of the 'novela reprivatizada' colludes with the idea of the free, autonomous individual, thereby lending force to the ideology of late capitalism which advocates freedom in the guise of subjection.

The literary preoccupation with identity is no longer centred on fixing or pinning it down, but on revealing and exploring its elusive, even non-existent, nature. Concerns with textual, personal or collective identity are found to be inseparable. This book is less concerned with the question of whether it is appropriate to talk of the identity of a literary text, of the literary text as having an identity distinct from a non-literary one, or indeed possessing an identity within a body of literature, as with the issue of whether such considerations can be discussed apart from questions of individual identity, authorship and subjectivity. For the Formalists, literariness is what constitutes the identity of a literary text, its particular arrangement of linguistic elements which together constitute a particular patterning. Indeed, we may feel that a text's identity resides in its formal features, which are static and immutable. Similarly, the individual may be said to possess identity through a set of defining, often physical, characteristics. Underlying this notion is the idea of identity as stability: the literary text is a self-sufficient artefact held together by its inner coherence; the individual is a unified being distinguishable from all others. Identity is furthermore evidenced in difference. In the case of the text, this means difference from other works of literature; in the case of the individual, from the rest of humanity. Such a view is, of course, open to challenge: literary discourse is not in every case distinguishable from everyday

13   See Gonzalo Sobejano, 'La novela ensimismada (1980-1985)', *España Contemporánea*, 1 (1988), 9-25.
14   See José María Mainer, 'La reprivatización de la literatura: el dietario como síntoma', in *España frente al siglo XXI. Cultura y Literatura*, ed. by Samuel Amell (Madrid: Ministerio de Cultura y Ediciones Cátedra, 1992), pp.23-24.
15   Manuel Vázquez Montalbán, 'La literatura española en la construcción de la ciudad democrática', *Revista de Occidente*, 122-123 (1991), 131.

language; texts share characteristics; individuals are both like and unlike others. Moreover, recent reception theory tends to undermine the notion of the text as fixed product and replace it with the idea of the text as process, realised only in the act of reading and, logically, realisable in different ways by different readings. The author is no longer unproblematically accepted as the authenticating voice behind the text, the creator whose intention accords the text its identity. Similarly, individual identity is not God-given and thereby universally authenticated, but exists in relation to other identities which seek to fix and stabilise it. The complex ways of dealing with this are reflected both in the novels discussed in this book and in the approaches to the novels on the part of its co-authors. Questions such as 'what is the balance then between the fixed and the fluid?', 'is there a core of identity which shapes external constructions of it?' and 'what makes texts or individuals cohere and what makes them dissolve?' inhabit all the texts under review. The ideals of the self and the text as centres of permanence and certainty are now so distant that we may feel that they are no longer a subject of legitimate concern. Yet the notion of their possibility still haunts us, and we can either constantly hanker after the 'core of identity', the 'real' meaning of a text, or its direct generic ascendancy, or we can speak of everything as relative, as having multiple meanings, plural identities, recognising and referring every now and again to the phantoms of past certainties. Alternatively, we can take a more pragmatic view, epitomised by Randolph Pope, writing about 'general problems of autobiography', when he says that 'to claim [...] that the truth cannot be defined is to hold on to a nostalgic definition of truth. We should understand [...] that under certain conditions, in a limited domain, and according to certain rules, we easily agree in [sic] what is truthful'.[16] Several of the novels discussed in the chapters which follow resist the urge to take contingency for certainty, avoid the 'well-rounded' character, and undermine generic categorisation, yet do not fully renounce the paradigms and conventions of traditional narrative.

Given the uncertainties surrounding questions of this kind, it may be suggested that identity is not a particularly helpful way of looking at either texts or persons. Concern with identity is a challenge to the very notion of identity. More accurately, it is a challenge to the lexical item 'identity' and is thus related to the wider question of language as constitutive category. In this regard, the writings of Emile Benveniste have been highly influential and it is with regard to identity that his ideas have a particular force: 'It is in and through language that man constitutes himself as *subject*, because language

---

16   Randolph Pope, 'Theories and models for the history of Spanish autobiography: General problems of autobiography', *Siglo XX/Twentieth Century*, 12 (1994), 214.

alone establishes the concept of the 'ego' in reality, in *its* reality'.[17] It is not idle to conceive of personal identity in terms of textual identity, for the processes of creation and deciphering are similar. What is important is to recognise that positions on questions of identity are intrinsically ideological, they participate in other struggles for freedom, control, democracy, struggles in defence of humanism, liberalism, feminism, and so forth. There still exists an important ideological division of opinion between, for example, the humanist view that man speaks language, creates with it, determines himself through it, and the structuralist premise that language speaks man, but again there are those, like Paul John Eakin, who eschew extreme formulations and hold simply that 'self and language are mutually implicated in an independent system of symbolic behaviour'.[18] Of the novels studied here, *Makbara* brings these differences into sharpest focus. Most of the others do not attempt its degree of defamiliarisation on a linguistic and literary level; they do not signal themselves as experimental or deviant, but they do appear to accept that meaning is a reworking of old meanings. They often parody or ironise other forms — the thriller, the autobiography, the *roman-à-clef* — rather than attempt to express a unique and autonomous interior psychological world of subjective experience. In terms of the self, the processes which may create the identity of the text, its creation, its socio-historical circumstances, its relation to other texts, the interpretations to which it is subject, apply in equal measure to the person. Susan Suleiman makes the point that: 'If Derrida sees the internal difference and continual deferring of presence as constitutive of the literary text, that is precisely how Lacan sees the human subject'.[19] The force of this point is that neither human nor textual identity is ever complete for it is subject to internal contradictions which are never resolved and thus fails to become concretised or fixed. Just as identity appears to be pinned down, some other dissonant feature emerges which contradicts or undermines it. Juan Goytisolo's *Makbara* embodies precisely this kind of textual instability. Identity is not an object but a continual process, a process which self-consciously strives towards, but never reaches, total intelligibility.

In relation to aspects of self and identity the reclamation of narrative writing is particularly significant. In the contemporary Spanish novel, narrative and

---

17 Emile Benveniste, *Problems of General Linguistics*, trans. by Mary Elizabeth Meek (Coral Gables, Florida: University of Miami Press, 1971), p.224.

18 Paul John Eakin, *Fictions in Autobiography* (Princeton N.J.: Princeton University Press, 1985), p.192.

19 *The Reader in the Text: Essays on Audience and Interpretation*, ed. by Susan R. Suleiman and Inge Crossman (Princeton Guildford: Princeton University Press, 1980), p.41.

the assertion of self often appear coterminous. Moreover, contemporary Spanish writing shows a marked penchant for the autobiographical, either in its explicit form, or as an element in the narrative unfolding. For Julio Llamazares, for example, language seems to be the only, if inadequate, means by which some core of identity is retained in the midst of flux and change. This is part of the premise underlying traditional concepts of autobiographical writing. It is the supreme construction of a life as narrative. It does not aim to be the whole truth, nor does it claim to be wholly fictional. Its truth is partly there in experience, its fiction is the representation, the creation of a pattern, the sense-making amid what is only a series of events in time. Another of the writers dealt with in this book, Antonio Muñoz Molina, has, since the writing of *Beltenebros*, based his writing on autobiographical material. His most recent work, *Ardor guerrero*,[20] is precisely about his experiences of military service. It has as its epigraph the Spanish translation of Montaigne's famous phrase: 'Así pues, lector, yo mismo soy la materia de mi libro', and in an interview the author comments that 'contar con naturalidad la experiencia propia fue como internarse en una mina de oro. [...] Estoy escribiendo el mismo libro. Un libro consistente en contar las memorias verdaderas de un protagonista falso'.[21] The aim of such writing may be to seek the enigma at the centre of being. It may equally be an assertion, in the face of what is sometimes seen as merely a contemporary fashion, that identity is more than an interpretation by others, created by their own strategies and prejudices, and that these interpretations are not themselves free of the pressures exerted by the text, or the person, and which exist independently of the interpretative act. In *Beltenebros*, the impression of a conscious mind is always present, working on the material of the world, juxtaposing selves, events and perceptions in a synchronic overlay which evades chronological time. The work of Muñoz Molina discussed in a later chapter is read as a particularly complex use of narrative in relation to the paradigm of possible attitudes to coherence and authority within a temporal framework. There is a sense, common in these novels, that the 'real' past and 'unreal' imagined time are equally powerful in the formation of the narrative we call our self. This refutation of a common notion is made most vehemently in Javier Marías's novels. The sense of not only the past but also the future as influencing the construction of the self is typical. The radically temporal self is no longer the sum of his or her past, but feeds off the future — consciously and constantly prefiguring new versions and possibilities. The fragmentation or rearrangement of chrono-llogy in

---

20   *Ardor guerrero* (Madrid: Alfaguara, 1995)
21   Ramón F. Reboiras, 'Antonio Muñoz Molina: El éxito en literatura es durar', *Cambio 16*, 1219 (1995), 72.

Makbara, which was so common in the 'experimental' novels of the 1960s and 1970s, implies a faith, now all but lost, that time can be controlled, the past redeemed in the present of the writing. This is of course the premise behind the autobiography, the official genre of self-writing. *Makbara* straddles change in thinking about the self as a narrative construct, as *La verdad sobre el caso Savolta* incorporates the turn between the experimental novel and the 'new realism'. The use of autobiographical and narrative techniques by Javier Marías, on the other hand, supports a different notion of the self as a narrative creation, and the seriousness of the moral discourse which underlies this support adds weight to the ingenuity and humour of his work, and surely contributes to his popularity. Narrative writing, as a particularly temporal mode of writing, involving constant choice and decision-making, procedural rather than descriptive, is particularly apt for current concepts of self and identity. In spite of what some critics see as a complete turning of backs on such socio-political concerns as were to be found in the novels of the fifties and sixties, the novelists under discussion do seem to have their fingers on the pulse of concerns which are in a different sense 'public'. If 'internalisation' were mere solipsism it is unlikely that serious books such as *Corazón tan blanco* or *La soledad era esto*, or lyrical works like *La lluvia amarilla* would attract the large numbers of readers that they do.

The third strand which we identified as informing the critical approaches taken here, and which can also be detected as an influence in the novels themselves, is an awareness of the importance of poststructuralist thinkers, such as Jacques Lacan and Jacques Derrida, in relation to the concept of the primacy of language. In Lacanian theory, the moment of recognition, when the infant becomes simultaneously aware of his/her subjectivity and the objectivity of others, marks the entrance into the 'symbolic order' of language. Furthermore, it is not fanciful to conceive of the scripted self in terms of the well-known Derridean idea that there is nothing outside the text. Derrida's exposition of the delay or 'différance' between the moment of perception, and the related idea that final meaning is always deferred, goes beyond the more acceptable notion that language simply conceptualises experience. There is no reality behind or before conscious experience which can be spoken about, no coincidence of word and world. This reduction of reference to illusion, and of experience to text does not mean, of course, that a text can mean anything. It can only mean in relation to other texts. The way we form our concepts of self works in the same way. A strong and coherent 'personality' tends to be accepted as the 'real' or 'authentic' person. Although the individual text is not, in practice (in the reading, that is) 'free', it can be in theory. It is just so with the individual self. We are only made possible of course by being born, by being written, but this is only a point of origin for the body and the material substance of the book — the network of meanings, cultures, language, transcends us. The liberal-humanist belief that some core of selfhood exerts pressure on our own and others' concepts or interpretations of who we 'really' are is so deeply engrained that it is not easy to relinquish, and persists to varying degrees in the work of writers studied here however much they strive to overcome it. Nevertheless, the poststructuralist critique provides a powerful position from which to challenge the view that 'writing the self' simply substitutes self as 'inner core' for self as life-story — a metaphor which maintains the traditional and relatively unproblematic relationship between experience, and writing the experience.

The idea, then, that the self is not given, but is in some measure constructed, permeates contemporary narratives, and results in explorations of possible, alternative, and multiple selves, stories we tell about ourselves or which others impose on us. The self can thus often appear as the site of competing narratives, so that writing the self becomes a pressingly urgent endeavour. From nostalgia for the old certainties of prescribed formulae to a knowing and sophisticated parodying of such roles, scripting the self in contemporary Spanish narrative writing takes on divergent forms, from the creation of postmodernist, fragmented collage to the search for coherent, if fictional, patterns in the new realism. Paradoxically, this new realism accepts the need for illusory patterning while postmodernism in some measure 'reflects' an absence of coherence and certitude. The new realism, if this is what it is, can be seen as a form of radical postmodernism.

While we have emphasised identity as a concern in much contemporary Spanish fiction, the writers of this book acknowledge the diversity of its conception and treatment. The book does not, therefore, adopt a conventional academic approach to the material, in the sense that it seeks neither to offer a supposed evolution of ideas and form nor to adopt a similar method in its treatment of texts and authors. From Juan Goytisolo to Belén Gopegui, the twelve novels by eight authors discussed here span two generations and a period of thirteen years. Successive chapters deal variously with individual texts, with the same texts from different perspectives, with several works by one or different authors. Rather than attempting to be representative of a general theme, the organisation of the book reflects the variety of approaches encountered in the novels themselves and their treatment of identity and writing the self. For example, the chapter on *Makbara* looks at the identity of the text as well as that of the protagonist. Several aspects of identity are discussed as aspects of *La escala de los mapas* and *La soledad era esto,* including the possibilities of writing from a gendered position. *Todas las almas* and *Corazón tan blanco* are examined as novels which deal with the concept of writing the self as an ongoing process throughout the two texts. Nevertheless, an attempt is made to illuminate these diverse approaches by cross-reference and by contrastive and comparative approximations to identity as diversely perceived. The book wilfully resists the imposition of a coherent identity on the writing of the period. Its main aim is to do justice to the novels themselves by expanding on the frequently expounded, but not, we feel, sufficiently examined opinion that they are 'returns to the subject' or novels of 'internalisation'. By concentrating on the question of textual identities, this book seeks to offer a fresh perspective on the current debate on contemporary Spanish narrative writing.

Part One
The Self Remembered

CHAPTER ONE
Nostalgia for a prescribed identity in
Todas las almas by Javier Marías.

RUTH CHRISTIE

With his first novel, *Los dominios del lobo* (1971), Javier Marías began a novelistic career which is still gaining momentum. The trajectory of his writing has been described as one of increasing maturity and he is now widely recognised as a novelist of some weight, both in Spain and abroad.[1] Besides eight novels to date, Marías has published a book of short stories, numerous articles and essays, and has translated various works from English, most notably Lawrence Sterne's *Tristram Shandy*.[2] Before the publication of *Corazón tan blanco* (1992),[3] the highly acclaimed 'best-seller' *Todas las almas* (1989)[4] was considered to be his best novel.

To investigate aspects of identity in Marías's work is to read it in a context which is shared widely by his contemporaries, and which has not been examined hitherto. *Todas las almas* is particularly interesting for an English reader, offering as it does an irreverent outsider's view of the hallowed University town of Oxford. And it is the nature of this 'outsider' factor which is especially relevant here, for the sense of unease which permeates the novel is due not only to the narrator's degree of marginalisation in relation to the customs and traditions which fashion Oxford University life, but also from

---

1   See, for example, Juan Antonio Masoliver, 'Espejismo en una galería de espejos', *Insula*, 546 (1992), 21-22: 'Álvaro Pombo y Javier Marías han sido para mí [...] los narradores más interesantes que han surgido en los últimos veinte años'. See also Michael Kerrigan, reviewing *All Souls* (*Todas las almas*) in *Times Literary Supplement*, 4675 (1992), 21: '*All Souls* is a dazzling example of the Oxford novel [...] it is genuinely enterprising, genuinely experimental, and if not itself immortal, certainly likely to outlive the usual monuments of post-modernism'.

2   Laurence Sterne, *La vida y las opiniones de caballero Tristram Shandy. Los sermones de Mr. Yorick* (*Tristram Shandy*), trans. by Javier Marías (Madrid: Alfaguara, 1978).

3   Javier Marías, *Corazón tan blanco* (Barcelona: Anagrama, 1992).

4   Javier Marías, *Todas las almas* (Barcelona: Anagrama, 1989). All page numbers in the main text of this chapter refer to this edition.

a network of distancing and separations within himself — it is a *mild* identity crisis, 'la historia de una perturbación' (p.69).

One way of placing *Todas las almas* within the discourse of the self is to review it briefly in the light of the title of *Corazón tan blanco*, tracing a thread back, through the dense web of writing on the concept, to Schopenhauer. The connection is to be made through Joseph Conrad, who was strongly influenced by Schopenhauer, back to Javier Marías, who recognises the influence of Conrad in his own work. The title *Corazón tan blanco* alludes to Conrad's *Heart of Darkness* (1902), as well as being a quotation from *Macbeth*. The concept of self embodies a cluster of identities which mark sameness to and difference from other individuals and groups. It is a vehicle for all the factors which we consider important in relation to who we are and where we stand in the world. The apparently constant aspects of our identity — race, gender, nationality, family — are all felt to be superseded by the permanence of the self 'in itself', which we feel stands behind, or is a receptacle for these constants, for memories and for personality, in some kind of synthesis of body and mind. But when approached, this self, like consciousness, cannot be found. It may therefore be useful and pertinent at this stage to mention just one metaphor for the self — Schopenhauer's 'glass globe':

> To reflect fully upon ourselves while we direct knowing inwards, we thus lose ourselves in a bottomless void, we find ourselves like a hollow glass globe, and while we thus wish to grasp ourselves, we seize with a shudder nothing but an unstable ghost.[5]

Schopenhauer overcomes the paradox of this image of the subject trying to know itself as object by identifying the self 'in-itself' with the will. The will, he says, is more real than anything else, and we can know it in a way we cannot know other things which only represent themselves to us.[6] (This claim that the self 'in itself' is in some non-empirical way knowable is the foundation for the cult of authenticity,[7] which has particular relevance here, as will be seen). But he claims the will as the source of evil, impossible to overcome, the force which drives us on through life, which he sees as a process of

---

5   Arthur Schopenhauer, *Die Welt als Wille und Vorstellung. Sämtliche Werke*, vol. ii (Wiesbaden: Eberhard Brockhaus, 1949), p.218n, (excerpt trans. by Vincent Pecora, *Self and Form in Modern Narrative* (Baltimore: John Hopkins University Press, 1989), p.74).

6   *Die Welt als Wille und Vorstellung*, vol. ii, p.218

7   Pecora, p.74

desengaño.[8] Conrad's figure of the 'heart of darkness' is an image of such pessimism. *Heart of Darkness* tells of the search for self of two men: Marlow, the narrator, and Kurtz, the imperialist adventurer. Kurtz, in his final breath, knows himself to be nothing, or ineffable, yet is still capable of horror at what he saw or did not see — his 'heart of darkness'. The sense of loss inherent in the title of Marías's novel when it is read as an allusion to *Heart of Darkness* is symptomatic of an emptiness which seems to afflict mankind in this latter part of the century, when not only the bourgeois subject, but also the self as a horrifying abyss has been deconstructed. The name Ranz, moreover — so similar to Kurtz — suggests the analogical contrast that is being drawn between the role of the relation between the narrators and these two figures in the two books. Horror depends on shock, and shock depends on not knowing, and yet we are so knowing in this postmodern world, and so self-conscious. To be self-conscious is, paradoxically, to see oneself as if from another's point of view, rather than being able to act spontaneously; to 'express one's self' or 'be oneself'. We have to find or invent new ways to shock ourselves, new sources for the strong emotions which are inherent to any sense of identity. Marías deals with the self as a centre which can no longer feel its own weight. The narrators of *Todas las almas* and *Corazón tan blanco* are somewhat jaded characters who are no longer able to found their identities on the old sources of emotion and fundamental relationships of the past, and who can no longer feel the *loss* of such certainties as a source of anguish. These novels, amongst other things, are concerned with whether new sources of identity and self can be sought out, or invented, and whether nostalgia for prescribed roles can ever be overcome. In theory, the idea that the self does not contain, but in some way *is* the experience we 'have' has long been current; there is no permanent transcendental ego which *has* the experiences, there is only experience which is always transitory. The self, we conclude, is the necessary referent of the 'I'. The coming to terms with the implications of such conclusions as they begin to affect the way we *act*, the passing of theory into practice, is one of the most significant reasons why questions of writing the self now play a major part in contemporary narrative writing in the Western world. No longer does the narrator search to 'find' him or herself, but rather to find out what 'self' can mean, or to recreate the self. The dissolving of the walls which kept the self intact has been very positive in that it has released new possibilities of being, but it has also been negative in that it has created great insecurity.

---

8   Arthur Schopenhauer, 'On the vanity of existence', in *Essays and Aphorisms*, trans. by R.J. Hollingdale (Harmondsworth: Penguin, 1970), p.54.

But the narrator of a novel can no more be identified with the self who experienced than the telling of the experience can be identified with the actual experience 'itself'. The postmodernist no longer seriously entertains the hope that the self can be reconstructed beyond the limitations of the language with which, it is suspected, it was constructed in the first place. As Stephen Frosh explains:

> For modernists [...] the self [...] is not a fixed entity: it is constructed out of the bits and pieces of experience and is in a dialectical relationship with social organisation. It is full of conflict, particularly between what is desired and what is encountered. But in the distance there is promise: not a certainty, but a chance that something more cohesive and supportive can be created. The postmodernist vision is, on the whole, different [... What] it contradicts is any sense that [...] on the individual level [...] there is something real and true lying behind the sense of self which is created within each individual.[9]

Yet more than a hundred years since the German philosophers were devising ways of rescuing the transcendental self from the reasoning of their own philosophies, we still find we cannot function without some analogous notion, inscribed as we are in the subject/predicate of language. Javier Marías writes from a postmodern awareness that our selves are creations we make in our negotiations with others, that identity is only a function of difference. But however far the narrators of his novels go in reassessing their relationships and their identities — and Marías seems to see awareness of the possibilities and extent of story-telling as the greatest hope, in that it brings a fuller recognition of the self as linguistic 'I' — nostalgia for the certainties of prescribed identities remains. It is, as James Fernández says in his book *Apology to Apostrophe*, a study of writing as self-representation in Spain: 'un conflicto ontológico no del todo superado por el hombre moderno: el 'hacer' del nuevo orden — mis acciones, mis logros, mi *curriculum vitae* — frente al 'ser' del antiguo — mi ascendencia, mi sangre, mis raíces'.[10]

According to the narrator, Javier Marías's novel *Todas las almas* is the story of a 'perturbación', due mainly to the fact that he is in Oxford, 'ciudad conservada en almíbar' (p.14), and not in his 'real' world, Madrid. The narrator's sense of unease is 'poco serio', he tells us. He does not suffer

---

9   Stephen Frosh, *Identity Crisis: Modernity, Psychoanalysis and the Self* (Basingstoke: Macmillan, 1991), p.31.
10   James Fernández, *Apology to Apostrophy* (London: Duke University Press, 1992), p.125.

from angst, but from 'una perturbación leve y lógica y articulada' (p.198). Behind this lack of seriousness, in the rootlessness he seems to experience, can be read a disquiet beyond the strangeness of Oxford, an unease which is postmodern in all its aspects. One of these aspects is loss of belief in the self as a stable centre of identity, and this may be read as one of the main causes of the narrator's disquiet.

Oxford, and particularly Oxford University, the setting of *Todas las almas,* is likely to make a foreigner feel particularly foreign; the system is so quintessentially English, so traditional and class-bound. The narrator comes to Oxford University for two years as a *lector* in Spanish. From the outset, he tells us, he feels 'perturbado', due particularly to the lack of any witness to his past. He says that whatever happens to him in Oxford will be as nothing in the entirety of his life, but from what follows it becomes plain that it is he who feels himself to be nothing. He shares no 'stories' in common with the people he meets, and he experiences a crisis — 'no muy seria' — of identity. Forced to fall back on his own inner resources, on the strengths of the autonomous self, he finds a vacuum which must be filled. His concern is to recreate a new sense of self, and he does this by searching for links with others — lovers and friends. It can be said that he tries to re-member himself, to bring his points of reference into line again, but lazily, for he is not really suffering, but merely uncomfortable, as a foreigner. In this sense his experience contrasts strongly with, for example, that of the Arab in Paris in *Makbara*, whose presence in the city, as John Macklin points out, represents'... a threatening occupation by the Other'. 'Otherness' in *Makbara* is conceived in terms of antithesis; Macklin emphasises the chiaroscuro effect on the narrative as a whole. These binary oppositions, first world/third world, white/black, clean/dirty, and so on, allow the foreigner's marginalisation to be used as a site of rebellion and demystification, as the hierarchy of such dualities is reversed. The maintenance of such a black and white vision, even though the hierarchy is reversed, does not really work as an attack on a postmodern society in which identity is not threatened or obscured by the 'other', but because it reduces everyone to the same level of consumer. As John Macklin makes clear, it is this kind of uneasy positioning of an idealistic perspective on a postmodern world which makes the textual identity of *Makbara* particularly complex. The romantic and nostalgic nature of the problems of both personal and textual identity as a rejection of consumerist capitalism in *Makbara* can be contrasted with the feebly nostalgic and romantic quest for identity of the narrator of *Todas las almas*. The chiaroscuro of *Makbara* and the radical 'otherness' of the Arab in Paris corresponds to a greyness, and a much slighter 'otherness' in *Todas las almas*. It is a 'lightness of being' which the narrator finds disturbing. It is the *lack* of absolute difference which feeds his nostalgia and creates the 'perturbación'. The conviction of the sense of displacement of *Makbara* is simply unease in the later novel, for although the narrator does not share 'stories' with his friends and colleagues, they do have many other things in common — they are all Europeans, all academics, all middle-class, and so on, so this being 'off-centre' does not offer the scope for reaction or rebellion of the 'marginalised' Arab in Paris. Carlos Galán Lores recognises a 'disconformidad con el medio en que vivimos' on the individual level in the postmodern Spanish novel, which he describes as 'neoromanticismo'.[11] However, such disconformity can only be called 'romantic' if the answer is sought in some kind of authentic lifestyle which 'el medio en que vivimos' suppresses. The demystification of such concepts of 'authenticity' is surely one of the most important effects of the nebulous concept of postmodernity. However, traces of such 'romanticismo' *are* manifest in *Todas las almas*, but it is recognised as a last gasp, and tends to be covered with bravado, as when the narrator says 'Para mí este territorio es territorio de paso, pero se trata de un paso lo bastante dilatado para que deba procurarme lo que se llama *un amor* mientras estoy aquí' (p.84). However, the nostalgia for the easy identity he seems to have lost and the temptation to fall back on prescribed models makes him, paradoxically, a creature fit for the 'ciudad conservada en almíbar' in which he finds himself. The slant between admiration and disdain for Oxford and its inhabitants is typically contradictory, but it is also symptomatic of the ambivalent attitude of a narrator who is unsure of 'himself'.

The most immediate way in which the narrator attempts to overcome or survive his crisis is in an affair with Clare Bayes, the wife of one of his colleagues. From his first meeting with Clare at a high-table dinner to which he is invited, it is clear that this is not going to be the story of a passionate sexual attraction, although we are told of his 'abierta admiración sexual' and her 'escote de excelente gusto' (p.53). His initial attraction recedes into high-table burlesque and the network of lustful or jealous glances and drunken stares, and the real importance of the relationship for the narrator is intimated: 'Entonces yo miré abiertamente al rostro de Clare Bayes y, sin conocerla, la vi como alguien que pertenecía ya a mi pasado' (p.62). He imagines that he sees the 'aparición' of his infancy in her eyes. In contrast to the opening of the novel, in which the narrator assures us categorically of the difference between the 'yo' who writes and the 'yo' who experienced, this reads as a romantic moment of nostalgic lapse. Clare, he says, has somehow seen his childhood, and allowed him to glimpse hers. Thus begins his attempt to forge an identity with her, as he tries to assuage his unease.

---

11   Carlos Galán Lores, 'Los más jóvenes de los jóvenes', *Insula*, 512-3 (1989), 14.

He goes on to describe moments from his and her childhood, bringing forward a story he hears from her later, the significance of which is not made clear until the end of the book.

But the relationship means something else for Clare, (what, exactly, we are never told, as the first-person perspective is strictly adhered to), and when her son, Eric, falls ill, she rejects the narrator in order to spend all her time with him. The narrator describes how one day, in the Ashmolean Museum, he sets about spying on her as she spends a day out with her father and her son. He is not jealous of the fact that they are enjoying Clare's company which is denied to him, so much as envious of the strong sense of continuity suggested by the striking family resemblance they share. The three almost identical faces are evidence of a bond beyond mere appearance — of a blood relationship from which, as a mere lover, he is absolutely excluded. Moreover, he attributes to Eric a sensation which he says he has never known, the certain knowledge that he is going to die, the experience of life as a fall into death. It is nostalgia for a sense of inevitability. To say one knows one is going to die and really to know it are two different things, and the narrator feels the not knowing it as a loss, caused, perhaps, by the very fact that he can articulate it. He 'reads' the family likeness as evidence of a natural identity which, in the case of the boy, is unquestioned and inevitable. There is an intimation of something which is expanded in *Corazón tan blanco* — that telling things makes them real, but also robs them of their truth. (The boy, it is assumed, has never told himself that he is mortal, it is an intuition with which the narrator endows him). But this nostalgia for certainty is a weak affair compared to Schopenhauer's identification of the self as the will to live, the transcendental subject which survives time. The narrator's nostalgia is for the meeker certainty of a sense of mortality. In the family of Clare Bayes he sees evidence of a metaphysical bond of identity in their physical likeness. From now on the narrator makes it clear that his desire for Clare Bayes is a desire to share this sense of identity, which is none other than a sensation of falling, a knowing that one is like others and will die because they have died. His desire now is to:

descansar de mi pensamiento que unifica y asocia y establece demasiados vínculos [...] Hablar con Clare Bayes, y proponerle algo, no despedirnos, no separarnos, que me permita hacer mía la sensación de descenso de la que participan todos y que yo aún no conozco. (p.198)

The concepts involved owe their genealogy to a Spanish philosophical tradition, as well as a broader postmodern one. Javier Marías's father, Julián

Marías, in his book *Reason and Life*,[12] written in Spanish in the late 1940s — a book which owes much to his mentor, Ortega y Gasset — discusses the importance of the meaningful horizon of death. He says that life is lived in anticipation of itself, that as adults we know our days are numbered. For the father this 'living in anticipation of the self' means that for a child, for example, life is vast, almost endless; nevertheless 'adult life' is an end that children can foresee, and they 'project' themselves toward it, some more precipitately than others. 'And then', says the father:

> death begins to function as a dynamic ingredient of living. This does
> not mean that the adolescent, for example, does not know that men
> die, and that he himself has to die; he knows it, but he does not reckon
> with it, that is to say, he does not live in view of death; it functions for
> him at such a distance that strictly speaking it is outside his horizon,
> 'beyond' him; it is the Greek Kalends, the "That's a long time yet"
> ["¡qué largo me lo fiáis!"] of Don Juan.[13]

The narrator of *Todas las almas* enviously attributes such knowledge — which is conceived more radically by Javier Marías than by his father, — to the boy Eric. Julián Marías goes on to say that man can only live in view of death, he needs to 'be in some belief with respect to the reality of what we call dying; because if it is not so, he finds himself completely at a loss to understand the very meaning of his life [...] which assumes its shape when it has to reckon with the certainty of a death'.[14] The desire of the narrator of *Todas las almas* to *know* he is going to die is a desire to feel alive, to feel the weight which lends life meaning, and to 'grow up'. This desire relates, in particularly Spanish terms, to *congoja*, or Unamuno's 'sentimiento trágico de la vida',[15] his hunger for immortality, and also to Ortega y Gasset's reversal of Heidegger's concept of 'being-towards-death'[16] as a will to live. The narrator of *Todas las almas* feels he does not live 'in view of death'. Javier Marías seems to be challenging the optimism of his father's mentor, Ortega, who said 'Mi nacimiento es un cuento, un mito que otros me cuentan pero al que yo no he podido asistir [...] en cuanto a mi muerte, es un cuento que ni

---

12   Julián Marías, *Reason and Life*, trans. by K.S. Reid and E. Sarmiento (London: Hollis and Carter, 1956).

13   *Reason and Life*, p.349.

14   *Reason and Life*, pp.375-6.

15   Miguel de Unamuno, *Del sentimiento trágico de la vida* (Buenos Aires: Espasa Calpe Argentina, 1941).

16   See George Steiner, *Heidegger* (Sussex: Harvester Press, 1978), p.78.

siquiera pueden contarme'.[17] The narrator would agree with this but cannot accept it, it leaves him feeling only half-alive. He is a kind of latter-day Don Juan, whose sexual conquests (for example) are not a challenge to the voice that says 'you will die and have to face the consequences of your actions', but rather a desperate attempt to evoke such a voice, which remains silent, and deprives the actions of meaning. '¡Qué largo me lo fiáis!' would be in the narrator's mouth not a mockery, but a plea for a way to feel those consequences as a real threat. He is a typical postmodern 1980s character; one of those who, according to Javier Marías's own words, are 'children who are unable to remember when they were once even smaller and can't imagine that they will ever be less so. Everything is so distant for them. They do not understand that the world didn't begin with them, nor that it could somehow survive without them'.[18] It could be said that the postmodern condition as found in *Todas las almas* is that of never growing up, in the sense described above by Julián Marías, and, paradoxically, of being aware of the condition. The disquiet the narrator feels is the result of a loss of the effectiveness of all those threats, dreads, weights and certainties that have kept us grounded and alive for so long, and against which the original and successive Don Juans were able to rebel, but which have been removed from the life of the postmodern and leave him floating, with no sense of his own significance.

The narrator would love to be able to forget language and *be* himself, to escape the lightness of his 'perturbación' and experience 'la sensación de vértigo, de caída y gravidez y peso, de falsa gordura y abatimiento' (p.23). In other words, he needs a direction, a certainty, a sense of something definite even if it is *knowing* that death is his destiny — this is what Clare Bayes, he imagines, can give him. But the body is the final frontier; the hard evidence of inherited features are signs of identity which cannot be appropriated. However, families and nationality can be adopted, and his final fantasies, which Clare dismisses as absurd, are to do just that. Nevertheless, her being another man's wife is part of the attraction, part of the romantic role he half tries to play, and again, his attempt to deny this reads as no more than bravado: 'nunca tuve por ella [...] una debilidad lo bastante prolongada o firme para estar en peligro de ninguna clase (si no era Edward Bayes, tampoco estuve nunca en peligro de suplantarlo)' (p.32). The narrator always talks about 'Clare Bayes' rather than 'Clare' as if, by rubbing in salt, he may begin to feel the wound. One's name is such a

---

17   José Ortega y Gasset, *Obras completas*, vol. vii (Madrid: Revista de Occidente, 1961), pp.496.

18   Javier Marías, 'The 1980s: Age of Recreation', trans. by J.J.Dunlap, *Encounters*, 2 (1990), 12-15.

blatant mark of identity, the surname marking the family group, which also distinguishes it from other families, the first name marking one's individuality within the family. For the narrator, the constant referral to Clare as Clare Bayes recalls also her husband, which would not, of course, be the case with a Spanish name. So by frequently referring to her in this way he never allows her to cease being her husband's wife. And significantly, it is the narrator (the nameless one) who always has to remind her what time it is when she is with him, who worries about her husband finding out about their affair. He desires Clare Bayes, wife of another, as well as Clare Bayes, daughter and mother; Clare Bayes whose name represents the difference and sameness which *are* the concept of identity. And perhaps, in both cases, there is more than a little desire to destroy, through their adultery, such signs of belonging, which he himself cannot share.

Rejected by Clare, and out of boredom caused more by his lack of a role, lack of work, and the tedium of the Oxford streets, he extends the romantic outsider role he has begun to appropriate. He begins to identify his own life with that of the (real) writer John Gawsworth, who spent his last years down-and-out in the streets of London, without a woman to curb his drunken ramblings. The link between Gawsworth and Clare is made clear as, after assuring the narrator that their affair is over and she has no intention of leaving her husband, Clare takes up the narration, (and the fact that the novel ends with Clare's story, rather than *his* story ending with the conquest of *her*, makes his quasi-romantic search even more of a failure) and tells the story of her mother's tragic affair. Her mother's lover, it turns out, was none other than the young John Gawsworth. She ended the affair by throwing herself from the bridge above into the river Jumna.[19] This story is transparently an invention of the narrator's, in contrast to the rest of the book which is easily taken for straight autobiography, thus it is instrumental in lifting the novel clear of the realist mode.

---

19   *Above the River* (London: Ulysses Bookshop, 1931) is the title of a short book by John Gawsworth. The protagonist has the following experience: 'The mist enfolded him lovingly - suddenly it parted and for one ecstatic moment transfigured, he beheld with blinding clarity the secret of his heart. A rapturous cry. A lurch. Silence.' (p.14) This allusion is rather distant, but contrasts dramatically with Kurtz's dying cry of 'the horror!, the horror!'. The coincidence between fact and fiction, and the network of allusions that it sets up between various texts, is typical of Marías, and evidence of a Nabokovian influence. The influence of Vladimir Nabokov is evident in the work of several other contemporary Spanish novelists (see, for example, Belén Gopegui, *La escala de los mapas*, p.121).

'Coincidences' of this elaborate narrative kind can never, in a sense, be the result of chance in fiction, as we all know that the author put them there. Their function is always complex. In this case, the narrator's artifice as he retells the story within a story upsets the notion that the author has ironically had the narrator give himself away — the wink to the reader behind the narrator's back that as readers of novels we are so familiar with is made obsolete as the narrator himself steps out of the realist, autobiographical frame. It is part of the deliberate attempt on the part of the author to complicate the relationship between, or the identities of, the author, the 'yo' that writes and the 'yo' who experienced, and the narrator. Also, the story picks up on the first reference to Clare's childhood in India, which was made when she and the narrator met at high-table, and this shaping device reinforces the relationship with Clare as also structured and contrived, the narrator's answer to his identity problem. And it explains Clare's deliberate choosing of a traditional and stable role for herself — she is not going to allow a romantic affair to ruin *her* life. In this way it also provides the narrator with a satisfactory if transparent escape from his position as rejected lover, in that it rescues his pride. He is not *himself* rejected by Clare, rather she is merely learning from her mother's mistakes. The narrative link between the two stories of adultery is not gratuitous, as the analogy can be made sense of through the other repetition of the three faces of Clare, her father and her son, representing as they do the idea of the family bond and the narrator's envy of it. There is a clear contrast between the tragic end of the mother's affair and the rational, unperturbed way in which Clare ends her own affair with the narrator. He returns finally to Madrid, and they do not even correspond. The suspicion is planted that the narrator would have preferred Clare to throw herself off a bridge also. Or that he himself could have fallen, like Clare's mother, 'con su sensación de descenso, con su sensación de carga, con su sensación de vértigo, de caída y gravidez y peso' (p.230). The dramatic nature of Clare's mother's death is the product of the strict moral code which protects the family, the centre of identity seen as so desirable by the narrator. She literally falls to her death. Absolute values produce strong emotions and dramatic actions — things which it seems that the narrator and Clare can no longer experience in their mundane affair. The only emotions the narrator seems to feel — envy and nostalgia — have to be read in his reaction to the family likeness in the faces of Clare and her relations. Love affairs such as that of Clare's mother belong only to that lost world which is only actual in childhood, 'cuando el mundo [fue] más mundo' (p.70), or perhaps to a past time when such things were taken more seriously. The postmodern narrator of *Todas las almas,* only able weakly to parody his romantic role in a mundane adulterous affair, and to reflect it in a melodrama, already has a 'corazón tan blanco' — a leeched as opposed to an innocent heart, which he would dearly have red once again.

Problems with their identities either in relation to other people's families or within their own are common to many of the protagonists of Marías's novels. Different strata of relationships — the blood relationship, the marital relationship, the sexual relationship, friendship — and the self as father, son, husband, lover, are re-assessed as prescriptions of identity and imaginatively reinvented. The narrators' desires for a family are complex in both *Todas las almas* and *Corazón tan blanco*. Strangely, in *Todas las almas*, as the narrator stalks Clare and her father and son through the museum, he never once draws consolation from his own family in Spain. Although we may think of identity as something formed in the past which still applies in the present, the narrator's past does not appear to succour him. Isolation and insecurity are what he feels *now*. Marks of identity, in other words, are of little use unless recognised by others. And the narrator's relationship with these others in Oxford is that of a foreigner; he is identified by his difference, even though, as we have seen, he is not *very* different and his foreignness is diluted. He takes a remark made by Clare to her son in the museum as a personal insult directed at him, spoken loudly so that he will overhear it. As they stand looking at the statue of Marco Polo, she tells Eric that he spent so long in China that he became 'un chino de ojos azules' (p.190). The narrator interprets this in terms of his own pampered, outcast state of mind, but as with his family in Madrid, he feels only nostalgia for an identity, and not consolation in the fact that he will shortly be a Spaniard back in his own country. The future as well as the past offer no consolation, for identity and being oneself are all to do with the illusion of presence, 'who am I?', not 'who was I?' or 'who will I be?' And between the lines can be read another comparative loss of weight — the contrast between fact that the narrator is not really an outcast, that his being away from Madrid is voluntary and transitory, and the real exile, the serious and meaningful pain of those previous generations, which was in fact a *mark* of their identity, and compared with which the narrator's 'perturbación' is trivial — and his sense of self lightened even further.

However, the narrator's nostalgic relationship to the family of Clare Bayes is more than a temporary reaction to a transitory state. In a short chapter half-way through the book, in which the narrative jumps ahead to the future, we find the narrator installed in Madrid with his new wife and son. But although it would seem that in the founding of his own new blood relations he may at last have found a role to play, a stable identity in the traditionally prescribed manner, the new baby causes thoughts which upset this interpretation. The baby's presence does not seem to worry him in any of the ways one would expect a new baby to worry its father — it does not make him jealous because it usurps his place in the mother's affections, it does not weigh him down with a sense of responsibility — for such things would contribute to his sense of the son's importance and hence lend weight to his new identity as father. But the new role also lets him down. The ease and lack of ceremony with which the child has appeared bothers him. 'Hace poco no *era'*, he says of the new son, and 'Ahora es un niño eterno' (p.108). The narrator realises that he has forgotten the child's existence completely for forty-five minutes, and this capacity to forget about someone who should be so important fills him with horror, for he realises that he will slip in and out of his son's consciousness in a similar way. He perceives his son as a threat to his identity, in that he foresees, not a continuation of his genes, the perpetuation of his name, a future consolation for his own death — all those things our progeny are supposed to bring us — but the realisation that he in his turn will be forgotten. He understands that lineage signifies not only identity as sameness and continuity, but also as repetition and passing.

In an interview for *Cambio 16,* Marías claims that:

> Los vínculos son tan fuertes por lo que hay como por lo que no hay; por lo que existe como por la ausencia de ello. Por ejemplo, es tan fuerte el vínculo con un hijo que nunca se tuvo como con el que se tiene [...] Al mismo tiempo existe la idea de la disolución; la negación de lo que ha sido muy cercano.[20]

It should be noted that he does not say 'por lo que existe como por lo imaginario' but 'como por la ausencia de ello'. This is consistent with Marías's description of his novels as stories of 'lo que pudo ser'.[21] He seems to be saying that the dividing line between fact and fiction is simply a question of chance, what happens in his novels could just as easily have been what really happened. The imaginary is conceived here as what could, or might have been, meaningful and possible, rather than in absolute terms as fantasy as opposed to reality. Thus the difference between what is imagined and what is brought to fruition becomes a relationship between the present and the absent, rather than between the real and the unreal. This aspect of the novels is examined more closely in another chapter, but it plays a particular role in relation to identity, self and the other, in the way the men and women of the novels form romantic relationships.

---

20   Interview with Javier Marías, 'He sido el joven Marías durante demasiado tiempo', *Cambio 16,* 1173 (1994), 81.

21   Interview with Javier Marías, 'La magia de lo que pudo ser', *Quimera,* 87 (1988), 24-31.

For example, the narrator of *Todas las almas,* as a stranger in Oxford, sees a girl on Didcot station with whom he forms a vivid, but completely idealised, sensual relationship. After taking up with Clare Bayes, he says that the girl on the station was merely someone to think about, almost an antidote to boredom. But when Clare rejects him at the end of the book, he reduces her also to something he needed to help pass the time: '[T]ener lo que se llama *un amor* en el territorio de paso, en *quién* pensar, esa fue la resolución, y fue el proyecto [...] [L]as relaciones no consanguíneas [...] jamás son fructíferas ni muy interesantes, y sin embargo parecen ser necesarias para el pensamiento [...] Para que no sufra de abatimiento' (pp.208-9). The tendency of love-affairs to disintegrate when they change from ideal to real is a theme that is explored in *Corazón tan blanco.* It is of course the most important and often written-about identity search in the modern novel, nevertheless it is reworked in new ways by Marías within the context of 'lo que pudo ser'. The romantic love affair, as everyone knows, promises an end to being alone, a fusion of identities, both physical and emotional, or perhaps forgetting the self in adoration of the other, in any case it is *the* prescribed method for happiness. In these novels the women are on the whole stronger than the men in terms of having worked out the meaning and the self-deception necessary to maintain a liveable illusion of self.

The concept of writing the novel to save past experience is not, in Marías's case, motivated by a redemptive belief. This can be explained by considering his statement that 'Si algo no es contado, es difícil tener constancia de que haya sucedido'.[22] The obverse of this is that what has been told, has also, in a real way, happened. One good reason the narrator/author is keen on 'saving' this particular story is to do with the fact that three of the characters in it are dead at the time of writing. The narrator, so envious of the gravity he read in Eric's face, had not attended a death, he lacked his 'own' dead. This is the story, it seems, of *his* dead, people he knew who died. He hopes by writing about them that the weight of their deaths will rub off on him, relieve him of the lightness of his 'perturbación': '[E]stoy haciendo ahora este esfuerzo de memoria y este esfuerzo de escribir, porque de otro modo sé que acabaría borrándolo todo' (p.69), he says. And it is this act of telling, finally, which is the core of the self. In telling of others we tell ourselves.

The problematic concepts of self and identity underlie the theme of 'perturbación' which sets the tone throughout *Todas las almas* and *Corazón tan blanco.* The points of reference which are used in relation to these problems are the eternal ones — the love affair, the horizon of death, friendship, the family. In *Corazón tan blanco* identity is conceived of and

---

22   *Corazón tan blanco,* p.69.

given more prominence as a concept of difference or uniqueness. But in this chapter an attempt has been made to read *Todas las almas*, insofar as identity is conceived, as a lost sameness. The narrator tries to recreate his understanding of himself according to a prescribed formula: a nostalgic attempt which fails. The new identities he tries to construct, be they lover or father or even romantic loner — the down-and-out Gawsworth figure — always run parallel to or intertwine with that of story-teller. As such narrator and author are drawn together in a curious double-act, which will be discussed in the chapter on autobiography.

CHAPTER TWO
Memory and oblivion: personal and rural identities in the narrative writings of Julio Llamazares

JOHN MACKLIN

Julio Llamazares is a writer who has enjoyed both critical acclaim and popular success with works that are an evocation of life in rural Spain in the period since the Civil War. His work is an exercise in memory, but not nostalgia, for he shares the conviction of Paolo Portoghesi, written from the quite different perspective of the postmodern architect, that 'It is not the cult of memory, but the loss of memory, which will make us prisoners of the past'.[1] In addition to two books of poetry, *La lentitud de los bueyes* (1979) and *Memoria de la nieve* (1982), a collection of articles, *En Babia* (1991), and an account of a local festival in León, *El entierro de Genarín* (1981), Llamazares has produced four narrative works, *Luna de lobos* (1985), *La lluvia amarilla* (1988), *El río del olvido* (1990), and *Escenas de cine mudo* (1994). These narratives, apparently very different, are united by a number of preoccupations such as the passing of time, the role of memory, landscape and place, and by a series of recurring motifs, images and symbols. There are also in these narratives undoubted autobiographical resonances, explicit in the case of *El río del olvido*, more implicit in the first novel, *Luna de lobos*, and we can discern a progression through these works whereby the authorial voice and the narratorial first person become increasingly indistinguishable. The link between the works, however, is provided by the concern with identity, which is explored through representation of a return to origins. In Llamazares's work, identity is not conceived of in terms of postmodernist linguistic constructs, but it is nonetheless experienced as precarious and evanescent, seeking solidity and security in the physical reality of the present and the reconstructed memories of the past. Whereas for postmodernism identity is inherently precarious in itself, for Llamazares it is precarious in the sense that it is threatened with disappearance. Nicolás Miñambres has written: 'Cualquier lector que se acerque a la obra de Julio Llamazares comprobará que el poder de evocación para poetizar recuerdos y vivencias a

---

Paolo Portoghesi, *After Modern Architecture*, trans. by Meg Shore (New York: Rizzoli, 1982), p.111.

través de la memoria poética constituye el objetivo fundamental de su obra'.[2] By establishing an indissoluble link between the individual and his community, Llamazares forges a narrative of rural identity, with roots in the Romantic ideal of living close to the land and which persists in a strong tradition of writing in twentieth-century Spain, from the 'paisajistas' of the early century to the rural novel of the post-Civil War period, but also one which, in its untroubled mimeticism, stands in contrast to more the audacious and problematical explorations of modern identity described elsewhere in this book. It should perhaps be pointed out that Llamazares does not see himself within the context of *nueva narrativa española*, a phenomenon about which he is largely sceptical. In an article written for *El País* (4 June 1991) and collected in *En Babia*, he writes:

> El fenómeno de la *nueva novela* es sin duda uno de los más curiosos de la vida cultural de los últimos años. Tras un largo diluvio en el que los novelistas españoles, eclipsados por la censura, primero, y por los latinoamericanos más tarde, vivieron años de vacas flacas (confinados en el arca de Noé del experimentalismo y condenados por ello al anonimato), de repente la situación dio un giro de 180 grados y comenzaron a acaparar las mejores cuotas del mercado editorial hispánico. El fenómeno coincidió con el despertar político, económico y social de la llamada España democrática y, paradójicamente también, con el *boom* de la *movida*, esto es, del diseño y de la imagen. Seguramente ocurría que, después de un largo tiempo en el que los españoles nos dedicamos a conocer la *verdad* que hasta entonces había sido vedada — y que supuso, por tanto, el apogeo del ensayo — volvimos a sentir esa dulce atracción de la *mentira* que es tan vieja como el hombre y que tiene en la novela su territorio más abonado.[3]

The success of Llamazares's work, in Spain and elsewhere, particularly in France, seems to bear some relation to its apparent simplicity. Set in a countryside far removed from the postmodern city whose typographies, as Judith Drinkwater demonstrates elsewhere in this volume, provide a metaphor for both alienation and identity, or from the sophisticated cosmopolitan world of Javier Marías, and free of the borrowed strategies of foreign models, his novels seem to inscribe themselves within a specifically Spanish tradition, most clearly seen in Unamuno's intrahistoric vision, in

---

2   Nicolás Miñambres, '*La lluvia amarilla*, de Julio Llamazares: el dramatismo lírico y simbólico del mundo rural', *Insula*, 502 (1988), 20.

3   Julio Llamazares, *En Babia*, p.118.

which a timeless world is recreated through memory as a refuge from the narratives of modernity. It is what Juan Marsé had in mind when he commented that in contemporary Spanish narrative 'la imaginación es memoria'.[4] These narratives are testimonies to a disappearing world written without irony in a carefully worked Castilian prose by a writer sensitive to the poetic power of words. Yet insofar as the reader constructs a narratorial persona from these texts it appears as in some way unrooted, marginalised, melancholic, even in its place of refuge. In this, he resembles other melancholic narrators whose 'malestar' or 'perturbación' are described in this volume, most particularly in the works of Marías. The effort to recall a way of life that has been lost, through industrialisation, through migration, or indeed through the apparently endless creation of dams and reservoirs which engulf villages and displace whole communities, transcends any social concern to become an attempt to fix identity, both rural and personal, through the weaving of a narrative built upon the complementary processes of memory and forgetting. But Llamazares's attitude is not one of hope, nor even of nostalgia, as he explains in an interview: 'Porque no hay esperanza y sin esperanza tampoco hay nostalgia, que es una esperanza hacia atrás en la que ni siquiera cabe la posibilidad de que el azar impulse su cumplimiento'.[5]

Julio Llamazares's first novel, *Luna de lobos*,[6] relates the story of a group of Republicans continuing the struggle against Franco, but effectively on the run, in the mountains around León. The author recounts in 'Adiós a Gorete', first published in *El País* and collected in *En Babia*, how he had heard the stories of these men in his childhood and how they took on mythical dimensions in his mind.[7] The main character is based on one individual, Gorete, who lived for eleven years, three months and five days in a cave near his village, completely alone. Some of the apparently most fantastic events of the novel have in fact a basis in reality, while the whole narrative is imbued with the legendary quality surrounding the stories of these men which have persisted in popular memory. In one sense, the novel traces a history of defeat and, to a degree, glorifies the sacrifice and loss of the vanquished of the Civil War, thereby creating a minor modern epic. Llamazares, however, has other preoccupations, for he is concerned with the progressive isolation and loneliness of these individuals, their loss of identity, and their desire to

---

4 Samuel Amell, 'Conversación con Juan Marsé', *España Contemporánea*, 1 (1988), 86.

5 José María Marco, 'Julio Llamazares sin trampa. Entrevista realizada por José María Marco', *Quimera*, 80 (1988), 24.

6 Julio Llamazares, *Luna de lobos* (Barcelona: Seix Barral, 1985). All references are to this edition and are incorporated in the text of the chapter.

7 *En Babia*, pp.94-97.

preserve it through maintaining contact with their village, family and friends. This in turn leads to an intense evocation of their rural environment, creating a curious dissonance between the violence and dejection of their situation and the peculiar rhetoric of this evocation. The link between defeat and returning to one's roots is articulated clearly by Llamazares in an interview with José María Marco in *Quimera*: 'Son gente derrotada, pero que encuentra en la derrota una estética superior a la del triunfo y además se aferra a unas raíces y a un paisaje que sabe que no existen tampoco porque son una imagen del deseo. Es gente condenada de antemano, que lo sabe pero que no por ello renuncia'.[8] Observations such as this suggest that Llamazares, while he cannot be inscribed within the deviant and often highly theorised production of other writers of his generation, is nonetheless touched by anxiety about the self and the world. Past and present, self and world, are, in Llamazares's telling phrase, images of desire. Each of his four narratives explores, seeks, recreates or explains the past. On one level, this is a kind of nostalgia: for the *maquis*, a desire to reintegrate into normal life, to be secure in the confines of family, community and place. More generally, a persistent sense in these works is a longing for a simpler, more primitive, life, whose narrative will offer an escape from the uncomfortable narratives of modernity. While major writers in Spain, and Goytisolo is the most distinguished example, explore personal and national identity as inseparable, the national assumes little importance in Llamazares whose work is entirely focused on the region, and especially the rural, which in some basic way seems the locus of identity, construed as stable, permanent and outside the flux of time and history. Llamazares's aim is not so much to preserve the rural way of life as to preserve its memory. To this extent there is a sociopolitical dimension to his work and it seems to confirm the force of Antonio Muñoz Molina's remark that 'Puede que una de las tareas de la novela española sea ahora mismo utilizar la memoria como una provocación contra la amnesia que patrocina el poder'.[9] The desire to capture the past through memory operates on several levels in Llamazares's first novel.

Luna de lobos is recounted in the first person and, despite the fact that it is a narrative of the past and covers a period from 1937 to 1946, is written in the present tense. This imparts to the historical text a kind of immediacy which underscores the intensity of the struggle for survival. Arguably, identity is totally absorbed in the struggle to survive. The text opens with an anonymous narrator who names the other characters — Ramiro, his brother, eventually identified as Juan, Gildo and the 'yo' of the narration, who is Angel.

---

8   *Quimera*, 80, 24.
9   Antonio Muñoz Molina interviewed by Constantino Bértolo, 'Insistencia', *El Urogallo*, 36 (1989), 58-59.

This 'yo' has the conventional function of authenticating the narrative. None of the protagonists is ever described and only the most rudimentary details of their previous existence is given. Indeed, the fullest description of them is given in the wanted posters which reduce their identities to a set of physical characteristics and a set of political allegiances. This is in contrast to the many vivid descriptions of the landscape, though this is often characterised by hostility, darkness and oppression. Death hangs over the narration from the outset, in the characters' flight before it, in their own identification with it, in its association with 'soledad', and in the death of the dog in the first sequence. Against this is set memory, recollections of home and the past, evoked by the meal in the peasants' house, 'la memoria atravesada por antiguos sabores familiares' (p.15) and then brought back by the sight of the village, 'un alud de imágenes' (p.18), 'los paisajes familiares que nunca había olvidado' (p.19). Identity is sustained by relationships — Gildo is identified by his birthplace and by the person he married (p.20) — but these have been broken by circumstances. Their isolation brings death, and the conditions of their lives, in the mine where they are hiding, eliminate memory, time, and awareness, which are the ciphers of identity. 'Es como si estuviéramos muertos. Como si, fuera de aquí, no hubiera nada' (p.27). Although isolation might seem the appropriate condition for confronting the 'essential' self, as will be the case in *La lluvia amarilla*, here it eliminates difference, removes choice and agency, leading to passivity and sameness. The sameness is reinforced by the use of the present tense and by a technique of repetition — of details, of preoccupations, of actions. What once distinguished these men as individuals no longer exists. A security of being would only, it seems, be assured by the existence of a continuity between former and present selves which would guarantee some kind of essence or integrity, whereas this core of identity is in fact compromised by a specific set of socio-political circumstances. They are refugees, men on the run, *maquis*, and this positioning of them, in relation to place, to family, to authority, also constitutes their identity. This raises anguished questions about the nature of identity, of the inaccessibility of the other. A desire for permanence, fixity, is undermined by transience and change. Angel, for example, no longer recognises the Ramiro he had known, or created, in the past:

A veces me resulta difícil reconocer en él aquel niño tímido con el que tantos días compartí los juegos de la escuela o el cuidado del ganado en las vegas de La Llánava. Me resulta difícil porque ahora, frente a mí, hay ya sólo un hombre lejano e inaccesible, un animal acorralado que sabe que, más tarde o más temprano, acabará acribillado a balazos en cualquiera de esos montes que ahora observa con mirada indescifrable (p.61).

Alienation has replaced community, which is now represented only in memory. In the final part of the novel, Angel is a stranger to those who should know him when, at the village fair, he mingles with others unaware of his 'auténtica identidad', imbued with the sensation of being someone else 'como si no fuera yo' (p.129), whereas those who are hostile to him, his enemies, 'ni un solo instante se olvidan de mí' (p.128). But this 'me' is only the fugitive, the only identity which is not condemned to oblivion is the inauthentic, the accidental, one. He can only find vaguely familiar faces among the crowd. They are now 'rostros imprecisos. Rostros borrosos [...] en los que sin embargo no me fue difícil descubrir el recuerdo lejano de antiguos alumnos y vecinos [...] Todos inalcanzables para mí, al otro lado del destino. Todos ajenos por completo a mi presencia junto a ellos' (p.130). With his final companions killed, he is confined within an almost total solitude and loses more and more of his humanity until ultimately he has to accept the inevitable and cut his final links with his family after the death of his father. His desire to retain his ties of kinship in abnormal circumstances fails and his continued existence in the boundary world between life and death, between community and isolation, is impossible. His defeat is summarised in the final line of the novel: 'Sólo hay ya nieve dentro y fuera de mis ojos' (p.153). This is also a kind of insight, for if the coordinates of identity are variable, if they can be removed in forgetting, that sought after kernel of being resides only in the consciousness of the individual and it too is shown to be unreliable.

In an interesting, if somewhat over-argued, article which draws heavily on the ideas of Michel Foucault on crime and punishment, in particular the notion of surveillance, Susan L. Martin-Márquez suggests that *Luna de lobos* 'is structured by a visual regime which could be characterised as panoptic'.[10] Foucault's analysis of Jeremy Bentham's panopticon emphasises the importance of surveillance in contemporary society and in *Luna de lobos* observing, seeing and being seen, hiding, are all central elements in the maquis' predicament. The Civil Guard observe from their strategically positioned barracks, the maquis observe the countryside from their vantage-points and seek to evade the gaze of their pursuers and persecutors. They can see, but are unseen. Martin-Márquez is able to demonstrate the importance of the visual sense in the novel and singles out episodes, for example, the killing of the Civil Guard through the eye, which cumulatively underline its importance. As Ruth Christie has demonstrated in relation to Javier Marías's *Todas las almas*, one's sense of identity is inseparable from being recognised by others. As Angel's failure becomes more apparent, his

---

10   Susan L. Martin-Márquez, 'Vision, Power and Narrative in *Luna de lobos*: Julio Llamazares' Spanish Panopticon', *Revista Canadiense de Estudios Hispánicos*, vol.xix, 2 (1995), 380.

powers of perception decrease: he is hidden in the darkness of the pit and eventually disappears from view as he goes into exile.[11] The theme, and the grammar of reference which accompanies it, is, as we shall see, continued in Llamazares's next novel.

La lluvia amarilla[12] is Llamazares's second novel and recounts through memory the final years of the life of Andrés de Casa Sosas, the final inhabitant of the village of Ainielle, in the Aragonese Pyrenees. The author's concern with the disappearance of rural Spain is well-known — he himself was born in the now vanished village of Vegamián in León — but this novel merely uses this phenomenon as its starting-point. It takes up the themes which were prominent in *Luna de lobos* — solitude, memory, community, death, nature, decline and decay — but in a much more concentrated manner. The narrative is still a first-person one, but much more intimate and intense and, while there is some narration of external events, the focus is essentially on the individual coming face to face with himself in a situation of extremity. This was also true of the earlier novel, but here we find a much more obsessive probing of the nature of identity and of the role of language, narration and memory in forging it. We are confronted here with a sustained focalisation of the narrative through the perspective of a character whose perceptions are limited, essentially by the force of his desire, but also by physical (both corporal and geographical) constraints. *La lluvia amarilla* is a classic exposition of the scripted self poised precariously between fixity and evanescence. While it could be said to be a kind of interior monolgue, it nevertheless lacks the random, associative quality of the inner life and partakes rather of the kind of internal structure we associate with writing. Writing, as Llamazares conceives it, is 'lo que queda del tiempo que pasa'.[13] *La lluvia amarilla* is an attempt to come to terms with the past, to attempt to know it and retain it, in the face of a desperate present, but this past can only be known through its traces, of which the ruins of the village are an appropriate correlative. While the narrative opens with a kind of certainty, in the emphatic future tense, as the protagonist narrates the discovery of his body after his death, certainties dissolve under the weight of loss and solitude. That the novel has these concerns is made apparent in Chapter 4. In the reconstruction of himself, Andrés relies on memory and is aware of its fallibility. Aware of 'la presencia obsesiva de mi cuerpo' (p.39) as a sign of the materiality of his physical self (which, incidentally, is barely described in

11 This theme, of being hidden and buried underground, is repeated in *El río del olvido* in the story of Eufemiano Díaz González, 'El topo de La Mata'.

12 Julio Llamazares, *La lluvia amarilla* (Barcelona: Seix Barral, 1988). All references are to this edition and are incorporated in the text of the chapter.

13 *Quimera*, 80, 24.

the text), he is doubtful of the reliability of his senses, especially sight. Llamazares's novels frequently allude to eyes, looks, sight, and accord a special importance to the visual, but here sight and memory are superimposed, as image is suspected of supplanting reality. In similar manner, the self is reconstructed as image: 'La soledad, es cierto, me ha obligado a enfrentarme cara a cara conmigo mismo. Pero, también, como respuesta, a construir sobre recuerdos las pesadas paredes del olvido' (p.40). This solitude is intense after the suicide of Sabina when unself-conscious experience gives way to an endless ruminating upon and patterning of existence: 'A partir de ese día, la memoria fue la única razón y el único paisaje de mi existencia' (p.40). Time dissolves into memory and reflection upon self leads to an inevitable dissociation from self: 'he vivido de espaldas a mí mismo' (p.41). Extreme self-consciousness leads to a loss of the unity of the self as Andrés asserts his non-being, his sense that it is not he who is wandering through the village, sitting by the fire, going to bed. Such a view implies a core of being which is mysterious, hidden and impenetrable and which is distinct from its apparent externalisation and certainly from its recollection in narrative. The novel points to a problematical sense of identity, at least a sense that one is intrinsically divided. While Llamazares does not exhibit a postmodernist distrust of language and seems to subscribe as a novelist to a broadly mimetic conception of narrative, he links memory and language as instruments of confusion: 'al igual que las palabras, cuando nacen, crean silencio y confusión en torno suyo, los recuerdos también dejan bancos de niebla en su alrededor' (p.41). Language and memory had earlier been linked in neighbours' fireside conversations during long winter nights (p.20), here serving as a support to community. Left alone, however, Sabina and Andrés rarely communicate: 'Parecía como si las palabras hubieran perdido de repente todo su significado y sentido' (p.24). Language is conventional, routine, inconse-quential, but in conditions of extremity its limited value is exposed and the power of silence assumes its full force.

If there is in the text an interplay between language and silence, other tensions also manifest themselves, such as that between topographical precision and hallucinatory states. The opening of the narrative traces the journey of the villagers to Ainielle to find Andrés, dead or alive, and the route, the positioning of landmarks and buildings, is carefully recorded. In Andrés's own wanderings through the deserted village, equal emphasis is placed on exact spatial references. Topography provides a kind of security. After the winter, which homogenised the landscape, the contours and outlines of the village and its surroundings are revealed. Emphasis is placed upon seeing these features and sight is crucial for identity in the sense of positioning oneself in relation to the world. As in *Luna de lobos*, the visual is given a peculiar prominence. For example, in a scene analogous to the killing of the Civil Guard, Andrés kills the boar with a shot through the eye (p.20). Alongside this, however, are Andrés's imaginings, first the sound of the dead Sara's breathing, precisely located in the room where she died, then the presence of the dead Sabina in the house during his bouts of delirium after being bitten by a viper. When the certainty of perception breaks down, the certainty of identity is called into question. It can be no accident that Andrés dwells on 'las últimas miradas de los muertos' (p.73) and links look, life and death. The way in which Andrés reacts to the photograph of Sabina is significant: the eyes seem to assure her continued presence in the house and he feels the need to avoid her gaze. The steeple of the village church is emblematic is this connection as it seems to characterise the destruction of Ainielle: 'el sólido bastión de la espadaña que todavía se yergue sobre la destrucción y la ruina de la iglesia como un árbol de piedra, como un cíclope ciego cuya única razón de pervivencia fuese mostrarle al cielo la sinrazón de un ojo ya vacío' (p.13). But perception in this work is indissolubly linked to memory which appropriates what is seen, familiarises it and interiorises it: 'Los ojos se habitúan a un paisaje, lo incorporan poco a poco a sus costumbres y a sus formas cotidianas y lo convierten finalmente en un recuerdo de lo que la mirada, alguna vez, aprendió a ver' (p.34).

La lluvia amarilla is not essentially an attempt to recover the past through memory, but a reflection on the workings of memory in the creation of self and identity. What constitutes Andrés is never fully defined as he approaches the status of the shadows which surround the fire in the house at night. The frontier between life and death is blurred as he wonders to which state he belongs. The subject of self-writing is in any case liminal, situated as it is between the private and the public, the personal and the social. The narrator's isolation, the fact that others have forgotten him, his blurred perceptions, all indicate a kind of death. For him, his identity is bound up with the continuation of his village and his fidelity to it, to which he needs to cling tenaciously, and which constitutes his purpose and being, but there are other perspectives on him, other constructions of his being. Madman is one, for he sacrifices family, comfort, sanity even, to retain his roots in the village to which he belongs, aware that his and its survival are intertwined, his death and its death are inseparable. Like *Luna de lobos*, *La lluvia amarilla* is filtered through the consciousness of an individual who is progressively isolated. Whereas the former novel includes action and narrative, and concedes a degree of objective validity to the world, the latter is almost entirely introspective, juxtaposing events, things, experiences and elements of nature into a final stream-of-consciousness before the onset of death. This is the meaning of the novel's title. In Llamazares's words, 'es una metáfora del paso del tiempo, de ese color que cogen las fotografías con el paso del tiempo. Aquel hombre, en su locura, piensa que es una lluvia que va mojando los papeles y las cartas y los calendarios'.[14] As he approaches death, he increasingly questions his own identity, is less and less secure in his own being, feels alienated from himself. He cannot bear to look at his own image in a mirror, to see himself outside of himself. He hears the dying words of others and realises that he is the intersection of the voices of others ('el eco de otras voces', (p.113)), not a unique individual. He loses his sense of unity and feeling of control over himself and over his world. *La lluvia amarilla* contributes to an important strand in modern literature which aims to explore, define, and perhaps even defend, the self. In its use of the first-person narrative, however, it must inevitably confront the limitations of that goal. The use of 'yo' irremediably locates the text in the present, cuts it off from the past it tries to recover. As a pronoun it is inseparable from the moment of narration, denied contact with the past, exists only in its own enunciation. Unlike the classic third person of realist writing, whose omniscience seems to authenticate the verisimilitude of the text, the first person is inherently uncertain, open to question, and ultimately self-referential. The only identity it can claim is the identity created by its own writing. The autobiographical project which is undertaken in *La lluvia amarilla* is inevitably circumscribed by the limits of the 'yo' which cannot escape the parameters of its present discourse, of its own scripting. It is grounded in the actuality of the body at the moment of the body's own dissolution in death. This awareness accounts perhaps for the particular potency of the novel, for its attempts to preserve the past intact, in a kind of insane fidelity, are shown to end only in the presentness of the moment of autobiographical articulation, in this case, death. In *Escenas de cine mudo*, this idea is developed further in that the fusion of the narrative voice and that of the author is almost complete.

Escenas de cine mudo is Llamazares's most recent novel, and he is insistent that it should be called so, despite its clear autobiographical features. In terms very reminiscent of Unamuno, he insists that 'toda novela es autobiográfica y toda autobiografía es ficción'.[15] This introductory note is signed 'El Autor' and stresses the links which connect the work to the author's own experience and to a particular reality. Llamazares is concerned in this work with the workings of memory, with the interplay between memory and oblivion, as he engages, through the contemplation of a set of old photographs, in the reconstruction of his childhood in Olleros de Sabero. While the theme is commonplace, the implications of Llamazares's creative

---

14   *Quimera*, 80, 24.
15   Julio Llamazares, *Escenas de cine mudo* (Barcelona: Seix Barral, 1994), Author's Note.

endeavour in terms of modern writing are interesting. Postmodern fiction has, for example, been very much concerned with cinematic representation (Salman Rushdie, Manuel Puig), and also with photographic models (Juan Goytisolo, Michael Ondaatje), exploring their potential and inadequacies. Llamazares finds an image in old rolls of film, lost in the projection room, for the workings of memory. Narrative is used as a means of understanding, one that is communicational (between writer and reader) as well as private. But whereas photographs are static, narrative is dynamic and the photographs, like the cinema posters, merely provide the stimulus for the weaving of a narrative, 'Sólo que éstas son las de mi vida y por eso, yo soy el único que les puede dar sonido y movimiento' (p.39). In the case of *Escenas de cine mudo*, Llamazares seeks to understand his own past, that of the author, and here too the novel connects with pressing contemporary concerns. Broadly, there are two ways of conceiving identity, either as something fixed and stable, an essence as a unique individual endowed with subjective integrity, or as a social or linguistic construct subject to fragmentation and provisionality, to being sited in different positions. The divide is between autonomous identity and social construct. The former is the individual of liberal humanism, in the words of Victor Burgin, 'an autonomous being, possessed of self-knowledge and an irreducible core of "humanity", a "human essence" in which we all partake, an essence which strives over history progressively to perfect and realise itself'.[16] The latter accepts the argument that identity is constituted as a matrix of subject-positions and subjectivity as linguistically and discursively constructed. This is the formulation put forward in poststructuralist critiques of the subject, and its predominance can be said to account in narrative for the movement from the notion of subject as a unified ontology to that of subject as a fragmented epistemology. We have, for example, become accustomed to post-structuralist or deconstructionist assertions of the death of the author, first shockingly expressed by Roland Barthes in 1968:

The Author, when believed in, is always conceived as the past of his own book [...] The Author is thought to *nourish* the book, which is to say that he exists before it, thinks, suffers, lives for it, is in the same relation of antecedence to his work as father to his child. In complete contrast, the modern scriptor is born simultaneously with the text, is in no way equipped with a being preceding or exceeding the writing [...] We know now that a text is not a line of words releasing a single 'theological' meaning (the 'message' of the Author-God) but a multi-

---

16 Victor Burgin, *The End of Art Theory: Criticism and Postmodernity* (Atlantic Highlands, New Jersey: Humanities Press International, 1986), p.32.

dimensional space in which a variety of writings, none of them original, blend and clash.[17]

It is clear from his practice of writing that such a notion would have no meaning for Llamazares, for whom the novel is an intentional act in which the various parts are interconnected and have a meaning within the whole. In the specific case of autobiography, which Llamazares is at least partly engaged in, it is precisely the integrity of the individual which provides the veracity or authenticity of the text in which personal testimony is embodied in transparent language. Moreover, Llamazares's intention is to recover a sense of what constitutes an individual, what makes him unique, and to discover the part played by memory in that process. In the novel he writes: 'la memoria es una mina oculta en nuestro cerebro. Una mina profunda, insondable y oscura, llena de sombras y galerías, que se va abriendo ante nuestros ojos a medida que avanzamos dentro de ella; una mina tan profunda como los hundimientos de nuestros sueños' (p.107). In terms of identity, writing is both affirmation and discovery. His activity as author is central to this process. That does not mean, however, that there are no indeterminacies in this process, for Llamazares is equally Unamunian in his inability to determine what is real and what is invention, what was seen and what was dreamt. Nevertheless, Llamazares ascribes this to psychological processes, the workings of consciousness, and not to any linguistic or cultural conditions, or to interplays of meaning, or to the fictional constructions of discourse. His life is like stills from a film 'a la que sólo puede dar vida el foco distorsionado de la máquina del tiempo' (p.39). His work, therefore, for all its conventionality, is concerned with the process of narrative reconstruction of a past and partakes of an essential quality of all narrative. As Peter Brooks puts it: 'We live immersed in narrative, recounting and reassessing the meaning of our past actions, anticipating the outcome of our future projects, situating ourselves at the intersection of several stories as yet not completed'.[18] In Llamazares's case, the urgency of writing his memories is to preserve them before they are totally lost in oblivion. Llamazares writes to combat the passing of time, which threatens identity. Death and the passing of time are the dominant notes of the text, inherent in its theme, and evoked constantly in the pages of the narrative: 'el paso del tiempo y la impotencia y la angustia de no poderlo parar' (p.49). Another opposition played with in the text is that between flux and stasis, between movement and contemplation. For Llamazares, life can only be apprehended

---

17   Roland Barthes, *Image - Music - Text*, selected and trans. by Stephen Heath (Glasgow: Fontana Collins, 1977), p.146.
18   Peter Brooks, *Reading for the Plot* (New York: Random House, 1984), p.3.

when at a standstill, but this apprehension is only partial, for all the movement in between has been lost. Again, a cinematic image is used to describe this, gaps or cuts in the film which appear only as darkness on the screen. The remembered parts of life are interspersed with lacunae of darkness, parts of a life that may be significant but which are entirely forgotten. The snapshots that are put together are thus a false representation, a partial identity, and when the lacunae become more frequent the possibility of intelligibility is lost. Llamazares's narrative therefore contains an acknowledgement of its own limitations, an acceptance that the identity being reconstructed through photographs and storytelling is only one of many possible versions. This perhaps accounts for the many moments of distance which recur in the work: between the photographs themselves which are related only by the narrative, but which are unconnected and even appear not to represent the same individual, between the present and past, between the author and the people he is viewing, as in the view on the bridge: 'El (abismo) que yo veo ahora se abre entre ellos y yo y es tan profundo y oscuro que ni siquiera la mirada del fotógrafo que, sin saberlo, comenzó aquel día me sirve ya para poder cruzarlo sin que el vértigo del tiempo me llene de nostalgia y de melancolía' (p.56). This repeated image of the void seems to underscore the frustration of the attempted recuperation of the past self, often likened to a phantasm, which the photograph seems to envelop in 'el ojo oscuro y mudo del abismo' (p.25). Although Llamazares seems to adhere to the notion of a centre of self, this is not without its problems and it seems perhaps safer to discern a more interesting equation in which essence is not denied but accepted as something on to which more is added, a kind of interplay between fixity and fluidity, in which the self is never definitive or precise, but is nonetheless more than the sum of a number of perspectives, interpretations or positionings.

Escenas de cine mudo, interestingly, begins with a brief social history of Olleros in what could appear to be the most objective part of the narrative, asserting a belief in the importance of both place and history. These are perhaps positioned in order to counteract the inevitable presentness of autobiographical writing which is linked inextricably to the present discourse of the enunciating 'yo'. The place of the past is in some way asserted first, even if it is in the suspect language of the social historian intent on offering explanations. Interestingly, Olleros is shown as the site of nature's resistance to exploitation, for all attempts at successful mining, with its attendant social ills (lung disease, environmental blight, displacement of families) come to nothing. Personal and social history are intertwined, but are equally shown to be distinct. Identity is neither stable, unitary, existing outside history, but neither is it merely a political, linguistic or cultural construct. It is on this background with these implications that Llamazares constructs his narrative based on an old family album. The attraction of photographs for the author is twofold: firstly they appear to halt the passing of time and, secondly, they accord a particular importance to the visual. In holding still the fleeting moment, the fortuitous, the incidental, the contingent, a photograph converts the past into a permanent present:

> En la lucha de los hombres contra el tiempo — esa lucha denodada e interminable que todos sostenemos sin éxito hasta la muerte — la fotografía se ha revelado más eficaz que la pintura o que la novela. Entrelazando el miedo y la maravilla, lo burdo y lo teatral, la fotografía, al revés que aquéllas, nace de lo cotidiano, de la humildad de la luz, de la anécdota, para hacer lo irreal real y lo fugitivo eterno. Tal vez por eso, las fotografías más verdaderas, más auténticas, son aquellas que reflejan escenas sin importancia o momentos de la vida intranscendentes (p.127).

Llamazares reveals himself here to be engaged on a quest for a realm that transcends time and history, aware of his alienation from the actual present (in his hotel room in Chicago, in Berlin, in Baghdad, scenes from his adult life which are woven into the narrative). Llamazares's fear seems to be one of a loss of origins, of a lack of connection between his present and past identities. It is a sense of loss which was seen acutely in the disappearance of the traditional, rural way of life. Narrative seeks to fix that past so that it can appear still to exist, or at least be shown to have existed. For this reason, the narrative, through photography, concedes special importance to the visual and links it to traditional mimesis. Realistic representation implies vision and reflection and language is conceived of as essentially iconic. From the earliest moments in *Escenas de cine mudo* the emphasis is on what is seen. The vision of the photographs evokes memories which are represented in images, even if these are at times blurred and unclear and the importance of this is that the unity of visual perception appears to guarantee the existence of the individual, to reveal his distinct identity. Identity depends on the connections which are established between the different photographs and on the continuities which link them in the narrative. Both narrative and photographic record are the means whereby the author represents himself to himself, and both are the instruments by which it is hoped that identity can in some way be pinned down. What the author realises from the outset, however, is that what the photographs provoke are to an extent arbitrary inventions and that the past reconstructed is not the past as it was. This is implied from the outset when the author refers to 'estas fotos que el destino me devuelve para hacerme recordar — o ¿inventar? — aquellos años' (p.16). If Llamazares is aware of himself as phantasmal, it is because of the unreliability of memory or, more properly, of language in which memory is manifest. The language of reconstruction is detached from the reality of being which, moreover, only exists as the reconstruction, only exists insofar as language grants existence to it. *Escenas de cine mudo* is posited upon a belief in the necessity of language to preserve identity in memory and at the same time on an awareness of language as a record of forgetting. Memory and oblivion are the twin poles of identity. This is an insight which Llamazares had already articulated in his previous work, *El río del olvido*,[19] which is a kind of primitive version of *Escenas de cine mudo*. Considering in his introduction the relationship between landscape and memory (the former 'sostiene las huellas del pasado' (p.7)), Llamazares is aware that memory is in the end always destroyed, a look is never the same, and a return to origins is always frustrated:

> La memoria y el tiempo, mientras yo recordaba, se habían mutuamente destruido — como cuando dos ríos se unen — convirtiendo mis recuerdos en fantasmas y confirmando una vez más aquella vieja queja del viajero de que de nada sirve regresar a los orígenes porque, aunque los paisajes permanezcan inmutables, una mirada jamás se repite. (p.8)

This is the same anxiety about vision as before, the fact that the unity of perception which would seem to guarantee a core of stable identity does not exist. The contemplation of the photographs leads to a position where a sense of self is both reaffirmed and undermined.

The self, then, seems to be asserted above all through its own scripting. Narrative establishes connections between events and rearranges them so that they seem in some way to have purpose. Llamazares's narrative seems to imply that exterior circumstances condition the self even if they cannot be said fully to constitute it. Just as the narrative began with a particularising of Olleros, the irruption of mining into rural tranquillity, so other points of reference are placed at various stages within the work which serve to anchor it in a specific temporal context, the assassination of John F. Kennedy, the first moonwalk, Franco's motorcade, and these, like specific dates, serve to link private and public and underscore the novel's constant appeal to experience. Yet there is the latent implication that experience is inseparable from representation, making *Escenas de cine mudo* the most self-conscious of Llamazares's works. Indeed, the main characteristic of each of these 'historical' references is their inherent fictionality. Kennedy's assassination is

---

19 Julio Llamazares, *El río del olvido* (Barcelona: Seix Barral, 1990).

the child's first real intuition of a world outside Olleros, but it has a remote, unreal quality. None of his school companions have heard of him or it. The moonwalk is derided by his grandmother as entirely fictional, a simulacrum enacted only on television but not in reality. Despite considerable expectation, Franco's passing near the village is fleeting and unnoticed and gives rise to rumour about the illusory nature of his public image. In all cases the reality is submerged below the concern with its mediation. These are pointers to a process at work in the text as a whole, an awareness that the scripted self is the only self that can be known and the suspicion that beyond it lurks a self that is forever unknowable and of which the script is but a pale simulacrum. Constructing the self upon photographs is to make a representation of a representation in a kind of mimetic *mise-en-abîme*. To it can be applied Nietzsche's remark: 'I am one thing, my writings are another'.[20] To an extent, this is also to say that writing the self is an exercise in creating one's public image, an extended fabrication, the turning of fact into artefact. In this work, Llamazares identifies himself as 'El Autor'. In *El río del olvido*, he signed himself 'El Viajero'. In *La lluvia amarilla*, the writing becomes quite literally a death mask through which a self will be evaluated and understood and in which a life will be justified.

For all its apparent simplicity, then, the writing of Julio Llamazares explores identity in ways which relate to more radical explorations of the self described elsewhere in this volume. In his concern with identity in narrative, he implicitly acknowledges the role played by language in the construction of subjectivity, a formulation mostly identified with the thought of Emile Benveniste: 'And so it is literally true that the basis of subjectivity is in the exercise of language. If one really thinks about it, one will see that there is no other objective testimony to the identity of the subject except that which he himself thus gives about himself'.[21] The world is intelligible only through language and it is only through language that the self is articulated. In terms of Llamazares's reconstructions of the past and the self, identity is always divided into the narrating consciousness and the self being narrated and thus the subject is always a contradiction, never fully constructed, a dynamic process rather than a fixed identity. A simple reading of the 'autobiographical fiction' of Llamazares would work to mask this division by addressing its 'I' to the 'you' of the reader implying a stability and intelligibility in both. As Catherine Belsey observes in another context: 'This model of intersubjective communication, of shared understanding of a text which re-presents the

---

20   Friedrich Nietzsche, *Ecce Homo,* trans. by R. J. Hollingdale (Harmondsworth: Penguin, 1979), p.69.
21   Emile Benveniste, *Problems in General Linguistics* (Miami: University of Miami Press, 1971), p.226.

world, is the guarantee not only of the truth of the text but of the reader's existence as an autonomous and knowing subject in a world of knowing subjects'.[22] But within the conventions of narrative, Llamazares explicitly questions some of the premises on which such a position might be validated. He does so, not by any radical approach to language or form, but by overtly questioning the security of the individuals who people his work, from the apparent epic of *Luna de lobos* to the more thematised exploration of representation, narrative and photographic, in *Escenas de cine mudo*. While the overt context of these narratives is one of coherence and stability, the processes of narrative disturb this consistency by subjecting identity to crisis, whether through defeat and exile, or through death itself, or the inexorable passing of time. The work of Julio Llamazares betrays all the urgency of the concern with the self found in much contemporary Spanish writing. Although this concern is worked out in a broadly realistic narrative framework, Llamazares's novels nonetheless explore, in compelling and obsessive narratives of personal identity in situations of crisis, the terrible precariousness of the ego seeking to affirm itself in memory, yet condemned to the insubstantiality of memory's inevitable corollary, oblivion.

---

22 Catherine Belsey, *Critical Practice* (London and New York: Methuen, 1980), p.69.

CHAPTER THREE
Place, memory and death in José María Merino, *El caldero de oro* and *Cuentos del Barrio del Refugio.*

JUDITH DRINKWATER

José María Merino is one of the foremost exponents of post-Transition fiction in Spain, although, in common with other writers of his generation, he resists categorisation, and insists on the spontaneous nature of literary production, rather than its dependence on socio-political circumstance. One of the particular challenges in the study of his work, as critics now point out, is the breadth and depth of its reach. [1] His literary output covers the decade of the 80s and beyond, and his earlier work is notable for three particular types of focus: firstly, for the way in which it looks outside, beyond the capital/city and to the regions, and specifically to León, his native province; secondly, for the way it reaches beyond Spain, and beyond the limits of existence in time and space, in its investigation of the identity of the peoples, both historically and geographically speaking, who have made up the population of Spain as it is today; and thirdly, for its investigation of the relationship of identity with narratives of the supernatural and the imagined, and with death. His later fiction takes a closer look at Madrid, where the author now resides, and continues to place identity in the context of place, memory and death. [2]

---

1   See Emilia Velasco Marcos, 'José María Merino, La complejidad de un proyecto literario', *Insula*, 572-573 (1994), 19-21.

2   His prose fiction comprises the 1976 *Novela de Andrés Choz* (Madrid: Magisterio Español, 1976); *El caldero de oro* (Madrid: Alfaguara, 1981); *La orilla oscura* (Madrid: Alfaguara, 1985); a trilogy of adventures for children on the conquest of America: *El oro de los sueños* (1986), *La tierra del tiempo perdido* (1987) and *Las lágrimas del sol* (1989), published together as *Crónicas mestizas* (Madrid, Alfaguara, 1992) and a further volume for children, *Los trenes del verano - No soy un libro* (Madrid: Siruela, 1992); *El centro del aire* (Madrid: Alfaguara, 1991); and three volumes of short stories, *Cuentos del reino secreto* (Madrid: Alfaguara, 1982), *El viajero perdido* (Madrid: Alfaguara, 1990) and *Cuentos del Barrio del Refugio* (Madrid: Alfaguara, 1994). All page numbers in the main text of this chapter refer to the editions listed here.

Throughout Merino's work runs the motif of the 'orilla', with its plural meaning of foreign shores, and of the 'other sides' of life and the human personality to be found in death, in paranormal experience, or in the labyrinths of the mind's workings. Like Javier Marías in *Corazón tan blanco,* Merino deals with the realms of 'lo que pudo ser', although in Merino's writing this is a dimension far stranger than that found in Marías; similarly, Merino shares with Marías and Llamazares a desire to reconstruct self-identity through memory. In common with Llamazares, however, Merino's concern is not with any sort of national identity, nor indeed with specific regional identities as they might be understood in the contemporary Spain of the autonomous regions. And whilst he does preoccupy himself with the individual identity and its constitution or fragmentation, this is less from the perspective of existential dilemma than from that of the collective identity or consciousness of peoples, and the way in which these interact with time and place.

Although, as I shall outline below, much contemporary criticism (rightly) places Merino at the forefront of the new literary trends in Spain today, there is a significant sense in which his writing participates in and revitalizes preoccupations which have previously been seen in Spain. In particular, his investigation of the strata which historically have contributed to the identity of her peoples has been likened to Unamuno's ideas about *intrahistoria*, and his identification with the landscapes and figures of León (although any association explicitly with Castilla as an entity is one which he would reject) cannot fail but evoke the turn of the century writings of Unamuno, Ganivet, Azorín and others who likewise sought the essence of the dominant centre of Spain.[3] An early documentary essay, *Los caminos del Esla,* published in conjunction with Juan Pedro Aparicio, certainly evinces an interest in 'real' landscapes and social conditions in León.[4] This is not to imply that Merino's writing is in any way conservative, or that he yearns for some antiquated *casticismo* in order to make sense of the present and forge contemporary identities. This is especially not the case since his fiction deals to a considerable extent with the impact on Spanish identity of the links with the continent of America, the other 'orilla', and its indigenous inhabitants, albeit in a manner which is radically different from the treatment of other cultures such as that of an iconoclastic writer like Juan Goytisolo in *Makbara*. Rather, Spain today is rapidly being integrated into an ever more homogeneous Europe and is once again aware of its proximity to North Africa, yet

---

3   This is mentioned but not discussed in full in the only monograph on Merino: Antonio Candau, *La obra narrativa de José María Merino* (León: Diputación Provincial de León, 1992), p.70.

4   Juan Pedro Aparicio and José María Merino, *Los caminos del Esla* (León: Everest, 1980).

simultaneously is divided (often against itself) by lines of demarcation which recall ancient historical boundaries and divisions. In these circumstances, Merino's narrative brings to mind, even if it cannot resolve, those issues relating to identity — place, and mythical, traditional, collective memories of places and events — which are so much a part of the individual psyche and yet so separate from it. What he seeks to do is not so much achieve a return to origins of the type analysed by John Macklin in his chapter on the work of Julio Llàmazares, as to demonstrate how the accumulation of past experiences and past sites of experience becomes a part of identity in the present, of what we are today. Yet there is more to his conception of the relationship between identity and place than this, for Merino deals not only with 'real', concrete, flesh-and-blood worlds which precede in historical time, but also with worlds which are exterior or parallel to this one, adding a further meaning to concept of the 'orilla' which appears in so much of Merino's work, that of dimensions of identity which exist coterminously with the everyday but which (in the normal run of things) go unperceived — hence his interest in doubles, ghosts and extraterrestrial beings.

In his writings about literature and in interviews, Merino comments on the demise of the experimental and social realist literature which was seen in the Spain of the 1960s and 1970s, but, as one commentator states, 'Merino no renuncia ni al realismo ni a la literatura'.[5] He writes within the boundaries of traditional forms — novels and short stories — which often seem deceptively transparent until the narrative is underway, and explicitly or implicitly makes reference to the literary inheritance of his writings, whether this be the journals of the *conquistadores*, travel writings, Cervantes's short stories, Spanish-American magic realism, ghost stories, adventure stories or science fiction. Merino has been said to be 'el novelista que con mayor intensidad ha renovado el realismo' in Spain: his approach, however, is not mimetic.[6] Instead, he adopts a multi-layered technique in his writing which allows for the interplay of dreams, memories, race memory, literary 'memories' and the imagination in the constitution of the consciousness through which the reader's impressions of the 'real' world in the text are mediated. This is not, however, purely fantastic literature, but a textual world which, whilst replete with everyday detail, and to that extent 'realist', is moved by forces which are not of it, the forces of the irrational or the unconscious. In Merino's own words with reference to *La orilla oscura*:

---

5   Antonio Martínez Menchen, 'La doble orilla de José María Merino', *Cuadernos Hipanoamericanos*, 439 (1987), 117.

6   Santos Alonso, 'La transición: hacia una nueva novela', *Insula*, 512-513 (1989), 12.

[...] aunque el aspecto de las historias era fantástico, resultaba que, al imbricarse para formar la novela, componían un entramado realista.

Me refiero, naturalmente, a ese realismo en que la verdad de los sueños tiene tantos derechos como la verdad de la vigilia. Pues, a mi juicio, no hay ámbito más apropiado que el de la ficción narrativa para que la realidad de la vigilia y la de los sueños se emparejan y engendran un nuevo ser, victorioso de la tiranía de esa lógica convencional que suele aprisionarnos, ceñida al día, al despertar, a lo cotidiano, que quiere convencernos, obligarnos a aceptar que el tiempo es lineal y consecutivo, que los lugares son exactos e inequívocos y los personajes — las personas — individuales, diferenciados y exclusivos.[7]

In a later interview, he stresses the part played by the imagination in the apprehension of 'reality', and as a consequence the linking of both through language in the novel:

La realidad se compone, por una parte, de hechos, relaciones y normas, pero, por otra, incluye lo imaginario, que es patrimonio de la novela, precisamente, lo imaginario construido mediante la pura materia de las palabras. La novela representa lo imaginario no compulsivo, acomodado siempre a nuestra medida; por eso asumimos la posible seducción de su lectura como algo plenamente integrado en la vida cotidiana, sin perjuicio de los elementos oscuros e inefables que a su través podemos conocer o intuir.[8]

Elsewhere Merino suggests that an element of the 'fantastic' in narrative is appropriate in the contemporary world of technological marvels in which the unseen exchange of information of all sorts itself represents a whole dimension of experience which is unseen but which impinges on everyday life: 'A mí me parece que lo fantástico define muy bien la asimetría del mundo en que vivimos; un mundo un poco fantástico: iluminación, flujo de la comunicación, la simultaneidad de las noticias'.[9]

In an article entitled 'Una estética para después del posmodernismo', Gonzalo Navajas presents the outline for the literature of the 1980s in Spain which he sees as constituting the new way forward, and which productively

7   José María Merino, 'Novelar después de todo', Nuevas Letras, 5 (1986), 28-32, quoted in Candau, p.35.
8   Quoted in Santos Alonso, 'La renovación del realismo', Ínsula, 572-573 (1994), 13.
9   'Encuentro de narradores leoneses', Ínsula, 572-3 (1994), 5.

unites the best of both the 'realist', mimetic, and 'postmodernist', experimental, modes in writing. He suggests that this evolution is not simply a rejection of past modes: 'Esa configuración no aspira a la destrucción definitiva del mundo previo en el que nada parecería recuperable'.[10] Instead, the new 'configuración' follows on from the 'fase mimético-didáctica de los años 50 y 60' and 'la fase posmoderna', and in this 'tercera fase se investiga la posibilidad de reformular (e incluso cancelar) la indeterminación ética y estética posmoderna tratando al mismo tiempo de no incurrir en las limitaciones de un programa social o moral estrecho e inflexible'.[11] The new trend 'reconsidera la transparencia y el equilibrio de la episteme clásica pero no para reproducirlas sino para reposesionarlas confiriéndoles dimensiones que incorporan la reflexión moderna'.[12] This third phase he terms one of 'nostalgia asertiva',[13] and Merino's work, with its emphasis on place and memory, would seem in many respects to epitomise this new tendency. The primary focus is on nostalgia, or a 'perspectiva nostálgica'.[14] As Navajas explains :

La nostagia revela la ineptitud o impotencia del sujeto para definir coherentemente el mundo y una aceptación de que la realidad debe percibirse más como se presenta al deseo y la imaginación que a la razón. Los hechos y experiencias pasados, transformados por la imaginación, tienen una presencia más prominente y emotivamente impactante que la realidad tangible [d]el mundo pero esa falsificación aparece como acogedora frente al presente que se concibe como inhóspito para el yo.[15]

Nostalgia can therefore be interpreted not as a mere yearning for what is past, but a deliberate re-evocation of that past, in the context of the specific places in which events occurred, in order to recast the present in its mould, to evoke its traces in the present. Similarly, this nostalgia is not simply an emotional veneer to the story which is told, but a reliving of the experiences of the past in order that their accumulation may lend depth and intensity to present events.

---

10   Gonzalo Navajas, 'Una estética para después del posmodernismo', *Revista de Estudios Hispánicos*, 25 (1991), 131.
11   Navajas, 132.
12   Navajas, 149.
13   Navajas, 132.
14   Navajas, 132.
15   Navajas, 132-133.

Eduardo M. Larequi García sees Merino's fiction as opening up the limits of reality: 'Merino no pretende abandonar el mundo "real", sino más bien ampliar sus fronteras [...] tres son, a mi entender, los principales elementos constitutivos de esta nueva realidad a la que Merino quiere dar entrada en su narrativa: el mundo de los sueños, las experiencias derivadas de la imaginación y el universo de la ficción, entendido como un mundo autónomo y capaz de competir y hasta interferir en la realidad empírica'.[16] Merino himself terms his interpretation of realism 'lo real imaginario', opening up the possibilities of fiction.[17] Candau refers to this technique as the 'ensoñación', the evocation of that state of being which lies on the borders between waking and sleeping.[18] But the 'ensueño' through which Merino's characters come to perceive the complexities of their existence, is also to be found — and obsessively so in Merino's latest collection of short stories — at the boundary between life and death, in the strange limbo of those who cross the threshold of death or experience or witness near-death experiences: and Merino's fiction is important for its exploration of identity, not in terms of the here and now, social circumstance, or personal crisis, but in terms of its outer limits, seen not as a barrier to comprehension of identity (as death so often is), nor through the blur of religious consolation, but as a transforming and mysterious process in which the self is fulfilled and achieves plenitude.

The two works of prose fiction through which I wish to illustrate the role of place, memory and death in the construction of identity are *El caldero de oro* — an early novel, set in the province of León across the centuries — and *Cuentos del Barrio del Refugio*, Merino's latest collection of short stories, which centre on present-day Madrid. Merino's preoccupations are the same in both texts — the fundamental role played by the 'ensueño' in everyday life, the establishing of identity by the recuperation of past experience, the importance of place in collective identity, the fine line between the two shores of life and death — whilst the second reflects the honing of his literary technique and of his conception of identity as rooted in the genesis of narrative and the narrative of place.

In form and structure, *El caldero de oro* is at first reminiscent of so many other texts which deal in pseudo-autobiographical manner, and in flashback, with the evocation by an older, city-bound narrator, of the passage from an

---

16 Eduardo M. Larequi García, 'Sueño, imaginación, ficción. Los límites de la realidad en la narrativa de José María Merino', *Anales de la Literatura Española Contemporánea*, 13 (1988), 225-247.

17 Quoted in Santos Alonso, 'La renovación del realismo', 13.

18 Candau, 1992, p.34. For example, in *El caldero de oro*, 'Pero todo es ensoñación, o no hay ensoñación alguna y soy realmente un hombre que agoniza, un guerrero herido mortalmente', p.195.

idyllic rural childhood to the disappointments of adulthood. It is reminiscent, too, in its opening sequence, of Kafka's *Metamorphosis* (which also plays a significant part in Millás's *La soledad era esto*, discussed in another chapter in this book), and indeed spontaneous change and evolution become a feature not just of the existence of the narrator, but also of the movement of the text as the different strata of experience are revealed through it to the reader.

It is nostalgia in the broad sense already described which predominates in *El caldero de oro*, and which is embedded in the story at different levels. The text centres on the motif of the 'caldero', an ancient artefact engraved with the figures of people, animals and objects, which represents the mythical past of the narrator's people. The action of the novel takes place in the few seconds between the appearance of the narrator, Chino, wounded in a bomb attack, in the first chapter, and his death at the close of the novel, and is accompanied by Chino's musings about the 'caldero', which may or may not 'in reality' have existed. Ultimately, its real existence is irrelevant, since what is important is the belief in its mythical status, which confirms the existence of the other narrator-characters in the novel, and the layers of history to which the narrator's consciousness has access. The novel functions by relating several stories simultaneously, and these levels of narrative combine to produce a sense of the identity of Chino as an individual but also as part of the mythical collectivity: he is at one and the same time a 'real' person, and also one of the historical figures who will join the others engraved on the 'caldero': his individual existence is only important in as far as it is the sum of, and subsumes and anticipates, the other identities of which it is composed and in which it will go on to participate. Simultaneously, multiple identities are produced which exist outside the person of Chino, however much his presence may be necessary to foregrounding them: the mestizo, the 'aindiado', the Moor, the Romans, the barbarian inhabitants of the Iberian peninsula, all of whom are part of the collective memory, are present in and through his consciousness.

Yet on the most immediate level, the story is a familiar one of the return from adulthood to childhood, and from the city to the country. A student turned aspiring actor, Chino works in an insurance company in Madrid, and upon the news of the death of his grandfather returns to the village where he spent his childhood summers. His childhood and the way of life in the village are evoked in detail: 'Y los recuerdos, a pesar de ser todavía muy confusos, me traían un regusto cálido, también primaveral y veraniego; estaban todos ellos envueltos en una atmósfera de placidez; sugerían vivamente olores y reflejos; aproximaban a mí cada vez más, una presencia que, aunque incoherente, irradiaba una plenitud diáfana que la trascendía' (p.36). Chino

decides to return to live in the village which confers on him an identity which
the urban environment cannot provide:

> Ser de la capital era ser de ninguna parte, y creo que fue por eso por
> lo que me vinculé con tanto fervor al pueblo del abuelo. El pueblo del
> abuelo quedaba exacto en la memoria, con sus sombras cambiantes,
> con sus distintas luces cada hora del día. Era posible llevarlo dentro
> con todas sus características, sin olvidar ninguna. Era posible
> recordar a todos sus vecinos. Era posible conocer las historias más
> relevantes, hasta tiempos lejanísimos (p.183).

In his grandfather's house, he sleeps with the housekeeper, appropriately
named Olvido, who represents the unfulfilled desires of his youth: sexual
fulfilment, like death, brings him a sense of total fusion with the rural world of
his ancestors:

> Allí, en la oscuridad, fui olvidando que ella y yo éramos dos seres
> distintos: me parecía asumir, con ella al mismo tiempo, en una
> sincronía unánime, una nueva identidad en la que también se
> incorporaba la habitación, la casa, la noche [...] éramos la madera, el
> ladrillo, la piedra, el adobe, el yeso, el cristal. Éramos la fábrica
> misma de la casa [...] luego estaba la tierra, y también era mi cuerpo
> (pp.55-57).

His memories blend with the layers of recollection which he experiences as
he lies dying as a result of his participation in a bomb attack on a dam which
is being constructed to collect the waters of the river which feeds the region
where the village is situated. He identifies with the generations of 'warriors'
— barbarians and Romans — who have fought to preserve their way of life in
the valley against invasion, and whose first-person narratives take over the
text at several points. Further voices which enter into the narrative are those
of an ancestor who participated in the colonization of Mexico, and the
'mestizo' of a later generation who returned to reestablish a life in the village.
These narratives are quite separate from that of Chino, but are always a part
of his consciousness and of the wider scheme of things: the constant
interplay of 'yo' and 'tú' heightens the sense of these fluid identities,
representing not just the 'I' inside addressing itself, but the dialogue between
simultaneous existences and modes of being. As the wounded warrior after
the Roman invasion hears the sound of wolves feeding on the dead on the
battlefield, he realises his place in a wider scheme of things:

Has sido lobo como has sido trucha, como has sido golondrina de pecho amarillo, y toro mugidor, y gallo de mil gallinas, y cigüeña, y rebeco. En el fluir infinito de la vida has sido muchas vidas distintas, vidas que no recuerdas pero que mantuvieron a través de los tiempos tu sustancia (p.50).

The landscape, the river and the beings within it are all a part of the same endless chain of existence in which Chino, as he lies dying, knows he will also come to form a link:

El cielo es también un enorme río, un río profundísimo, eterno. Acaso las nubes serán guerreros alguna vez, porque las almas no perecen y, cuando atraviesan la laguna del olvido y llegan a los confines de la tierra, les espera otra reincarnación, incorporarse de nuevo al ciclo de la vida, que fluye continuamente, como un manantial, como las fuentes cuyo cauce es el musgo ancestral (p.191).

Yet behind all these strands of narrative runs the doubt that any of the events described occurred at all or that any of the figures evoked existed: 'Todo se mezcla: las cosas verdaderas y las soñadas. Lo que de veras sucedió, y lo que no se sabe si sucedió, y lo que puede suceder' (pp.193-194).

In *Cuentos del Barrio del Refugio*, Merino turns his attention to the inhabitants of the city. He revisits the Cervantine tale and the ghost stories of Edgar Allan Poe in a metafictional approach to narrative and its genesis which directly reflects his account of an identity tied up with the accretions of urban life over the centuries, and which can in the fullest sense of the word be said to be metaphysical.[19] The return to Madrid and the setting of the stories in the nineteenth-century 'barrios' of the city, quite apart from the questions which it may raise as to why so many contemporary novelists seem to have gravitated towards the geographical centre of Spain, presents a different focus to that of the city as a site of alienation, as seen in Millás's *La soledad era esto*, or as the site of sinister underworlds, as depicted in Múñoz Molina's *Beltenebros* or Montero's *Te trataré como a una reina*.[20] Merino's 'barrio' is primarily a community of individuals not dissimilar to the rural communities observed in his earlier narrative, whose personal dramas are tenuously interconnected by virtue of their physical proximity in

---

19   In the story entitled 'El derrocado', reference is made (p.72) to a volume of Edgar Allen Poe which was left as a legacy to the narrator.

20   Merino deals with the issue of the novelist and the capital in his frequent allusions to the writers with whom Madrid is associated, and in the story 'Los libros vacíos'.

neighbouring streets. There are constant passing reminders throughout the stories of these links: the translator in the first story, 'El caso del traductor infiel', notices two budgerigars perched on a nearby balcony (p.29), which later turn out to be the (re)incarnations of the dead mother and son of the final tale, 'Pájaros'; Rosa Mari, the narrator of 'La costumbre de casa', ends with a reference to 'la muerte de mi profesora doña Isabel, una vecina de la misma calle' (pp.52-53), whose tragedy is later recounted in 'Materia silenciosa'; the 'anticuario' who comes to buy up the household contents of the dead Doña Isabel is presumably the same person who participates in the story 'Tertulia'; and those gathered for the 'tertulia' in the story of that name comment on the viability as a story of the preceding tale, 'Para general conocimiento', which recounts the visit to the 'barrio' of an extraterrestrial being. Just as the inhabitants of the quarter are given identity by virtue of the interweaving of their existences, so also the city has a complex life of its own which contributes to this. The Madrid of *Cuentos del Barrio del Refugio* is a city whose inhabitants are ever mindful of its origins. The successive ages through which the city has passed are laid down as if they were geological strata, all existing simultaneously and in the same place, superimposed upon and superseding each other. The 'anticuario' in 'Tertulia' muses on the changes wrought by time in the city, in order to make the point that it is only through the medium of concrete objects that the past can survive to tell its tale:

Pensad lo que, ya esfumado para siempre, ha ido siendo la vida de este barrio, de este lugar, los bosques donde se cazaban los jabalíes y los corzos y los lobos que servían de blanco vivo en el establecimiento que acabó dando título a la calle de la Ballesta, la laguna cuyo recuerdo queda sólo en el pez solitario que originó el nombre de esta calle, las grutas y las pozas que marcaban el terreno con tanto carácter que acabaron incorporadas a la actual toponimia. Primero el bosque agreste, luego las casas de recreo, los conventos, las chifladuras conventuales de los iluminados, los quemaderos de la Inquisición, los palacios para la gloria del dispendio, y siempre gente bullendo de aquí para allá, en días de dolor o de juerga, según su papel en el mundo, la francesada, los chanchullos de aquel García Chico del que habló Galdós, [...], las bombas de la guerra civil sobre la gente que necesita su pedazo de pan para sobrevivir. De todo eso no queda ya siquiera un eco, pero yo consigo encontrar un brasero, un crucifijo oscuro [...] mostrando su vigencia como una venganza de lo inanimado, de lo que [...] es luego fiel contraste de nuestra brevedad y nuestra pérdida (pp.154-155).

Underneath the layers of history lie compacted all the pain and tragedy of the successive generations who have lived and died in the 'barrio'. When the fabric of the city is disturbed — in the process of restoration, demolition, the clearing out of old houses — the previous experiences and emotions resurface to trouble the existence of the present-day inhabitants, as occurs in 'Fiesta', when a group of teenagers takes over an old building, and disappear leaving only a heap of crumbling bones behind them, or 'Tertulia' in which a nobleman decides to do up his family house, only to discover reflected in a mirror uncovered in the restoration 'todas sus tragedias familiares' (p.158). In a parallel movement in individual lives, the physical environment in which they live forms the link between past and present selves: the protagonist of 'El caso del traductor infiel' has gone back to the 'barrio' where he lived as a student: 'Habían pasado bastantes años desde sus tiempos de estudiante [...] y el futuro había resultado estar compuesto de una materia muy parecida a la que formaba la realidad cotidiana de aquellos años' (p.10); the niece returning to her dead aunt's house in Madrid perceives that 'la casa de la tía Isabel parecía mantenerse inmutable, verdadera protagonista del tiempo, absorta en su espeso silencio y en su aliento a madera vieja' (p.190). And it is in endless circular walks or searches in the streets of Madrid that the protagonists unravel or weave their stories and tragedies, as in the case of Mestre in 'Bifurcaciones',[21] or the distraught, bereaved mother in 'Pájaros'. So it can be said that what is demonstrated is not the social construction of identity of the type posited in the chapter on Montero's *Amado amo* in this book, but a construction of identity on a far grander scale which is bound up with the fabric of the city and the environment, as well as with the inventions of the mind.

The identity of self in *Cuentos del Barrio del Refugio* also rests, in true Cervantine fashion, in the narrative itself, and in the power of language to create, deform and destroy identities. The self-conscious nature of the literary text is frequently made explicit in these tales: as Emilia Velasco Marcos points out: 'el autor expone su taller, sus herramientas, los materiales en bruto y [las] sucesivas fases de desbaste y pulido'.[22] The narrative which the narrators or protagonists of the successive tales construct becomes their identity, and in different ways the narrators — or the protagonists from whose point of view the tales are related — become the subject of their own narrative.

---

21   This title recalls Jorge Luis Borges' short story 'El jardín de los senderos que se bifurcan'. The influence of Borges is also apparent in the work of Javier Marías (see footnote 21, Chapter Eight).

22   Velasco Marcos, 'José María Merino, La complejidad de un proyecto literario', 19.

In 'El caso del traductor infiel', the gradual transformation of the protagonist/translator into the subject of the narrative mirrors the transformations which take place within the text. The translator takes a dislike to the main protagonist, a sophisticated female detective called Kate Courage, in the series of novels which he is translating, and to make the job more interesting deploys his professional talent, through his choice of terms in translation, in order subtly to transform and coarsen her character. In doing so he provides a model for the manipulation of character which prefigures the way in which he will also become the subject of writing. A letter of protest from a friend of the author of the Kate Courage novels is followed by a threatening letter from the author, and the appearance of a sinister visitor to the translator's flat. Finally, the translator is mugged in the street late at night. Later in the week, a manuscript of a further novel called 'El caso del traductor infiel', arrives. In it, a Kate Courage who conforms more to the behaviour patterns established for her by the translator in his translation than to the original character in the book, searches the streets and finally arrives at the translator's home just in time to see his body being put on a stretcher. At this point in the story, the translator regains consciousness after the mugging (the episode of the new manuscript having apparently been a dream), and is taken to hospital. He is on the road to recovery when Kate Courage presents herself at his bedside and the tale ends with the protagonist's realisation that 'su confusión empezaba a ser la única realidad posible' (p.39). The story is, of course, about the just desserts of a dishonest translator, but it is also about the creation of identity, as the translator himself becomes a character in a story over which he has no control, the layers of which superimpose each other until the 'true' thread of the story is lost.

In 'Fiesta', the principal character, who has pretensions to being a novelist, spies on a party being held by a group of teenagers in the apartment block opposite his own. The narrative is punctuated by his awareness of the narrative possibilities of the scene which he is witnessing: 'Ahí hay un relato, pensó de pronto él' (p.58), although it is never clear whether what he witnesses is 'real' or the result of the distortions of his imagination. He goes over to investigate the sudden silence and apparent disappearance of the youngsters, and imagines the tragedies which may have occurred in the old building: 'Pretendía imaginar relatos sin comprender que su propio relato se le escurría, subrepticio, se le escapaba sin que él pudiese entender la lógica que podía enlazar los distintos elementos' (p.66). At the close of the tale his partner comes to the window of their flat to look for him, but fails to hear him when he calls: like the lost teenagers, he too has perhaps slipped beyond human perception, out of the text and across to the other 'orilla', caught up in the dangerous web of the narrative which he has constructed.

Memory and death play cruel tricks in 'Bifurcaciones', when Mestre receives an invitation to a reunion of his university classmates, and slips into a state of 'ensoñación' which involves layer upon layer of memory, apparent recollection of imagined events, and present reality: his family seated around the television at home, his first meeting with his wife, his passionate encounter with a student friend from his youth, Irene, his memory of what his relationship with Irene could have been when they were students, his attendance at the reunion of his old university classmates. He is aware throughout his daydream of the unreality of what seem to be very real memories, and experiences:

la rareza de su intuición, sin atreverse a imaginar que, como Irene, la mujer y los adolescentes que parecían estar ante él eran también figuraciones arrancadas de una memoria casi desvanecida, y que él mismo no era sino el último intento de subsistir de un pensamiento errático, al borde de la desaparición (p.88).

In the 'ensoñación', he meets up again with Irene, the idol of his student years, confesses his passion for her and sleeps with her. As he talks of his life and family to her, he is struck again by the uncertain status of his memories, especially since her recollections of their relationship as students are obviously different from his: 'sintió de nuevo inquietud ante la sospecha, esfumada en el mismo momento de suscitarse, de que aquella imagen no se correspondiese con su experiencia personal sino que fuese sólo una figuración inconsciente, provocada al azar entre los millones de ellas vistas a lo largo de su vida, en el cine o en la propia tele' (p.94). And when he attends the reunion, there is no Irene, no picture of her on the graduation roll of honour: it transpires that she died in a boating accident shortly after leaving university. He remembers how he met Irene when they went to collect their exam results, and how in reality he then left and never saw her again. In his 'ensoñación', however, he recognises that 'el encuentro en el vestíbulo era un misterioso punto de bifurcación, donde su memoria parecía titubear' (p.103), and goes back in his memory, taking the alternative route to the one he chose in reality. He dreams of what would have happened if he and Irene had entered into a relationship: this strand of the narrative ends, inevitably, at the point of their death in the boating accident. Mestre, returned to 'reality', finds himself looking at the graduation photographs, but this time it is his face that is missing rather than that of Irene. The tale ends as Mestre's wife interrupts the reverie. '[C]omprendiendo que no es posible desandar con acierto los laberintos de la memoria' (p.111), he tells her about the invitation to the reunion. Once more in this tale, Merino's use of multiple layers of narrative creates doubt as to which is the 'true story'; Mestre's sexual encounter with Irene is presumably a dream, it seems apparent that he has not yet attended the reunion, and it is unclear in consequence whether it is Irene, or indeed Mestre himself, who is dead.

Probably, it matters very little either way whether Mestre is 'dead' or 'alive', or what is important is the sense in Merino's writing that individual identity is tied up with the fleeting moment, experienced, recaptured, but then lost in the maelstrom of memories and consciousness which is apparently shared, but never truly shared, by one or more individuals across time. Disconcertingly, this sense of self is most strongly experienced, in the *Cuentos del Barrio del Refugio* as in *El caldero de oro*, not in terms of the individual but at moments of fusion with other identities, either in sexual encounters (which in classical tradition are equated with or are a metaphor for death) or at the point of death. Mestre experiences with Irene 'una exaltación intensa, casi dolorosa, hasta que el espacio que les rodeaba pareció desmoronarse y desaparecer' (p.99), and the sexual climax transports him to 'un lugar donde el tiempo no podía prevalecer' (p.100), whilst Chino's full sense of himself, or his multiple selves, reaches plenitude in the instants preceding his death. All that is left of identity on this 'orilla', on the shores of life to which there is access, is the written word, the scripted self: 'El tiempo se consume pero los poemas resisten, pensó'.[23]

---

23   The quotation is a part of the reflections of the protagonist of 'Viaje interrumpido', p.218.

Part Two:
Re-siting the Self

CHAPTER FOUR
Autobiography as fiction in
Todas las almas by Javier Marías.

RUTH CHRISTIE

We have seen how José María Merino uses a 'multi-layered technique' to overcome the logic 'que quiere convencernos, obligarnos a aceptar que el tiempo es lineal y consecutivo, que los lugares son exactos e inequívocos y los personajes — las personas — individuales, diferenciados y exclusivos'.[1] Merino believes in narrative fiction as an ideal medium for realising these aims, for exploring the complexity of experience. Marías, on the other hand, exploits the 'multi-layered' nature of experience to cause confusion about fiction. We are presented with an undifferentiated author, narrator and protagonist in what is ostensibly an autobiographical novel. What the work of both novelists demonstrates is that concepts of identity and self are an essential element of the complex relationship between experience and language.

The genre *par excellence* of the scripted self is autobiography, and it is as 'autobiografía, pero como ficción'[2] that *Todas las almas* will be read in this chapter. The concept of giving an account of one's own life is so basic an aspect of identity and of autobiography that we tend not to question its validity. We all feel that we have an autobiography within us, and even if it is never 'set in writing', it is somehow already there as a series of memories, a continuity which is integral to our sense of self, a tale waiting, not to be told, but *re*told. The generic status of autobiography depends on the maintenance of a clear division between the fictional and the real, most particularly in the sense that the autobiography, as opposed to the fiction, has *already* happened. Autobiography is considered to be 'the inquiry of the self into its own origin and history'.[3] *Todas las almas*, in the particular way it

---

1   See Chapter Three, footnote 7.

2   Javier Marías, 'Autobiografía y ficción', in *Literatura y fantasma* (Madrid: Siruela, 1993), p.62.

3   Michael Sprinkler, 'Fictions of the Self: The End of Autobiography' in *Autobiography: Essays Theoretical and Critical*, ed. by James Olney (Princeton, New Jersey: Princeton University Press, 1980), p.342.

mixes the fictional and the autobiographical, undermines this first premise, and problematises the idea of a life as the story of a self waiting to be written, exploring as it does so aspects of identity and experimenting with new possibilities of 'scripting the self'.

In Marías's book of collected essays and lectures, *Literatura y fantasma* (1993), in which he discusses his own work at length, there is an essay entitled 'La muerte de Manur'.[4] In this essay Marías discusses his novel *El hombre sentimental* (1986),[5] in which he mixes the three planes of 'lo vivido', 'lo soñado', and 'lo imaginado'. He explains that his intention in that novel was not that the difference between these planes should be blurred, but that they should all have the same value for the reader, and should equally form part of the same story. However, he is talking about the 'lived', 'dreamed' and 'imagined' of the narrator, planes which all belong to the fictional world, or the author's 'imaginado'. In *Todas las almas* he takes the further step of including his own 'lived' in the novel. Having thus 'mixed' the two worlds, it becomes impossible to bracket together the ontological planes as simply as before; the reader cannot unquestioningly accept this extra dimension as of equal value, or 'part of the same story', for she/he is steeped in the belief that they belong inherently to different worlds. With *Todas las almas* the novels of Javier Marías enter a new phase of self-consciousness in the broadest sense, for he has not written directly of his own experience before: 'Al menos no lo había hecho *a sabiendas* de ello, que era justamente la forma en que tenía que llevarlo a cabo sin remedio en *Todas las almas*'.[6] The briefest knowledge of the facts of his life — and what we are told on the jacket of *Todas las almas* will suffice — is enough to make the reader realise, after the first couple of pages, that the novel is to some extent autobiographical. Marías himself took up a teaching post in Oxford, as does the narrator. How could he *not* write about himself and his own experiences there? This question begs others, such as whether 'semi-autobiographical' or *roman à clef* are satisfactory descriptions of this novel, and if not, then how does it subvert the various concepts and conventions of autobiography?

Todas las almas undoubtedly works within and against traditional autobiographical conventions. In his essay 'Autobiografía y ficción', Marías claims that he is drawn to write autobiography as fiction, an attraction which resulted directly in the writing of *Todas las almas*. However, there are important omissions in this essay; implicit questions which are not answered. Marías suggests three basic ways of confronting non-fictional material The first is to disguise it as fiction, the second is to present it as autobiographical,

---

4   *Literatura y fantasma*, p.73.
5   Javier Marías, *El hombre sentimental* (Madrid: Alfaguara,1986).
6   Javier Marías, 'Quién escribe', *Literatura y fantasma*, p.84.

and the third is to mix the two. It is the third method that interests him. But he offers no explanation as to why he rejects the first two, apart from calling them 'formalist', and·neither does he explain why he chooses the latter, apart from calling it 'más interesante y novedosa'. When trying to work out the evidence for what really happened and what did not in *Todas las almas,* the reader finds her/himself confused. In the essay, the following convoluted summing-up of his reasons for such a conscious mixing of fact and fiction only results in a similar *mise en abîme*:

> Es decir, que lo relatado le sucede a *él,* el autor, y al mismo tiempo *no* le sucede a *él,* el autor, en la medida en que en realidad no ha sucedido, ni a él ni a nadie en absoluto; aunque en la medida en que sucede en su obra de ficción, sea a él, el autor, y a nadie más a quien sucede. Se trata de una *mise en abîme* en la que ahora no podemos detenernos ya más. Deben de estar ustedes cansados. Sin embargo creo que es en esta delicadísima fórmula donde se encuentra la posibilidad de acometer la empresa que [...] cada vez me tienta y me interesa más [...]: abordar el campo autobiográfico, pero sólo como ficción.[7]

Why does Marías decide to 'abordar el campo autobiográfico, pero sólo como ficción'? The first two categories he mentions are rarely as clearly defined, as he himself admits: 'No se me escapa que este tipo de mezclas entre lo vivido o conocido y lo imaginado o inventado no tiene nada de particular; es más, seguramente es la base misma de la mayoría de las novelas que en el mundo son y han sido'.[8] But there is a vast difference between the unproblematic and the subversive mixing of the elements of 'lo vivido' and 'lo imaginado'. It is expected that inevitably there is a great deal of autobiography in the most fictitious work, and the converse of this is also conditionally to be expected. Fiction has long been thought of as a mass of 'acceptable lies' marked as such by means of various conventions, which distinguish it from 'unacceptable' or 'real' lies. But the earliest novels had to pass themselves off as histories before the concept of fictions which were not 'real lies' became accepted; the other reality of the fictional world has not always been the imagined world we accept today. And the division between fiction and reality has become far less comfortable and increasingly confused during the last twenty-five years. We may now even consider novels and lies *both* as fictions, the term 'lies' being an indication of cultural or social unacceptability rather than signalling their 'real' state of untruth. Writers such

---

7   *Literatura y fantasma*, p.69.
8   *Literatura y fantasma*, p.84.

as Randolph Pope consider this question of 'lies' as crucial in the definition of the autobiography. Pope states that lying is impossible in the novel, which can only contradict itself, whereas truth as verifiable is a defining feature of the autobiography. He adopts a highly pragmatic attitude to 'truth', as has already been mentioned.[9] Whether 'truth' watered down in this way still deserves the name is open to question.

As stated above, the division has been essential for the maintenance of autobiography as a genre and for the concept of autobiographical writing. And although in theory vast changes may have been made to our concepts of reality and fiction, truth and lies, in fact we only reluctantly relinquish the idea that in certain genres — autobiography being one of them — we will be told the truth; the opposition 'reality is, fiction *seems to be*' still holds. The explanation for 'mixtures' of fact and fiction has been that if a little reality is glimpsed in the world of fiction, as in the case of 'autobiographical writing', then all the better, since it goes to show how predominant the 'real' is, how fiction cannot but reflect it And in order that the reverse should not seem like a contamination, the elements of fiction that autobiography sometimes 'contains' have been considered as weaknesses on the part of the author, lapses in memory, rhetorical inaccuracies rooted in a human and understandable desire to exaggerate or hide certain facts. Two extremes which would seem to have threatened the ontological divide have not really been considered as such *because* of their extremity. These are fictions which are presented as autobiographies, such as the picaresque novel, *La familia de Pascual Duarte*, — the list is of course lengthy in Spain alone — and the argument that *all* fiction is and must be autobiographical, in that any person, place or happening described in fiction must originate in the experience of the author. In the first case the disguise seems obvious; an appeal can be made to history — how could such an uneducated man as Pascual Duarte, for example, write such polished prose? And if all fiction is in a sense autobiographical, this has been ascribed to the origin of words in the world; they mirror what goes on there, fiction being a distorting mirror in that characters and settings are 'composites' of real people and places, rearrangements which enable a more universal message to be communicated. Autobiography, in so far as it distorts, does so in the name of individual truth, it does not tell 'acceptable' lies as fiction does. By such means the fictional and the factual as conceived in relation to autobiography have been kept separate. If so many permutations have not seriously threatened the separation between the written self as real and as fictional, how and why do postmodern novels such as *Todas las almas* apparently pose such a threat? By looking at 'how' we can perhaps make more sense of

---

9   See Introduction, note 16.

'why', and thus be in a position to better understand Marías's attraction to 'abordar el campo autobiográfico, pero sólo como ficción', and the consequent implications of this for the 'scripted self'.

A conventional opening for western autobiographies is an explanation of why the task is being undertaken. The author must have some reason for wishing the reader to know that this is an account of a real life, and these reasons are usually to be found in the first few pages, when justifications and apologies are made. Again there is a long history of different gambits in Spanish literature alone, from the desire to tell of a religious conversion, or to apologise or confess, to the ironic excuses and mock-didactic reasons of the picaresque and the many other 'false' life-stories that allude to them, to the self-conscious avoidance of seeming egoistical. The gambits are various, but the convention is the same, and contributes to the reader's recognition of the autobiographical genre. An interesting and peculiarly fitting example can be found again in the work of Javier Marías's father. In the context under discussion, the opening of *Todas las almas* can be read as a challenging allusion to the Introduction that Julián Marías makes to his own *Una vida presente: Memorias,*[10] published in 1988, a year before *Todas las almas*. The father apologises for his autobiography by firstly quoting Ortega and the duty to 'devolver a la vida lo que ella nos ha dado',[11] and secondly by claiming that 'hay que *tomar posesión* de lo que se posee, y el hombre no puede hacerlo más que *diciéndolo*'.[12] Then he goes on to describe some of the difficulties of writing one's life story, for example 'Al hablar de uno mismo, hay que hablar de otras personas, y es dudosa la licitud de ello'.[13] The implication of this apology is that he may misrepresent them, and the unspoken concern is the contamination of autobiography by fictional material. His worry originates in a belief that in speaking of himself, he speaks from and about some inner sanctum, impossible to do, obviously, in the case of others, to whose inner selves he has no access; he can only speak about them as part of the outer world, as others. It is an affirmation of selfhood, and it implies a belief that to speak of oneself *is* valid, and that the self can be truly represented *only* in the autobiographical act. The impossibility of speaking of the inner sanctum without speaking of the outer world does not seem to shake Julián Marías's faith in this act.

Javier Marías turns convention around. *Todas las almas* begins:

---

10   Julián Marías, *Una vida presente: Memorias 1 (1914-1951)* (Madrid: Alianza, 1988).

11   *Una vida presente*, p.9.

12   Ibid., p.10.

13   Ibid., p.11

Dos de los tres han muerto desde que me fui de Oxford, y eso me hace pensar, supersticiosamente, que quizá esperaron a que yo llegara y consumiera mi tiempo allí para darme ocasión de conocerlos y para que ahora pueda hablar de ellos. Puede, por tanto, que — siempre supersticiosamente — esté obligado a hablar de ellos. No murieron hasta que yo dejé de tratarlos. De haber seguido en sus vidas y en Oxford (de haber seguido en sus vidas cotidianamente), tal vez aún estuvieran vivos. Este pensamiento no es sólo supersticioso, es también vanidoso. Pero para hablar de ellos tengo que hablar también de mí, y de mi estancia en la ciudad de Oxford.[14]

Where the father adopts an attitude of modesty, the son's claims seem arrogant, although his tone is in no way boastful. The reasoning of this ambiguous narrator at first seems extraordinary — to claim that if he had stayed in Oxford the others may not have died does indeed read at first as superstitious and vain. Such conjectures are 'superstitious' because they invest the subject with a power over others which it is impossible to prove it does not have, and they are 'vain' because belief in such power would place a very high value on the subject. Such superstitions arise because we cannot go back and make different choices. Because time is linear we can never go back and check whether the coincidence of our lives with the lives of others, for example, is determined at some point by walking under the ladder instead of around it, or if it would have happened anyway. This impossibility seems to fascinate Marías, who, as has already been mentioned, says he writes his novels as a way of exploring the realm of what could have been, but was never realised — 'lo que pudo ser'.[15] Nevertheless, the statement 'para hablar de ellos tengo que hablar también de mí' is a reversal of his father's affirmation of his faith in his own selfhood. His father regards having to write about others as in a way impinging on his self-writing: because they are also subjects like himself, it is impossible to write truly about them, so they are seen as necessary but regrettably unreliable characters in the otherwise true story. Javier Marías, in making the 'yo' ambiguous, in openly mixing fact and fiction, is writing from a belief that to write about others is the same as writing about oneself. We are all involved in each other's self image, and it is only through others that we have any concept of who we are. Perhaps one of the reasons why Javier Marías does not choose the 'memoirs' or autobiography 'proper' method of self--

---

14   *Todas las almas* (Barcelona: Anagrama, 1989), p.9. All page numbers in the main text refer to this edition.

15   See Chapter One, note 21.

writing is founded in a loss of belief in the self as inner sanctum, and in the concept of autobiography as an inward-looking and self-centred process.

After explaining why he is writing his memoirs, the father goes on to elucidate what he considers to be the main function of the book:

> Es menester, en la medida de lo posible, evocar el pasado reconstruyendo, no la circunstancia en que aconteció, sino sobre todo el yo, el *quién* que hizo y a quién le pasó eso que se va a contar. Si no se consigue hacerlo, todo se convierte en una falsificación, en una suplantación del que fue, del que ha ido siendo, por el que escribe.[16]

The conventional autobiography assumes that to all intents and purposes the author or writer, narrator and protagonist of the past — the 'real world' context of the story made present in the book — are one and the same. In this quotation, Julián Marías alters this by suggesting a difference between the 'yo' that writes and the 'yo' who experienced and acted. But, as with the example discussed above, in which his faith that the authentic self can be known is not shaken by his realisation that to write about himself he must also write about others, so here his differentiation between the 'yo' who was and the 'yo' who is does not lead him to the radical conclusions to which it leads his son. The quotation from *Todas las almas* above continues with a complex and categorical statement which is a subversion of the autobiographical genre as a search for identity or the authentic self. The ontological status of the 'yo' is expressed as highly problematical, and we are warned in these lines that this will be no conventional autobiography or autobiographical novel:

> Aunque el que habla no sea el mismo que estuvo allí. Lo parece, pero no es el mismo. Si a mí mismo me llamo yo, o utilizo un nombre que me ha venido acompañando desde que nací y por el que algunos me recordarán, o si cuento cosas que coinciden con cosas que otros me atribuirían, o si llamo *mi casa* a la casa que antes y después ocuparon otros pero yo habité durante dos años, es sólo porque prefiero hablar en primera persona, y no porque crea que basta con la facultad de la memoria para que alguien siga siendo el mismo en diferentes tiempos y en diferentes espacios. El que aquí cuenta lo que vio y le ocurrió no es aquel que lo vio y al que le ocurrió, ni tampoco es su prolongación, ni su sombra, ni su heredero, ni su usurpador. (pp.9-10)

---

16   *Una vida presente*, p.12.

Autobiography has come to be considered an attempt on the part of the author to discover his identity, it is a statement about who he really is and how he came to be this person, discovered in the act of writing. 'Autobiographers are not reporting on the process of their singularisation, they are performing it', and autobiography is an attempt to 'be received whole by those who read him'.[17] In the modern autobiography, worldly experience, whether positive or negative, has tended to be portrayed as a means of growing towards the mature state from which the autobiographer writes, towards the 'authentic' self in Julián Marías's scheme of things, rather than an obstacle with which he struggles in order to reach a state of true self-knowledge. Self-knowledge for the modern autobiographer consists of understanding properly the formative experience, and this means the double feat of 'evocar [...] el *quién* que hizo y a quién le pasó' whilst also writing and looking back over one's life as the person who inevitably 'lo haga desde su perspectiva actual'. The self may not be 'complete' but it is the sum of a lifetime's worthwhile experience. ('Mi vida real' says Julián Marías, 'se ha ido depositando en mí, capa tras capa, una densa *experiencia de la vida*').[18]

This is very different from the older, essentialist concept of autobiography. The history of this concept is traced by James Fernández in *Apology to Apostrophe*.[19] In this concept of 'autobiography by subtraction' experience is considered an *obstacle* to authenticity. From his studies of the *Confessions* of Augustine, through the autobiographical writing of the mystics and such secular autobiographers as Blanco White, José Zorrilla and Armando Palacio Valdés, Fernández concludes that they all have attempted to write about places or moments *beyond* the struggles of historical, social or political existence; places or moments which they identify as authentic, but somehow lost or just out of reach. This essentialist concept of autobiography has been less amenable to the reading public, and may not always have been recognised as autobiography at all. A radical example of this aspiration is the lyric poem of Valéry, 'La Jeune Parque', discussed by James Olney, and described as 'pure' autobiography[20] — the pure expression, that is, of a consciousness apart from what it is conscious *of* — pure form without impure narrative or historicity. The self is always there, a transcendent presence behind the roles we play, a 'feeling of an eternal present'.[21]

---

17   John Sturrock, *The Language of Autobiography* (Cambridge: Cambridge University Press, 1993), p.291.
18   *Una vida presente*, p.16.
19   Fernández, p.289.
20   James Olney, 'The Ontology of Autobiography' in *Autobiography, Essays Theoretical and Critical*, pp.249-57.
21   Olney, p.255.

The 'yo' of autobiographical writing refers traditionally, then, either to the writer, ('authentic' and 'fulfilled', or not, as the case may be) of the history or story, who is the sum of his experience, or to the essential and unchanging self that lies behind, and has, the experiences. In either case, it refers to the voice which transcends and authorises itself as it speaks. The myth of the present moment which sustains the possibility of identity between word and world, and which lies behind redemptive concepts of literature, is perhaps impossible to relinquish in that it is also accountable for the final kernel of self which we feel remains when all the old constants have changed. But in terms of telling or of writing the self, there is always a division or delay which destroys the identity within. Which is *the* self — the speaker or the listener — when we talk to or about 'ourselves'? The feeling that hearing others speak and hearing ourselves speak is a radically different process of understanding is an illusion.[22] The suggestion by Julián Marías, that the 'yo' who experienced in the past is other than the 'yo' who writes is only an intimation of this radical concept of the double within the self. But he is merely implying that the transcendental self is capable of change. In *Todas las almas* it is impossible to hear a transcendental voice, or to know on whose authority the 'yo' speaks. The ambiguity of the author's/narrator's voice is symptomatic of a postmodern awareness of this inability to be only the speaking or writing self, of a flickering between speaker and listener that lies at the centre of our identity.

Todas las almas is not an autobiographical novel in the sense that it mixes fact and fiction in the name of fiction; the author is not drawing from his own experience to produce a fiction, so much as drawing the fictional into his experience of the real. To read the way Marías uses autobiographical conventions as attempts to deconstruct the autobiography 'proper' is mistaken, yet in using certain of these conventions to expand the range of significance of the novel he automatically reduces the grounds on which autobiography as a genre is founded. For example, following the apology or explanation, the autobiographer conventionally begins by recalling his earliest memories, and tells the story of his life, mentioning those people, events and experiences he considers to have been particularly instrumental in forming the person he is at the time of writing. In order to underline the importance of certain people and places, and to emphasise their reality, photographs from the author's past are often included. These are usually of the autobiographer's parents and siblings, herself as child, himself as a youth, the house where he or she was born, and so on. The inclusion of photographs in a novel is unusual. In the centre of *Todas las almas* we find

---

22 See Jacques Derrida, *Of Grammatology*, trans. by Gayatri Chakravorty (Baltimore: John Hopkins University Press, 1976), p.3.

two photographs of John Gawsworth, one of him dressed in his RAF uniform, and one of his death mask. There is apparently no reason for them apart from the fact that Marías happened to have them and thought he might as well let the readers see them as well, as he himself suggests.[23] Yet they do parody the convention of highly significant family photos in that they are signs of a kind of ontological bleeding between fiction and reality which Marías refuses to suppress. We are influenced in our lives by both real and fictional characters, by people we meet and people we only hear and read about. Why should the blood relationship be presumed the most important? The inclusion of these photographs indirectly contradicts the bravado, discussed above, made manifest by the narrator in such statements as 'las relaciones no consanguíneas [...] jamás son fructíferas ni muy interesantes' (pp. 208-9).

Far from being a novel in which he simply mocks the system and has affairs, the narrator meets people — notably Cromer-Blake and Toby Rylands — who have faced up to, if not come to terms with, a reality which is for him still a fiction. (A remark made by Toby Rylands, as he tells the narrator of his feelings as death approaches, that '[l]o grave de que la muerte se acerque no es la propia muerte con lo que traiga o no traiga, sino que ya no se podrá fantasear con lo que ha de venir' (p.161), is only one of many ideas or sentiments that are taken up in *Corazón tan blanco*, in this case, the concept of the 'futuro abstracto'). *Todas las almas* is a novel of coming-of-age, or of realising what this can mean, in spite of the fact that Marías 'himself' was in his late thirties when he wrote it. The idea of not reaching maturity until one understands that one is going to die, that death is a future reality, relates closely to Julián Marías's central tenet: that of life as a project. In *Reason and Life* he says: 'Man's being is [...] a poetic reality, a product of fiction; I need to invent or conceive my life, in order to be able to live it'.[24] Ortega y Gasset, his mentor, had said before him that 'What a man does, he does definitely in view of [...] the imagined personage he intends to be', and 'life exists in plenitude only when one binds oneself under the impulsion of necessity to a particular outline; this is what is properly called authenticity',[25] or in Unamuno's words: 'Para cada alma hay una idea que le corresponde y que es como su fórmula'.[26] And after thirty years Julián Marías still maintains the same basic concept. In *España inteligible*, published in 1985, he still maintains that the most important element in all human life, either

---

23   'La magia de lo que pudo ser', 26.
24   *Reason and Life*, p.255.
25   Quoted by Julián Marías in *Reason and Life,* p.340.
26   Miguel de Unamuno, *Ensayos*, vol.vii (Madrid: Aguilar, 1958), p.54.

individual or collective, is the project.[27] To live is to choose from amongst possibilities. Reason, by which one justifies one's choices, is the proper human form of life, he says, and 'life [...] consists in preferring'.[28] For Julián Marías the important thing is to make the right choices — the authentic ones. He uses the same basic concept to explain the history of Spain — the 'project' of the Reconquest, of course, being his most obvious example. He combines the concept af authenticity and the notion of life as a project in the idea of 'vocation'. He recognises, however, that 'I am the personal author of only a part of my possibilities: the majority of them are received by me from my social surroundings', (these would presumably include chance and necessity as well as prescribed roles) but nevertheless he feels that 'I project or cast before me a figure of life to which I feel myself called'.[29]

It can be argued that Julián Marías is talking here about the project or vocation as a horizon which we work *towards*, (although in the case of his application of his theories to the history of Spain, he obviously writes with hindsight), and that it is nothing to do with autobiography, which is, we feel, always a looking *back* on a life. However, it is not difficult to relate the father's philosophy to the son's postmodern stance on writing the self. The autobiographical process as practised in the modern age is a circular one in which the author believes he authorises his own discourse — we know ourselves by understanding our experience; but the experiences we consider significant in this process are chosen by the selves we search to know. A correlative of the tail-biting nature of this process is that the very concept of autobiography, of the possibility of writing one's own life-story, may actually be instrumental in creating the experiences which form it. The fictionalising process described above goes on in the instant of action. The concept of autobiography is not universal, and we in the West have learned to experience self-consciously to an extraordinary degree. Paul de Man has suggested that the autobiographical act produces and determines the life, rather than viceversa; that is, that the self is the effect rather than the cause of language.[30] Geoffrey Galt Harpham 'normalises' this paradox thus: 'lives that at some point issue in autobiography are typically lives lived in anticipation of that fact, lived in consciousness of their own narratability'.[31] One need not be an autobiographer to live as if 'in anticipation of that fact',

27 *España inteligible* (Madrid: Alianza, 1985). See Chapter 30.
28 *Reason and Life*, p.330.
29 Ibid., p.226.
30 Paul de Man, 'Autobiography as Defacement', *The Rhetoric of Romanticism* (Columbia: Columbia University Press, 1984), p.69.
31 'Conversion and the Language of Autobiography' in Olney, *Autobiography, Essays Theoretical and Critical*, p.42.

and to a great extent, we all play, as outlined above, a double and alternating role of author and reader of our own actions — both in retrospect, and in anticipation — we imagine what we are going to do before we do it, to the smallest detail, we review with the hindsight of a few seconds, we watch ourselves in the act, as it were, in the self-conscious moment. We all do what Julián Marías himself suggested, that we need to invent or conceive our lives in order to be able to live them, although such a remark may have been interpreted more metaphorically then than today. The autobiographical act goes on most of the time anyway. The generic act of writing one's life-story maintains the forms and conventions of picking out after the event what are now much discussed as 'turning points',[32] but the rehearsal and choosing of them *a priori* goes largely unremarked. In Julián Marías's scheme of things they would be the choosing of 'authentic possibilities'. For Javier Marías and his narrators the loss of the present moment, the flickering between being speaker and listener, actor and observer of action, seems to have penetrated and spread through their lives, depriving relationships of intensity, and creating a self-consciousness which turns all actions into parody.

The narrator's encounter with Muriel in *Todas las almas* is an example of 'life lived in anticipation of that fact'. In the most intimate physical moments with her he finds himself not only thinking about what he is doing rather than enjoying doing it, not 'distraída', as she is, but translating the experience as it happens into words; not only thinking rather than doing, but thinking about thinking about it — becoming the author reviewing his past almost immediately, rather than from the distance of years. He is surprised at what is happening to him, at the physical intimacy — 'tengo la polla en la boca de Muriel' (p.145) — after only having known her for three hours. But he makes no moral comment; he does not make a confession of the incident, for example, which would be a conventional autobiographical way to treat it — as a self-forming episode. In fact it is more likely to invite condemnation from the contemporary 'politically correct' reader than collusion or understanding — demeaning to women, despite the context. It is not presented as an incident in the life of the narrator, from which he draws conclusions and increases his self-knowledge, nor as an experience so pleasurable physically that the double 'self-conscious' self disappears in a timeless experience of being, but rather the opposite — an incident which,

---

32   See Sturrock, 1993, p.43, in which he describes as a 'turning point' the moment in *Confessions* when Augustine interprets a child crying 'tolle lege, tolle lege' as a divine command, and goes and reads in the Bible the words which finally effect his conversion. It is a pivotal point in the narrative, and such devices are often referred to as 'turning points' in the critical discourse of autobiography.

because it is not an everyday happening, distances the narrator from himself, he 'stands outside himself' and tells himself what is happening as if he were another. The release, or change of state from this heightened sense of division comes only at the very last moment. Emphasising that perhaps the self can only escape words and thoughts at such moments of intense physicality as the peak of the sexual climax, the last sentence of the section reads: ' — Te deseo — dije. "Te deseo", pensé, y dejé de pensar después de este pensamiento' (p.149).

Marías has much to say on the identification of author, narrator, and himself. However, his essays and interviews comment on his fictional work whilst not explaining it. The myth of 'intention' has been demystified along with many other myths as part of the 'epistemological poetics of modernism'.[33] Such questions need not concern us here, they are taken as read. But articles and interviews even more than autobiography are considered to belong on the 'real' side of the boundary between fiction and reality. And it is surely reasonable if not essential for meaningful discourse to expect that in an interview or essay the author will say what he really thinks. The intertextual relationship between Marías's novels and his other writing often undermines the conventional manner in which the author normally speaks 'about' his work. In several published interviews he contradicts himself and shows inconsistencies, just as contradictory ideas often run together in his novels; each speaker seeming to 'tener la razón' whilst he or she holds the chair. Such inconsistencies are perhaps not intentionally subversive so much as resistent to the erection of a false boundary between what he calls 'el pensamiento literario'[34] and his novels. An essay such as 'Autobiografía y ficción', as we have seen, figures, rather than explains, the novel in which he puts the theory into practice — the point is that the relationship between fiction and reality *is a mise en abîme,* not that the author makes it so, and can explain how he does it. A different kind of example is an article in which Marías describes the different places he has lived as either conducive or not to writing. Describing his physical circumstances in Oxford, he says he rented:

una casa piramidal de tres pisos, en la que tenía tanta comodidad y espacio que hube de inventarme ante la casera a 'mi mujer y las niñas' para justificar la ocupación de un lugar destinado a *familias* universitarias. Mi mujer y las niñas (nunca supe cuantas tuve)

33 See Brian McHale, *Postmodernist Fiction* (London and New York: Methuen, 1987), in which he argues that the essential difference between the modern and the postmodern is one of epistemology/ ontology.

34 *Literatura y fantasma,* p.127.

estaban siempre a punto de llegar o acababan de marcharse, porque 'mi suegro, *you must know,* vive solo y su salud es delicada'.[35]

There are several reasons why this passage is interesting: firstly because the phrase 'una casa piramidal de tres pisos' is, apart from the word order, identical to the description in *Todas las almas.* One example such as this would be in no way remarkable, but the frequency with which such repetitions of phrases and descriptions from his fiction appear in his 'non-fiction' indicates, I believe, the non-suppression described above. In a more conventional essay the author would have used different words, or would have indicated in some other way such as quotation marks, the difference between his fiction and his non-fiction. This passage is also another example of *mise en abîme.* In *Todas las almas* this 'invention' of a wife and children is not described — not in this context anyway — so whether or not he intends to, Marías is here adding something to his novel, stretching and blurring the boundaries between it and the 'non-fiction' of the interview, and casting more shadows over its status as autobiography/fiction. Not only is he adding something that he did not include in the novel, but this something is itself apparently a fiction.

The narrator *does* tell of his wife and family in a later chapter. Marías explains in 'Quién escribe' that in order that the reader should not identify author and narrator, he sets one chapter in the future, in which the narrator is married with a child — 'el único dato comprobable que impide o impediría una total identificación entre el Narrador y autor por parte de un lector cualquiera, cercano y conocido o desconocido y anónimo, que quisiera establecerla'.[36] This subterfuge, he explains, conserves simply the ambiguity of the identity of the narrator, because to have called the narrator, 'Juan', or given him red hair, would have been to make identity between himself and the narrator impossible, whereas he, Javier Marías, *could* have married and had a child. The reader, he says, may easily forget the declaration of the first paragraph — that the 'yo' who writes is not the 'yo' who had the experiences — or take it as rhetorical. His intention was that the reader should not *necessarily* take the narrator for the author (or vice-versa). To take seriously Marías's claim that this chapter is a way of reminding the reader that the narrator and the author are not one and the same is to come to the conclusion that he is indeed ridiculously vain (and he does, after all, admit to being 'vanidoso' in the first paragraph of the novel). To imagine that the reader, as he suggests, will go to such lengths to try to find out whether Javier Marías is really a tall, red-haired man, is yet another

---

35   Javier Marías, 'La inspiración ocupa lugar', *El Libro Español,* 331-2 (1986), 4.
36   *Literatura y fantasma,* p.90.

subterfuge. The novelist must rely, of course, on the reader remembering what has gone before. Surely what he is saying between the lines is that the notion that the double-act the author performs as writer and reader of his own book — that when he writes he is himself, but he can read it *as if he were* another reader — is a mistaken belief. The 'diferencia sustancial' between the narrator married and with a son (which Marías says could have happened) and the narrator as a tall, red-haired man called Juan (which Marías says could not have been the case) is indeed important, but not as far as the reader who does not know Marías is concerned. It works in that it allows *him* to believe in his own narrator as either 'quien yo pude ser pero no fui', or as 'Nadie o Cualquiera, o por lo menos en Otro-además-de-mí'. Thus the narrator could go on accumulating more and more of his own characteristics as the novel progresses, without it being an autobiographical account. It allows him to recreate himself, to explore the 'yo', not as a centre of identity, but as an immensely complex system of referral, and in so doing to explore the fictitious and the real as aspects of the self; to experiment, it could be said, with new possibilities of autobiography.

To use conventional terminology, he is exploiting the difference between the self as a *roman à clef* character and the conventional autobiographical self. The *roman à clef* and the autobiography at first seem to have a lot in common. The *roman à clef* seems to be a mixture of fiction and autobiography which declares itself as such to certain knowing readers. We feel they both point outside themselves to the 'real' world, but the essential difference between them is that in the case of autobiography this illusion can be wholly produced through convention, whereas in the *roman àclef* it depends completely on the reader. The reader does not even need to have heard of the autobiographer to believe she is reading about a 'real' person, and the *roman à clef* may read as completely fictional if the people or places are not 'recognised'. Marías prevents himself/the narrator from being read as either a conventional autobiographer or a *roman à clef* character. But in so doing he demonstrates that the self apart from these two manifestations — apart, that is, from the self as signifier — is ineffable or non-existent. If he had written of himself in Oxford conventionally, written the narrator as himself, doubtless the narration would be somewhat different, and if he had simply 'disguised' himself wholly, called the narrator 'Juan' and had him tall with red hair, then the novel could be read as 'part true, part fiction', and no more questions asked about his identity. But by problematizing the identity of the narrator, what becomes important is not what is 'contable', the 'material "verídico"',[37] which may or may not be interesting, but the telling itself. Marías says that:

---

37   *Literatura y fantasma*, p.65.

mi interés de escritor no es muy distinto de mi interés de lector: como tal quiero verme forzado a pararme a pensar, y mientras eso suceda no me importa demasiado lo que me vayan contando. Pues al fin y al cabo, lo que es *contable* en una novela es sólo lo que se puede decir también en unas pocas e intercambiables palabras. Las novelas, sin embargo, suelen tener muchas palabras, y esas, justamente, nunca son intercambiables.[38]

To write as one reads, not in order to express and try to communicate something already there, but in a continuous '*atenerme* a lo ya escrito[39] is surely bred out of a sense of the double nature of the self, a loss of faith in the present moment, and an embracing of the idea that only in the actual telling does anything, including the self, become real.

Todas las almas is a transitional novel within Marías's body of work in relation to self, identity, and the possibilities of writing the self. The idea that 'autobiography' and 'autobiographical writing' are distinguished by the extent to which the 'I' is wholly referential in the former and only limitedly so in the latter, and that in fiction the 'I' is not self-referential at all, may be cast to the winds. But the story is, nevertheless, on one level, that of an uprooted young man who attempts to strike fresh, if shallow, roots, and fails. In spite of the declaration with which it begins as to the difference between who writes and who experienced, narrator and author — the fragmentation and ambiguity, that is, of the 'yo' — there is clearly to be read, as we have seen, a nostalgia for certainty, and a desire for identity and continuity, even if it is only a lingering desire. The novel looks back to possibilities of unity and union in the romantic relationship, but it also contains the seeds of a different idea of selfhood, which is explored in Marías's concept of 'lo que pudo ser'. This self is not conceived as an essential being whose trajectory through life is determined by who he is, by his essential nature, nor is it a wise or otherwise sum of experiences, whose learning or refusal or inability to learn from these experiences determines the action he takes, but rather a time-bound creature condemned to follow a narrow path amongst an infinity of possibilities. The self is conceived of as a fund of potentialities which, because of its fallen condition, is condemned to follow through only one of these possibilities in 'real' life. This one-trackedness of life has been made acceptable through the notions of self which have predominated. We imagine our lives are somehow inevitable, otherwise the choices we make, the things we do are meaningless. By reviewing a life as a series of events and experiences which resulted in the unique self which is doing the

---

38   *Literatura y fantasma*, p.93.
39   *Literatura y fantasma*, p.92.

reviewing and remembering, it is given value. 'Lo que pudo ser' is a concept which restores value to fiction, which acknowledges life, that which is or was, as just one version, an option, of what could have been. From this point of view the fact that the real life narrative was played out, whereas the others were never more than potentialities, does not in itself lend it any particular value. So another reason why Marías may reject the forms of writing mentioned above, and choose to write autobiography *as* fiction, with no attempt to hide the one or the other, may be that he rejects the idea that autobiography has a greater narrative *value* than fiction. What happened and what might have happened are given equal value in terms of determining, or being determined by, the self. The resulting mood is, of course, that of postmodern unease which permeates all the novels in question, and which is also due, as stated above, to the fact that there is no *angst,* only 'perturbación' in these books. Much of the agonising over the lost self is taken as read. Marías's novels, at least those under discussion here, are not searches for identity, but deal with the *possibility* of identity.

CHAPTER FIVE
Double identity: memory, duplicity and dissimulation in Antonio Muñoz Molina's *Beltenebros.*

JOHN MACKLIN

Beltenebros,[1] published in 1989, is Antonio Muñoz Molina's third novel, following *Beatus Ille* (1986) and *El invierno en Lisboa* (1987). Like the latter novel, which earned Muñoz Molina the Premio de la Crítica and the Premio Nacional de Literatura in 1988, *Beltenebros* was made into a film, with an international cast, directed by Pilar Miró, and released in 1991. On one level, the subject of the novel, which concerns an assassin sent to eliminate a traitor to the party, appeared ideal for translation to the screen, while its cinematic construction and *film noir* atmosphere already contained the seeds of a successful filmic realisation. On the other hand, the text's obsessively introspective nature and relative absence of plotting, together with its heavy reliance on verbal artistry, were impediments to successful translation to the screen, calling for greater freedom and inventiveness in adaptation. As a novel, however, this combination of features successfully underscores a number of recurrent themes and preoccupations which characterise the fiction of Antonio Muñoz Molina. These may be summarised as the nature of artistic and political commitment, time, memory, relationships and the boundaries of the self, all of which are concentrated on questions of self and identity. If *Beltenebros* appears to constitute Muñoz Molina's particular contribution to *novela negra*, a genre which enjoyed a particular vitality and popularity in the years of the *transición*, the peculiar structure of the plot, accurately, if not very originally, described by Vicente Gallego as 'un juego de espejos',[2] provides a framework for an exploration of identity in a world in which identities are false and uncertain, lacking the solidity conferred by shared values and cultural consensus and in which the indeterminate self is partly enacted by the unreal relations of modern life overlaid by the constructed reality of cultural reference, which figures prominently in the

1   *Beltenebros* (Barcelona: Seix Barral, 1989). All references are to this edition and are incorporated in the text of the chapter.
2   Vicente Gallego, '*Beltenebros* de Antonio Muñoz Molina', *Insula*, 514 (1989), 19.

novel through the use of novelistic and filmic antecedents. This phenomenon, which involves a reconsideration of the liberal humanist assumptions
about origins, creativity and self, has been described in its extreme form by
Douglas Crimp in the following terms: 'The fiction of the creating subject
gives way to the frank confiscation, quotation, excerptation, accumulation and
repetition of already existing images. Notions of originality, authenticity and
presence [...] are undermined'.[3] Muñoz Molina's appropriation of the
conventions of other genres, however, owes less to imitation and parody than
to their suggestions of illusion and fictiveness. His own views on *novela
negra* are characteristically forthright: 'Eso de la novela negra es una
tontería. *Novela negra* es un término espurio'.[4] Nevertheless, the
conventions of the genre, as we shall see, function within the novel, along
with those of the sentimentalised, romantic fiction typed out by the older
Rebeca Osorio, as a metaphor for the irreality of life's patterns, for the
construction of identities, for the provisionality and conventionality of sense-
making.

    Beltenebros recounts the story of a courier-cum-assassin, Captain
Darman, who is charged with the task of eliminating a traitor to the
Communist Party in the Spain of the 1960s by leaders in exile in Eastern
Europe, an assignment which repeats almost exactly one he had carried out
some twenty years earlier. This process of repetition establishes a number of
duplications and parallels throughout the text which, on one level, enable
Darman to see that the earlier assassination, like the present one, was of an
innocent man. In this sense, the protagonist's trajectory is one of enlight-
enment, of discovery, and conforms to the pattern of detective or spy fiction
in which an enigma is resolved. More importantly, however, the play of
parallels involves a process of memory and reconstruction in which the
material restored finally disappears, like the falling body of Ugarte in the final
sequence, into the enveloping darkness. The figure of darkness is evoked in
the epic title of the novel, which recalls, enigmatically, the alias of Amadís de
Gaula, with associations of valour and heroism which might apply initially to
the narrator-protagonist only to be transformed into a sinister and deadly
identity, that of the real traitor, Valdivia/Ugarte. The title not only introduces
the theme of multiple identities, but also that of the quest, for Beltenebros is
the name assumed by the knight in various adventures including his search
for a woman, Oriana. This duplication in character, coupled with the idea of

3   Douglas Crimp, 'On the Museum's Ruins', in *The Anti-Aesthetic: Essays on
     Postmodern Culture*, ed. by Hal Foster (Port Townsend, Wash: Bay Press,
     1983), p.53.
4   Juan Francisco Martín Gil, 'El que habita en la oscuridad. Entrevista con Antonio
     Muñoz Molina', *Quimera*, 83 (1988), 27.

the quest, is present also in the identification of Andrade, Darman's present victim, with Walter, his previous one. This pattern suggests, moreover, not just the repetition of history's mistakes, but also the impossibility of uniqueness, whether in events, persons or places. The principal female character, Rebeca Osorio, partakes of this multiplicity, for she is reprised in another character of the same name, who turns out to be her daughter. The clandestine world of spies and secret agents which is evoked in *Beltenebros* is ideally suited to this game of false or hidden identities and it parallels the world of the author, that other creator of identities and weaver of fictions which beguile, confuse and tantalise. The author himself has commented on this analogy, though only in terms of the part played by observation: 'El espía tiene una identidad y un oficio secreto, que es mirar lo que ocurre a su alrededor, pues bien, eso es lo que hace el novelista; contemplarlo todo con los ojos bien abiertos y, si no se comporta así, no puede salir una buena novela'.[5]

The first sentence of the novel: 'Vine a Madrid para matar a un hombre a quien no había visto nunca' (p.7), apparently innocuous and factual on first reading, appears in retrospect to underline the establishment of a relationship on the basis of non-relationship, to stress the importance of seeing, as distinct from knowing, while the tense of 'vine' creates a curious temporal ambiguity, and indeed a spatial one: from where is the narrator narrating? Moreover, the sentence suggests a control beyond the first-person narrator, wresting from him his authority as a maker of his narrative, emphasised in the anonymity of 'Me dijeron su nombre' (p.7). False and real names become ciphers of authenticity and inauthenticity, of the world of fiction and the real world, juxtaposed in the reality of Atocha station and the sentimental novels read by the fugitive. The doubtful parameters of time are suggested by the stopped clock (later in the novel Darman's own watch is trodden upon and smashed), the newspapers of different dates, the indications of former activity, all pointing to 'un error en el tiempo, no un anacronismo, sino una irregularidad en su paso' (p.9). Chronology and place are markers of identity, in narratives as in life, but here they are distorted, dysfunctional, so that the definite identity suggested by a photograph of the intended victim, given to Darman for the purposes of identification, seems curiously limited, suggesting too the missing identity behind the camera, the momentary, unknown relationship. A similar phenomenon is the association later of Luque with his photograph and police file which serve to identify him in a functional way. It is no surprise that photographs return with remarkable frequency in so much contemporary fiction. The wanted poster of Angel in Llamazares's *Luna de*

---

5   Juan Cantavella, 'Antonio Muñoz Molina. El que no entra en la literatura por amor a ella se equivoca', *Diario de Cádiz,* 12 March 1989, p.15.

lobos has a similar effect, and the photographs of *Escenas de cine mudo* both confirm and distort identity.

This kind of relationship is sustained in various modes of communication and non-communication repeated throughout Muñoz Molina's narrative. Darman receives messages via postcards, undertakes journeys at the behest of anonymous officials, is collected by unknown people, is ignorant of the task he is undertaking. Later, he is tempted to make a telephone call to his house in Brighton, thereby establishing a link between two places not otherwise linked, like 'dos desconocidos que leen simultáneamente la misma noticia en el periódico y nunca se cruzarán ni se verán' (p.35). Darman is intrigued by the existence of odd relationships, in a manner reminiscent of Javier Marías's characters. Collecting his key for his gun in the left luggage locker makes him aware that he is retracing the steps, in reverse, of the agent who left them for him: 'Repetir inversamente sus pasos me vinculaba a él en una indeseada simetría' (p.62). Darman's characterisation is like this, contingent, random, one of non-characterisation, of remoteness, distance, lack of commitment or, as here, arbitrary connections. He is characterised by lack of fixity, and this is epitomised in his involuntary travels, his geographical displacements at the behest of others. In the modern world, plane travel seems to encapsulate rootlessness and sameness, in that it makes all journeys between all places virtually identical. The airport is a place outside time and space, a modern construct which, though given the name of the place it serves, is not that place, but all places in which 'ni el tiempo ni el espacio son del todo reales' (p.13), creating a sense of 'provisionalidad y destierro' (p.14). Florence airport exists for Darman as a network of reminiscences in which faces and experiences merge, though all are seen with the same detachment and coldness. Darman appears in the guise of the postmodern existentialist, aware but surprisingly devoid of anguish, a man who sees the world as pure contingency and coincidence as a proof of that contingency, and who 'había perdido el hábito de la desesperación' (p.18). This absence of despair makes his compliance with destiny easier. It may be the absence of the concrete, of substantiality, in both persons and places that encourages Muñoz Molina, in denying his novel's affinities with *novela negra*, to stress its Kafkaesque qualities: 'yo me propuse hacer una novela abstracta, tipo Kafka, sin casi referencias concretas. Esto es una especie de parábola fría'.[6] This abstract quality is what makes the writer deny his work's affinities with *novela negra*, understood as a concern with contemporary social and political issues in a kind of new realism and emphasise instead its psychological and nightmarish qualities.

---

6   Juan Angel Juristo, 'Antonio Muñoz Molina. Para hacer la literatura hay que huir de la vida literaria', *El Independiente*, 7 July 1989, 30.

This nightmarish quality, bordering on paranoia, is evident from the first pages of the novel. The novel's epigraph, taken from *Don Quijote*, foreshadows this: 'Unas veces huían sin saber de quién y otras esperaban sin saber a quién'. Enigma and mystery surround the opening flashback, which occupies the first five chapters of the novel, and these contrast strangely with the precision with which everything is narrated, thereby imparting to the text an ambivalent quality of certainty and uncertainty at the same time. Identity is presented in terms of the same ambivalent qualities, and much of it is constructed through memory, of feelings (the 'sagrado rencor' which remains from his earlier life), of faces (the usher in the cinema), of songs ('Bahía'), and of an odd mixture of presence and absence, of being and longing, of a desire for movement and a desire for stasis, for the fleetingness of the moment and the length of eternity. Identity is not fixed, but positioned between apparently antagonistic states, multiplied and doubled. Repeatedly in the text, Darman reflects on the self as a process of perpetual transformation. In the hotel room, he is no longer the person at the airport, his appearance has changed: 'cada ciudad, pensé, cada viaje, nos transfigura a su medida, como un amor reciente' (p.24). This is no simple naturalism in which the effect of the environment is shown to condition the individual in a simple deterministic pattern of cause and effect, but a view of identity as subtly shaped, progressively reconstructed, willingly and involuntarily imposed. This still suggests, of course, that there is a core of identity to be transfigured, to be worked upon. This is also related to Darman's circumstances in that the ageing assassin is losing his edge. In the past Darman fixed faces in his mind, fixed identities, now he is unable to do this: 'Ahora los rostros y los lugares se modificaban cada minuto en mi imaginación como arrastrados por el agua, y mi memoria era a veces un trémulo sistema de espejos comunicantes' (p.40). Living so long in a world of deceit and dissimulation has dissolved certainties. The world of secret agents is a simulacrum of everyone's world, and this is underlined by further analogies in the text. Luque, for example, acts out the fiction of the young activist and confers on Darman an identity which confirms his aspirations and current world-view. His acquired identity merges into a kind of non-identity: 'Yo no soy nadie' (p.28), and for Darman in turn he ceases to have any material form: 'pareció desvanecerse como una sombra sin cuerpo' (p.28). The irredeemably fictional nature of this world is typified in the belief in words — as orders, as directions, as addresses — which circulate and perpetuate this illusory reality: 'Creían sobre todo y casi únicamente en eso, en la eficacia mágica de las palabras escritas e inmovilizadas en consignas, en su clandestina transmisión. Palabras impresas en el papel o en el aire, murmuradas en el oído de alguien que las guardaría y las repetiría, intangibles viáticos escondidos en maletas de doble fondo' (p.29). Javier

Marías similarly uses the same phrase of whispered words in *Corazón tan blanco* to indicate their meaning beyond the intention of the speaker. In this case, the duplicity of words, their compliance in falsehood, is underlined. Other characters will use words to conjure up reality. Rebeca has 'una supersticiosa necesidad de nombrar a Andrade, para que existiera así fuera de ella y su invocación alcanzara una presencia objetiva' (p.135). Earlier Darman had reflected on the use of the word 'ejecución, como decían ellos siempre, puritanos de palabras, acuñadores tenaces de palabras que no aludían nunca a la realidad, porque su único propósito era excluirla o conjurarla para que pareciera a otros sueños, los suyos' (p.59). Luque believes he uses them monologically, avoiding their 'doble fondo' and making them submit to reality, and relates to Darman on the basis of non-communication. But Darman's encounter with Luque the young activist is also a confrontation with his former self, or a fear of confronting his former self. His refusal to respond to him is a rejection of that self, with its political and existential certainties, its solidity and security. In the final pages of the novel, as Valdivia talks endlessly to him, rationalising the past, Darman again is aware of the limits of talk: 'hablar en la oscuridad era como estar muerto y acordarse de los vivos repitiendo en el simulacro de la conversación palabras antiguas y perdidas, nombres lejanos de fantasmas que no existían en el mundo' (p.235). Darman does not want his identity to correspond to the narrative of his own acts when those acts have been narrated by others. He plays a central role in his own creation: 'Yo mismo me multiplicaba invisiblemente en otros hombres', and these are shed, forgotten, discarded, relegated to a curious kind of non-existence: 'En torno a mí se movían las sombras de un porvenir que se volvió pasado sin existir nunca' (p.41).

All the characters seem to some degree to be implicated in the game of mirrors. The narrator notes that Rebeca 'era capaz de ser varias mujeres en el curso de un día, mujeres desconocidas, simultáneas, idénticas, como repetidas en espejos' (p.94). Darman interposes a veil between himself and what he does by continual acts of simulation. On one level, he is called upon to fulfil roles he does not choose while, on another level, he refuses total identification with these roles by living largely in his imagination and by refusing communion with others. He has developed the art of fictionalising to its highest degree of sophistication to the extent of consciously feigning the roles in which he is cast. Although he has been a successful assassin, and others categorise him as such, he has shed the skins of his former selves. Nevertheless, *Beltenebros* is the narrator's autobiographical, albeit fictional, reconstruction and the reader is likely to ask what kind of simulation enters into its making. If all is imagination for Darman, none of this narrative has claims to truth. So much in his world is a construct, so unreal is the world of assassins and spies, that only the presence of fictional works, those of

Rebeca Osorio, alerts him to the possibility of reality. Otherwise, he can separate his inner life from his outer, and he can do this almost unconsciously, without the exercise of his will. He can see that the others act out roles too, but unknowingly, without his kind of self-consciousness, imitating instructions they have been given or even 'normas tal vez aprendidas en las películas de gangsters' (p.38), aspiring to be heroes. A similar phenomenon occurs when Darman is brought to meet the party officials. They appear fixed into sameness, first in appearance and dress and then in gestures and looks. Their static, sedentary world stretches out into the world beyond, which they construct, relying on the evidence of information, relayed and written down, through the powers of their deductive reasoning. But this reasoning is of course fiction-making, the creation of narratives used to buttress their sense of self or sustain their view of the world. Bernal's construction is more important than reality: 'es posible que sólo concediera a la realidad una importancia secundaria' (p.51). Their task is filling gaps in their knowledge — names, motives, actions — and in so doing attempt a shadowy realisation of themselves. The difference between them and Darman is that he believes in change, they in stasis, illustrated in a simple exchange. 'Ya no soy el de antes — dije —. Todos cambiamos', to which Bernal responds, 'Nadie cambia. Ni ellos ni nosotros hemos cambiado' (p.48). Here there is a deep-seated need to believe in fixity and permanence as guarantors of the security of the world they inhabit. Andrade had always been a traitor, if only in potential. He was now fulfilling his destiny. By contrast, Ugarte, in his search for security and survival, escapes fixity by being invisible, by having no face: 'ningún detenido le ha visto la cara' (p.49), 'la vida oculta de aquel hombre sin cara' (p.232). The importance of looking and seeing is constantly emphasised throughout the text in a way which recalls the importance of surveillance and evasion in Llamazares's *Luna de lobos*. Bernal envelops Darman within his look, keeping him within 'el círculo de su posesión' (p.47). Darman will go to Madrid undetected: 'ni siquiera te verán' (p.47). When Darman sees the photograph of Andrade, he is linked to him by his look, which sums up the mystery of his being, more important than the reasons which led him to his acts of betrayal, more important than the proof or otherwise of his acts of betrayal. Darman seeks something deeper in Andrade, some hidden impulse, some quality of sadness, of a void at the core of his being. There exists a gap between the persona and reality, and identity is located in that gap, forged out of nothingness. In a further symmetry, the search for, and killing of Andrade, becomes a search for himself which he appears to identify with that void: 'Yo era nadie, un muerto prematuro que todavía no sabe que lo es, una sombra que cruzaba ciudades y ocupaba en los hoteles habitaciones desiertas, leyendo, cuando se desvelaba, las instrucciones a seguir en el caso de un incendio. Yo era exactamente igual que ese hombre de la fotografía que me estaba esperando en un almacén de Madrid. Por esa única razón vine a buscarlo' (pp.53-54). Darman's identity merges with that of his victim. In this way, Darman asserts a kind of control, ascribes a motivation to his acts, frees himself from the rigidity of the role in which he is cast. But his identity remains curiously engaged and compromised, for he finds himself, thinking about the killing in the plural ('habíamos ejecutado') and using their word, entering their linguistic domain. Darman's narrative identity rests on this interplay of differentiation and identification, of symmetries and asymmetries. His way of disengaging from the unreal world of his masters is to maintain himself in a state of availability, of constant openness. His extreme self-consciousness is manifest in his frequent sombre reflections on his own state: 'yo era un lento fantasma que fingía que iba a matar a un hombre y se internaba en la mentira como en una selva de espejismos' (pp.56-57). His clandestine world is a play of mirages and doubles, a duplicity which extends to his own self. As he arrives in Madrid he seeks his face among the crowd in a mirror and when he finds it 'pareció la de otro, tal vez quien de verdad soy sin saberlo, el doble que viajó a Madrid mientras yo permanecía acogido a la penumbra de mi tienda' (p.59).

Reality appears similarly mysterious and multifaceted, and the individual can merely perceive and conceive similarities and congruences in life, the interpenetration of apparent opposites, chance and fate, predestination and contingency, which are alike as 'un hombre y su doble' (p.70). It is a pattern which is constantly repeated. Rebeca has her 'doble' (p.95), the night is 'duplicada' (p.72), the stuff of memory as time follows its inverse course, turning present into past. Darman's actions are carried out as if they had already been completed as future is repeatedly converted into past. Darman recognises his similarity to his victim who is 'como yo mismo en los espejos, un fantasma de otro, una existencia conjetural y perdida' (p.70). Not surprisingly, mirrors are a recurrent motif in the text, growing metonymically out of its locations: bars, airports, hotels, dressing-rooms. In Chapter 8, the whole scene between Darman and Rebeca is conducted through mirrors, as they see themselves and each other refracted through the distance of glass and time ('mirándome ahora en el espejo', 'mirándome en el cristal', (p.100), 'absorta en el espejo' (p.101), 'permanecía fija en mí, en el espejo' (p.102), etc.). Just as Rebeca had been isolated from the present and from reality as if in 'una urna de cristal invisible' (p.93), like the transparent film which insulates Darman from the world, they are related across 'toda la vacía extensión del tiempo' (p.100). Eyes serve a similar function, as Darman sees his face duplicated in hers, the abysmal depths of his identity. Like the man in the warehouse, whom we do not yet know to be Ugarte/Valdivia, the receding mirrors of his identity fail to fix on a steady image. Ugarte revels in his multiple identities, refusing suggestively to accept Rebeca's claims of recognition. Darman constantly juxtaposes his different lives, aware that he has regressed to a past which overwhelms his present life: 'el pasado restablecía lentamente su poderío sobre mí, enajenándome de mi propia vida, la real, la que me esperaba en Inglaterra' (p.88). His self undergoes a process of dissolution. Aware that he is travelling incognito, this fact becomes an emblem of his whole existence, graphically conveyed as he sits in the darkness of the club with other unknown faces so that 'hasta la identidad se me desdibujaba como uno cualquiera de aquellos rostros acogidos a la sombra, desconocidos y pálidos sobre las lámparas azules' (p.91). As he enters Rebeca's dressing-room and sees his features reflected back at him, he becomes aware of the anguish of non-differentiation: 'En nada me distinguía de los otros' (p.99). Likewise the narrator in *Corazón tan blanco*, struggles to conserve what he considers to be his own identity which the state of marriage threatens to engulf. Darman is ambivalently poised between selfhood and anonymity. His attempt to forge his own identity is constantly thwarted by the roles in which he is cast, by the patterns which have been drawn elsewhere and to which he is made to conform. In *Beltenebros*, these patterns are drawn from the cultural constructs of literary, cinematic and performing models, which replace as much as replicate the orders of the world.

Antonio Muñoz Molina has explained his attraction to the world of the spy novel, especially John le Carré and Graham Greene, as well as real-life spy stories such as that of Kim Philby, and observed how these appeared to relate to a particular set of historical circumstances in the period of Francoism. The novel echoes, through Darman, the existence of an underground opposition and takes up a theme more explicitly treated by Llamazares in *Luna de lobos*. In Muñoz Molina's novel, however, the Communist Party, with its secret and closed infrastructure, seemed a natural breeding ground for betrayal: 'La traición ocurre sobre todo en las sociedades cerradas, en organizaciones que la propician dentro de un mundo marcado por la doblez. Siempre tiene que haber personas con doble identidad y es mucho más interesante una persona así, que no aquéllos con una identidad sencilla'.[7] History is an oblique presence in the novel. In the words of William Sherzer, 'la historia funciona para crear y encuadrar el argumento, mientras que a la vez retrocede constantemente para permitir a los personajes y al narrador la recreación de esa misma historia, creando de esta manera un significado más plural y trascendental'.[8] However vague

---

7   Cantavella, 15
8   William Sherzer, 'Tiempo e historia en la narrativa de Antonio Muñoz Molina', *Revista Contemporánea*, 4 (1992), 54.

may be Muñoz Molina's historical reconstruction of the Madrid of the 1960s, one critic at least[9] has seen the presence of Julián Grimau in two characters, in the personality of Darman and in the physical appearance of Andrade, and Walter is said to have been inspired in real activists, like Quiñones and Trilla, who came to Spain in the 1940s to organise the party. Muñoz Molina talks with admiration about this kind of solitary activist: 'En nuestra guerra civil, el franquismo y la resistencia europea, en los movimientos de rebeldía europeos desde los años treinta hasta la Segunda Guerra Mundial, hay unos seres inexplicables, como el Walter de mi novela, que está copiado de varios personajes reales. Es decir, gente que en los treinta se dedicaba a hacer la revolución, a ir por ahí cambiando el mundo [...]. En esta clase de comportamientos hay un misterio. El misterio, que he tratado de reflejar en la novela, de la lealtad y de la traición'.[10] The author himself recalls an incident in which someone he knew was accused of being a police informer and felt the attraction of 'esa confusión y doblez, muy novelesca'.[11] His choice of the name Beltenebros as the codename for the real traitor reveals the symbolic significance of the theme for him. In an interview he states: 'Puse *Beltenebros* porque me encantó la sonoridad de la palabra. Tiene algo misterioso. Como se sabe, es el nombre que adopta Amadís de Gaula cuando quiere transformarse. Como la novela trata de una transformación vista a través de la clandestinidad, el nombre me pareció de lo más apropiado. La clave de la novela es, pues, la identidad secreta'.[12] Against a background of the stereotypical ingredients of assassin, traitor, *femme fatale*, double agent, and a dark, mysterious underworld in which the reader is progressively ensnared, Muñoz Molina enacts a drama of identity, which is shown to be shifting, fluid and precarious. In a novel which adheres to generic conventions and which aims at implicating the reader in a broadly mimetic narrative, apparently divorced from the estrangements and defamiliarisations characteristic of postmodernism, Muñoz Molina nevertheless exhibits a strikingly postmodern approach to character and, concomitant with this, a concern with simulation as constitutive of the self and the world.

---

9   Francisco García-Moreno Barco, *La narrativa española a la luz de la crítica posmodernista: El caso de Antonio Muñoz Molina*, PhD dissertation, Michigan State University, 1992.

10   Ignacio Vidal-Folch, 'Muñoz Molina: la novela ha de ser útil hasta la obscenidad', *ABC*, 15 March 1989, p.18.

11   Miguel Angel Trenas, 'Muñoz Molina: la literatura es una sociedad secreta', *La Verdad*, 7 March 1989, p.15.

12   Juristo, 15.

An important dimension of this is the novel's generic indebtedness. Although Muñoz Molina, as we have seen, denies affinities with the world of *novela negra*, it is undoubtedly the case that his work is replete with echoes of cinematic antecedents, as was also the case with *El invierno en Lisboa*. The novel shares with *film noir* an atmosphere gripped by fear and paranoia and a world characterised by deceiving and dissimulation. Critics have often given a mythical reading to *film noir*, seeing the protagonist's entry into the dark and frightening world of the city as a descent into hell, and this is equally applicable to *Beltenebros*, an impression reinforced by the novel's title. A number of other features appear to link the novel and the filmic genre on a superficial level: the autobiographical narrative of a male hero, the repetition of past events, the use of flashback, the constant use of darkness and shadow, the city as menacing, the choice of locations (the small-time, shadowy world of bars, clubs, hotels), the use of set pieces, such as the musical numbers, or the drugging of the hero, both linked to the inevitable role of the alluring woman. As in *film noir*, the use of flashback adds to the sense of fatalism which hangs over the narrative and approximates the text to the confessional mode in which the narrator works out his own anxieties. Here the anxieties relate to a crisis of identity, and are worked out in relation to social and gender stereotypes, and to the passing of time. Thus, in addition to the superficial affinities, *Beltenebros* relates to *film noir* in more profound ways. It takes up obsessive concerns of the genre, questions of control and loss of control, desire and conscience, the need to recall and forget, to repeat and to exorcise, all part of the psychoanalytical undercurrents of the genre, which have, incidentally, provided fertile ground for feminist critics.

Darman is an ambiguous figure, a man who crosses frontiers and enters dangerous worlds. His return to Madrid is constantly referred to as his return to the 'interior', as he moves away from the contemplative life of the antiquarian bookseller, a possible family man, to the active life of the potent killer. This duality is further complicated by another duality, that of the young assassin, invulnerable, strong and secure, and the older man, tired, uncertain and weak. The two women, the duplicated Rebeca Osorio, focus his crisis. In another striking way, these characters combine stereotypes of *film noir*, for Darman is both the young man and the middle-aged man, usually competing opposites, and Rebeca embodies both the alluring, dangerous female and the protective feminine figure, living out an eccentric domesticity in protecting the victim. Woman here is again shown to relate deeply to man's insecurities about his own identity. Andrade is not afraid of Rebeca's betraying him, but more profoundly he fears 'su misma existencia y la perfección de su piel y su manera de mirarlo, la casualidad ya inflexible de haberla conocido y de pertenecerle sin remedio' (p.133). Woman somehow offers the security of possession, but also the anxiety of loss of freedom. In the club he shares her with others, just as her public performance reveals her dependence on another, the powerful man, perhaps Valdivia, as she gives pleasure, vicarious and voyeuristic. He also shares her physically, as she is a callgirl, unlocking men's fantasies in a fashion analogous to her mother's fabrication of fantasies in melodramatic fictions. The movement from melodrama to *film noir* is a movement from the home to the street, from the chaste to the carnal, from the innocent to the perverse. This movement functions as a means of escape from control, a means of being in charge of one's own life, as distinct from being possessed by a man.

Although *Beltenebros* is essentially Darman's story, told from his point of view and making his destiny that which concerns us, his search for his victim is refracted through his relations with the other characters and it becomes too a search for Rebeca Osorio, who represents the unknowable in a world of action, conspiracy and violence dominated by male figures. Her apparent function in that world is merely to defer for a time the killing of Walter and Andrade, but her more profound role is to throw into focus some of the contradictions of that male-dominated world. When she is dancing in the club, for example, and becomes aware of Andrade's presence, it is precisely his weakness which gives her a kind of strength, and man is made to act as a prop for the woman, in a striking reversal of roles: 'Imaginarlo débil y entregado la fortalecía' (p.138). Her dancing, moreover, implies movement and freedom, and liberates her from static poses in which woman is objectified. It is significant that in the film of the novel, she reprises a number from *Gilda*, in which it was performed by Rita Hayworth and which acts as a challenge to male supremacy, contesting his attempts at female containment. It is of course an 'act' in a double sense, a performance to beguile others and an implicit assertion of her freedom from control. Rebeca Osorio is the focal point which links all the lives in the novel and therefore becomes central to Darman's recovery of the past, interposing herself between him and his mission and becoming, in the fashion of *film noir*, an obstacle to the male's quest. She becomes also part of his quest, for she represents the enigmatic, the mysterious, in his pursuit of knowledge and certainty. His desire to remember and repeat is a desire to exorcise and forget, and Rebeca becomes an obsession: 'Para olvidar yo tenía primero que saber: para curarme de la venenosa ofuscación del deseo era preciso que pudiera cumplirlo hasta su mismo límite, y marcharme luego para siempre y no volver ni recordar' (pp.156-57).

Darman's quest, in its repetitions and circularities, leads to a merging of identities as he recognises that the world becomes the imposition of plots by others. The room in which he awaits Rebeca is timeless showing no 'indicio de pasado ni de porvenir' (p.109), a kind of eternal present. Andrade takes on the features of Walter in Darman's imagination, just as the symmetry of his death sentence reveals the world to be successive reductions to patterns which are imposed, not natural, in an endless play of mirrors reflecting 'rostros duplicados y lugares irreales y lisos como la superficie de un espejo' (p.111), all surface and no depth. Rebeca 'se ocultaba tras el nombre y la figura de otra' (p.112). The face, which is the hallmark of individuality, the assertion of identity, is again wilfully obscured in the novel. Walter's face is blown away and disfigured in blood, Rebeca's is hidden behind the make-up and style of the 1940s, Valdivia's is never seen, except in terms of reflecting glasses and the light of a cigarette. Darkness enshrouds all, like the anonymous faces, indistinguishable from one another, which watch the stage-act. People are as fictitious and as invisible as those imagined in Rebeca's sentimental novels, the products of imagination and untruth. Rebeca at one point appears to Darman as 'un simulacro de otra mujer que no existió' (p.167). This is what Darman feels about the unreality of his own life, constantly crossing boundaries, frontiers, in which the life left behind ceases to exist, partakes of the unreal quality of memory. Always in a state of transition, aware of other lives, he is increasingly conscious of the unreality of all of them: 'sentí que estaba transitando de una vida hacia otra, y que ninguna de las dos era verdad. Todo se diluía como la noche en el alba' (pp.152-53). All the faces of Darman's adventure merge into one, the driver in Florence, Bernal, the hotel receptionist, Luque, Andrade, the doorman at the *boîte*, finally to become that of 'Rebeca Osorio, su deseada y futura falsificación, volviéndose hacia mí desde la oscuridad del pasado, desde el recuerdo otra vez acuciante de la noche última' (pp.153-54).

The sense that life is beyond one's control is replicated in all the characters. In Rebeca, Darman comments on 'una obediencia sonámbula a los designios de otros' (p.167). A repeated feature of Darman's own characterisation is his sense that he is controlled by someone outside of himself: 'Alguien que no era yo me suplantaba y decidía mis actos' (p. 154), or by a double which is distinct from the conscious mind: 'yo o ese doble oscuro que nos usurpa las decisiones' (p.155). The pattern of the novel is one of duplications, so that it is driven as much by architectural as by existential considerations, even if these defy the logic dictated by his intelligence which rebels against the 'vanas duplicaciones del azar' (p.186). Nevertheless, when he comes out at Atocha, 'la duplicación del tiempo cobró una certidumbre de viaje circular' (p.186), so that ultimately he has a sense that 'el tiempo retrocedía como una película proyectada al revés' (p.191). The Universal Cinema, where he had coexisted with Rebeca Osorio and Walter, and the club, where he encountered the young Rebeca, are separated by time but joined in space, so that the unreality of the past merges with the mystery of the present in a world without the certainty of precise spatial and temporal references. It is this mixture of coincidence and pattern which appears to fascinate Muñoz Molina, the randomness of events and the pattern which logic and memory seem to impose upon them: 'Recordar es inventarse el tiempo. El pensamiento se mueve siempre en el tiempo, pero construye otro tiempo. La conciencia tiene unos territorios muy extraños y a mí me gusta que aparezca el azar, pero al mismo tiempo que parezca el destino, el tiempo tiene una arquitectura, una simetría. Las novelas no son ni estilo ni contenido, son fundamentalmente tiempo.'[13]

It is in the Universal Cinema that the novel is brought to its dramatic climax. The real revelation is not that Valdivia has taken the identity of Ugarte, but that Rebeca Osorio is alive and typing imaginary novels separated from the world by her madness. Her madness is a refusal to remember, a denial of the horrors of her past: 'negándose a ver y acaso también a recordar, muerta en vida, naufragada en la amnesia' (p.218). In a more general sense, Antonio Muñoz Molina has talked of the collective refusal of memory: 'En España no existe el pasado, no hay conciencia de Historia. En el fondo la postmodernidad y la llamada nueva novela significa: Mire no hay pasado, no hay nada detrás. Hay que contar lo inmediato porque no sabemos nada del pasado. El problema es que al ignorar el pasado no hay quien entienda el presente'.[14] Darman too had refused to remember, taking on his assumed and false life in England, with a counterfeit family and an alien tongue: 'había dedicado mi vida a no recordarla para no morirme de culpabilidad y de amor' (p.219). The novel's game of symmetries is complete, and the play of duplicities is exposed. Memory gives reality to events and places; loss of memory erases them: 'Uno cree que los lugares y los rostros dejan de existir cuando no los recuerda' (p.190). Resurrection of memories reveals the layers of reality under the layers of simulation. Valdivia's simulation of loyalty led to the fiction of Walter's betrayal and to its repetition in Andrade's. Andrade was cast in a role of victim of deceit, which was his real role:

Porque había nacido para víctima del heroísmo o del fraude, para culpable inmolado de los errores de otros y de cada uno de sus propios actos, de su inocencia inútil, de su tardío y torpe amor por una mujer que ni siquiera tenía una existencia real porque era la copia y la falsificación de otra, igual que él mismo había sido condenado a

---

13   Amalia Iglesias, 'Antonio Muñoz Molina. Todas las buenas novelas son tratados morales', *Diario 16*, 7 March 1989, p.30.

14   José Manuel Fajardo, 'Antonio Muñoz Molina. En España nos gusta ser genios', *Cambio 16*, 902 (1989), 122.

repetir la biografía y la desgracia de un héroe muerto veinte años atrás (p.222).

Valdivia/Ugarte dies in the darkness of the cinema, taking with him the 'identidades plurales' (p.232) which he had consciously created, leaving the others with their uncertain identities which are reflections of his. It is no exaggeration to claim that *Beltenebros* uses the conventions of the spy-thriller, with its false identities and illusory worlds, as a simulacrum of the insubstantiality of the person, of the absence of a centre to the self, of the mysterious darkness at the core of being.

CHAPTER SIX
'La soledad de las islas': towards a topography of identity in Belén Gopegui, *La escala de los mapas*, and Juan José Millás, *La soledad era esto*.

JUDITH DRINKWATER

The two novels chosen as the focus of this chapter deal in very different ways with obsession, with fin-de-siècle malaise, and the solitude, isolation, fragility and insecurity of the individual. Millás's novel is one of several by a successful, established author whose work concentrates on the construction of identity in the literary text, and in particular on the motif of doubles and alter egos.[1] Gopegui's is an extraordinary first novel with a unique perception of the links between language and interpersonal relationships. The trajectories of the novels are, in a sense, opposed to each other. *La soledad era esto*, neo-realist and confessional, traces the self-realization of a bored, middle-class Madrid housewife, Elena Rincón.[2] She lives a life of alcohol- and drug-induced idleness, but after the crisis of her mother's death, comes to a state of awareness and self-identity — and liberation from social convention — through the diary account which she pieces together of her mother's parallel life, and her own journal in which she learns to express her sense of self. In *La escala de los mapas*, a lyrical monologue of obsession and desire, the protagonist, Sergio Prim, pursues an unsuccessful love affair with a younger woman named Brezo.[3] He battles with the hermetic language by means of which he attempts to encapsulate his experience, but fails to translate it into a satisfactory relationship with her: only inside his head or outside the text can he locate the focus of his desire.

---

1 Millás's other novels include *Cerbero son las sombras*, 1975; *Visión del ahogado*, 1977; *El jardín vacío*, 1981; *Papel mojado*; 1983; *Letra muerta*, 1983; *El desorden de tu nombre*, 1988; *Volver a casa*, 1990; *Tonto, muerto, bastardo e invisible*, 1995.

2 Juan José Millás, *La soledad era esto* (Barcelona: Destino, 1990).

3 Belén Gopegui, *La escala de los mapas* (Barcelona: Anagrama, 1993). Gopegui has written a further novel, *Tocarnos la cara* (Barcelona: Anagrama, 1995).

A closer look at the critical discussion about late twentieth-century Spanish narrative is appropriate here. The two short fictions under analysis in this chapter would seem share the characteristics of 'deshumanización', 'ensimismamiento' and 'reprivatización' which have been provided as critical labels for modern Spanish narrative, if by these terms we refer to the ontological concerns of the narratives and the problematical relationship between the individual, desire and the environment which both describe. The so-called 'novela deshumanizada' discussed by Pablo Gil Casado is the egocentric literary vision which is the product of consumer society, and characterized by a sense of disillusionment in the face of false appearances. The protagonists of such narratives, with their burden of neurosis, 'andan incesantemente de un lado para otro, en busca de una identidad o tratando de escapar a un destino adverso o meramente anodino'.[4] Gonzalo Sobejano, in coining the term 'novela ensimismada', sees contemporary narrative in paradoxical terms: it is: '[la] novela que no quiere ser sino ella misma, novela y sólo novela, ficción y sólo ficción, sin por eso negarse a un enlace con la realidad del mundo, de la vida y de la conciencia', and which offers the reader 'la exaltación no de un mundo, sino de una conciencia de un mundo (en las *soledades* del individuo aislado)'.[5] José María Mainer analyses the 70s and 80s phenomenon of the 'reprivatización de la literatura', playing on the socio-economic connotations of privatization and the hermetic, greed-driven economy of the 80s. He writes of:

la refundamentación de un ámbito íntimo, *privado,* a costa de otros valores. Murió de consunción la trascendencia *social* en los años finales de los 60 [...] sobrevino una literatura obsesionada por sí misma, en permanente trance metaliterario, donde el sujeto enunciador vivía bajo continua amenaza de desposesión. [...] A la *reprivatización* económica — que ha concluido con el mito del estado benefactor y ha exaltado la iniciativa individual — ha de corresponder una *reprivatización* de la literatura: en lo que tiene de uso y disfrute por parte de autores y lectores.[6]

---

4   Pablo Gil Casado, *La novela deshumanizada española (1958-1988)* (Barcelona: Anthropos, 1990), p.56.

5   Gonzalo Sobejano, 'La novela ensimismada (1980-1985)', *España Contemporánea. Zaragoza*, 1 (1988), 12.

6   José María Mainer, 'La reprivatización de la literatura: el dietario como síntoma', in *España frente al siglo XXI. Cultura y Literatura*, ed. by Samuel Amell (Madrid: Ministerio de Cultura y Ediciones Cátedra, 1992), pp.23-24.

The dominant tone of discussions such as these is a negative one, suggesting the abandonment of proper social concerns in favour of a literature of selfishness and self-obsession. The implication is that, in literary terms at least, the move from political and ideological resistance in the 60s to the consumer free market of the 80s and 90s, whilst it may have resulted in greater autonomy and choice for the individual, has also brought with it a loss, whether this be of values, intellectual identity or social relevance, as well as a tendency to dwell on personal rather than social concerns.

Features such as diary writing, the confessional mode, or the retreat into a world of 'private' language mentioned by the critics discussed above as symptomatic of the inward turn of literature, are indeed to be found in the texts under review. They are present, however, not as escapes from grappling with 'reality' on the part of the authors or characters, but as instrumental in the probing of the construction of the individual and self-identity. It is precisely because such features are a commonplace of realist or modernist literature that they may be dismissed as overworked or hackneyed modes of writing, when in fact they constitute the most basic element of identity, which is the urge to narrate the self. In a contemporary society dominated by ready-made images and forms which the majority use as patterns to imitate, as John Macklin suggests in his discussion of popular genres in his chapter on *Beltenebros*, the return to diary writing, to one's own narrative, is a return to a primitive but primordial way of attempting to comprehend and apprehend both self and environment. What makes these narratives distinctive is their attempt through 'mapping' — and in a significant sense language understood as a 'map' or set of signs and symbols which must be interpreted — to redefine, shape, and capture that identity in the time and space of the narrative. Both novels examine the process of the individual, private, or secret construction of being and the world, in contrast to the way in which identity is shaped or distorted by outside influences, as is the case, for example, in Rosa Montero's *Amado amo*. They do this by insisting upon issues of real and imagined spaces/places, and the protagonists' attempts to rationalize these spaces — especially that occupied by the city — by means of maps, networks or systems, and to find escape routes from their predicament as a part of the process of fixing their identity and that of others in time and space. Both texts demonstrate a fluid and overlapping metaphorical relationship between the city and other geographical terrains with their maps and systems; the body with its distinct members, attributes, functions and infirmities; and identity and language. The mapping of the land, like the mapping of the body, represents the assertion of self over the unknown. Ultimately, therefore, through the interweaving of metaphor, whose significance lies beyond the primary meanings of the words and referents which constitute it, identity in both texts is seen as a sign, a function of language, and is of necessity a flux whose meaning is always open to question, is endlessly deferred and lies beyond articulation. The efforts of the protagonists/narrators of both texts to create or recreate themselves or each other through language are constantly thwarted, and whilst Elena's final blinding vision of the solitude '[que] irá incorporeizándose una forma oscura y bella como la del diablo' (p.181) suggests a coming to terms with the world which she has recreated through language, Sergio Prim's ultimate realization that his identity and existence and those of Brezo are reduced to words on a page and that beyond those words lies the refuge or 'hueco' he has been seeking, leads to the conclusion that indeterminacy and infinite space must be accepted as the only basis for identity in *La escala de los mapas*.

The obsession with space/place and language/identity found in *La soledad era esto* and *La escala de los mapas* is also one of the delineating features of postmodern culture, and it is a preoccupation such as this which ties contemporary Spanish narrative in with broader currents in western literature and provides a more contextually relevant, if not more positive, focus for Spanish writing than the critical approaches outlined earlier. Postmodern culture, according to Steven Connor, is fixated on the idea of compiling lists, drawing maps, ordering knowledge, in order to construct a 'vision of a cultural heterotopia, which has no edges, hierarchies or centre', and which brings with it 'a crisis of self-definition'.[7] The postmodern writing subject takes refuge in a private, self-governing world, in 'the building of textual worlds'.[8] She inhabits a 'pluralistic ontological landscape', wherein the expression of desire through language becomes the only lived reality.[9] In such a landscape, as Patricia Waugh states, 'Self is an endless gathering of fragments of experience'.[10] Frederic Jameson addresses the process whereby identity is acquired in late twentieth-century post-capitalist society, when fragmentation may cast the individual out into a solitary orbit yet at the same time provide the conditions for the formation of a unique identity: 'each group coming to speak a curious private language of its own, each profession developing its own private code or idiolect, and finally each individual coming

---

7   Steven Connor, *Postmodernist Culture. An Introduction to Theories of the Contemporary* (Oxford: Blackwell, 1989), p.19.

8   Connor, p.125.

9   Brian McHale, *Postmodernist Fiction* (London and New York: Routledge, 1987), p.36.

10   *Postmodernism. A Reader*, ed. by Patricia Waugh (London, New York, Melbourne, Auckland: Edward Arnold, 1992), p.8.

to be a kind of linguistic island, separated from everyone else'.[11] In both *La soledad era esto*, and *La escala de los mapas*, the idea of the linguistic island, the solitary space, shapes the text and our understanding of it. Of her own body — and by extension the diary she is setting down, and the text of the novel in which it is embedded — Elena's mother writes: 'Hay quienes dudan entre definirlo como un continente o como una isla, y ello se debe a que posee las complicaciones de los continentes y la soledad de las islas', and refers to its 'zonas desérticas' (p.118). For Elena, solitude brings with it total isolation, but also the possibility of starting again from nothing on an ontological desert island:

> Pues la soledad era esto: encontrarte de súbito en un mundo como si acabaras de llegar de otro planeta del que no sabes por qué has sido expulsada [...] La soledad es una amputación no visible, pero tan eficaz como si te arrancaran la vista y el oído y así, aislada de todas las sensaciones exteriores, de todos los puntos de referencia, y sólo con el tacto y la memoria, tuvieras que reconstruir el mundo (pp.133-134).

Sergio Prim writes of his 'isla desierta' (p.30), the solitary spaces of his mind where he imagines or invents Brezo, and time and time again reiterates his sense of his own solitariness and that of those around him: 'el aparato innecesario de mi soledad' (p.38); 'la soledad del viajero' (p.129); 'Antes no les miraba [a los viajeros de las ocho de la mañana], apartaba la vista de ese espejo de soledad, sudor y ruina' (p.202). The motif of the island surrounded by stormy seas is used more than once to underline this expression of solitude, and to suggest the idea of the individual marooned in a hostile world: 'Una ciudad en donde llueve se aísla, una oficina cuyos ventanales muestran ráfagas de agua movidas por el viento parece de otro mundo' (pp.39-40); 'Un hombre llega a su apartamento, cruza la puerta y no halla ciervo ni dintel, y le parece que el paisaje de su calle pudiera pertenecer a Irlanda o Córcega pues flota a la deriva en un océano que también flota a la deriva en un océano que ...' (p.190). A variant on the theme is the snowbound village: 'Sergio Prim era un pueblo de Burgos cuando nieva: territorio aislado' (p.135).

The texts shed light on the work of closed groups, the 'linguistic island' — entrepreneurs, doctors, psychoanalysts, geographers, detectives — who assume or appropriate the responsibility in late capitalist society for the design, building and manipulation of the physical environment, and dictate

---

11   Frederic Jameson, 'Postmodernism and Consumer Society', in *Postmodern Culture*, p.114.

the models of 'society' and the individual psyche to which protagonists and readers alike are subject. The 'professionals' employ 'scientific' procedures in order to reveal or shape the identity or reality of people, objects or ideas in the world. But the experience of Elena Rincón and Sergio Prim shows that knowledge of this type does not constitute a definitive lever on fact nor does it provide any certainty about the existence of the individual or of others. In Elena's case, the detective who informs her of her husband's double-life with his mistress and his shady business deals, also makes pointed comments about the nature of Spanish politics and business life, which has been transformed so radically from the hope and action of the Sixties to the complacency and corruption of the Eighties: the detective may not possess the key to Elena's 'liberation' but he is able to demonstrate to her the dissolution of the social class to which she belongs. Sergio Prim's professional life as a geographer does nothing to help him in his quest for the 'hueco', and Maravillas Gea, his psychologist, is equally ineffective in curing him of his obsession. In societies such as those depicted in these novels, the solitude of the individual is radical and the exclusiveness of different social groupings such that it enhances rather than breaks down that isolation.

If the commonplace of ontological enquiry found in both these narratives is a feature of (post)modern literature, so too is the backdrop of the city, which traditionally has served as a metaphor for the restrictions of urban society and for the isolation and marginalisation of the individual who is asphyxiated by urban life, the 'hombre pequeño' (p.33), in the words of Gopegui, or, as the critic Ignacio Echevarría would have it, the 'conventional woman', since he chooses to condemn the '[c]onvencionalidad [...] del personaje mismo de Elena' in a review of La soledad era esto.[12] Another critic comments on the way that there is in literature 'an overt linking of the city with cultural and personal anxiety, a growing despair over the increasing difficulty of achieving a balanced relationship between the individual person and his social environment', and these urban surroundings serve to throw into relief the 'small men', like Flaubert's Moreau or Joyce's Bloom, 'who are unable to cope with their urban environment or with themselves'.[13] Elena Rincón and Sergio Prim live out their stories in Madrid: both of them carefully catalogue their movements through named streets and quarters, echoing the toings and froings of the characters of the Galdosian novel through the alleyways and underworld of the nineteenth-century capital. But these texts are not classic realist novels, nor what the critic Andres Amorós calls the 'novela urbana,

12   Ignacio Echevarría, 'Otra mujer' (review of La soledad era esto), Quimera, 98 (1990), 67.
13   Burton Pike, The Image of the City in Modern Literature (Princeton, New Jersey: Princeton University Press, 1981), p.xiii; p.100; p.101.

que intenta comenzar a reflejar nuestro mundo de hoy, el de las ciudades españolas en la Democracia'.[14] Ultimately the urban setting serves not as a social document, but to suggest the physical and social parameters of contemporary life, inclusion in and exclusion from the social world, in much the same way as the streets of Oxford enable the narrator of Javier Marías's *Todas las almas* to construct his identity in a foreign city. The motifs of the map and the labyrinth which punctuate both texts are a part — even if an obvious one — of the attempt to fix and chart the nature of individual identity in society, and their ambiguous status is a reflection of a generalized anxiety: 'The inhabitant or visitor basically experiences the city as a labyrinth [...] He cannot see the whole of the labyrinth at once, except from above, when it becomes a map. Therefore his impressions of it at street level at any given moment will be fragmentary and limited [...]'.[15] The order of the map and the labyrinth, both of which are referred to in the two texts, is constantly undermined by the threat of disintegration which is implicit in it: they only make sense from above, so that those who enter the streets or the maze are bound only to have a partial knowledge of where they are and where they are going. Similarly, self is an apparently reducible concept from the 'outside' — from the vantage point of the philosopher, psychiatrist, psychoanalyst or religious guru — but a labyrinthine series of roundabouts, cul-de-sacs and dead-ends when experienced from within.

La soledad era esto centres on the obsession of the protagonist, Elena, with her 'bulto intestinal', the symptom of a psychosomatic disorder, which is the physical manifestation of the ontological doubts which assail her and which she cannot expel from her body or rationalize. The disorder of her body is fuelled by her dependency on drink and drugs, and hampers her personal development in much the same way as similar bodily disorders (illness, fainting, amputation) limited the existence of the nineteenth-century female literary protagonist. The body is exposed in *La soledad era esto* — much in the way that it might be in a Galdós novel — as being a '[map] of power and identity', its apparent naturalness representing a cultural construction or set of cultural expectations, its disorders as well as its orders having to be unlearned in order to free the individual from its shackles.[16] As Barbara L. Marshall writes, 'one of the key aspects of 'subjectivity', of 'consciousness', of 'identity' — be it classed, gendered or raced — is coming

---

14   Andres Amorós, 'Novela española 1989-1990', *Insula,* 525 (1990).

15   Pike, p.9.

16   D. Haraway, *Simians, Cyborgs, and Women: The Reinvention of Nature* (London: Free Association Books, 1991), p.180, quoted in Gillian Rose, *Feminism and Geography. The Limits of Geographical Knowledge* (Cambridge: Polity, 1993), p. 32.

to terms with, or learning to inhabit, one's body', and it is this which Elena sets out (unwittingly) to do.[17] Her rejection of conventional bodily trappings (long hair, neat suits), and her shaking off of hypochondria at the close of *La soledad era esto* represent, for all their triteness, a coming to terms with this bodily aspect of existence, and the assimilation of the body into a sense of identity, the unity of body and 'soul' or 'sensibility'. Elena's obsession with her body is worked out through the parallel with her mother, who reveals in her diaries the existence of a cancerous lump in her breast, which she conceals and which eventually kills her. The mother's predicament is the corruption of the body from within, by the hidden enemy. But there is, and markedly so in Elena's case, a corruption of the mental faculties as well, since the malaise is a secret obsession which invades the minds of the two women. Elena's mother and Elena compose journals in which they analyse the discomfort and illness experienced through the physical body and its contact with the world, and through this analysis they attempt to establish their identities and their position with regard to others. Their bodies are the maps which define, or should define, the limits of what is outside and what is inside, and it is through 'writing' their bodies that the self inside can be liberated.

In her diary, Elena's mother elaborates on the metaphor of the body as city, and the image of urban containment serves to express her feeling of alienation from, and simultaneous entrapment within, her body:

> Realmente, un cuerpo es como un barrio: tiene su centro comercial, sus calles principales, y una periferia irregular por la que crece o muere. Yo no soy de aquí, de esta ciudad que denominan Madrid, capital de estado [...]. El caso es que llegué a este barrio roto que tiene una forma parecida a la de mi cuerpo y una enfermedad semejante, porque cada día, al recorrerlo, le ves el dolor en un sitio distinto. Las uñas de mis pies son la periferia de mi barrio. Por eso están rotas y deformes (p.48).

The city and the body merge into one as she looks down from her window, but the scene bears no more relation to reality than does a map to the land it purports to describe, and the identity of the body and the social world are called into question: 'Como vivo en un piso alto, he visto la ciudad como quien contempla un cuerpo tendido. Esta ciudad es un cuerpo visible, pero la visibilidad no es necesariamente un atributo de lo real. Quizá no exista ni existamos nosotros' (p.130). Elsewhere, she sees the body as geographical terrain, a wilderness mysterious and uncontained: she refers to the

---

17   Barbara L. Marshall, *Engendering Modernity. Feminism, Social Theory and Social Change* (Cambridge: Polity, 1994), p.113.

'glaciaciones, terremotos y estallidos internos' which have shaped it, and to different parts of her body which she alludes to as 'superficie hostil', 'un matojo de hierba', 'una caverna' (p.118).[18]

For Elena, too, obsessed with her imagined intestinal blockage, the body is like a city or society, in that its forms of organisation are menaced by corruption and degeneration:

> pensé en mi propio cuerpo, que al fin y al cabo es un sistema, y tuve que admitir que gracias a la composición de los alimentos, localizada en el aparato digestivo, nos podemos mover y crecer, aunque también morir. Luego pensé en la enfermedad, sobre todo en la enfermedad de mi madre [...]. Aquella corrupción, localizada en su pecho, la libró de otra enfermedad más fulminante. Leí en algún sitio que un cuerpo convenientemente enfermo, igual que una sociedad convenientemente corrupta [...] previenen al organismo de invasiones parasitarias de mayor entidad (p.48).

Elena's mother, as already mentioned, considers her body as if it were a geographical entity, with a definable topography to be mapped out. Elena applies the idea of the map to the events in her life, or rather her interior life, and concludes that there is no correlation between life or identity and the narrative of self which the individual constructs:

> Yo sé que un diario de este tipo es una suerte de mapa esquemático en el que se relatan los aspectos más sobresalientes de la propia vida. Sin embargo, en mi imaginación, el diario es la vida misma. Alguna vez leí algo acerca de quienes confunden el territorio con la representación del territorio (el mapa); tal vez eso es lo que me sucede (p.115).

Ultimately the fabric of existence consists not in what sustains it from the outside — the body, the exterior world which can apparently be mapped — but the inner workings of consciousness itself.

The text is dominated by the idea of frontiers, lost homelands, impenetrable barriers, which emphasise the chasm between the inner and the outer self, and between the individual and others. Elena and her brother inhabit their own separate spheres, and find it impossible to return to the

---

18 For comments on this, see also Isolina Ballesteros, *Escritura femenina y discurso autobiográfico en la nueva novela española* (New York, San Francisco, Bern, Baltimore, Frankfurt am Mein, Berlin, Wein, Paris: Peter Lang, 1994), pp.157-158.

'primera patria' of their childhood, 'un territorio común en el que el intercambio habría sido posible todavía' (p.54). During a night of insomnia, Elena faces 'la frontera del terror', and becomes aware of the part played by her mother, as a self, an identity, in bridging the gaps between material objects, conferring sense on the physical world: 'el viejo orden, la antigua armonía, la sintaxis familiar que evocaban la butaca y el reloj y en la que su madre había jugado el papel de cópula, de unión' (pp.57-58). Later, we are told that Elena fears that she will 'convertirse ella misma en su propia madre atraída por aquel conjunto en que ella, en aquellos momentos, actuaba de cópula o de unión' (p.85), as she occupies the space in which her mother once sat. The only point at which time and space coincide, and identity asserts itself over the external world is in language itself: 'Sujeto, verbo, y predicado, gritó atravesando el salón en un movimiento de pánico' (p.58): it is only through language that Elena achieves some sort of order, some sort of map in her life, the possibility of writing her body, a 'realidad propia en que retirarse a vivir' (p.131), and in this she recognises her debt to her mother: 'me mostró el estrecho pasillo y las mezquinas habitaciones por las que debería discurrir mi existencia, pero al mismo tiempo me dio un mundo para soportar ese encierro o para hacerle estallar en mil pedazos' (p.131).

    La soledad era esto is prefaced by a quotation from Kafka's Metamorphosis: 'Es que deseaba de verdad se cambiase aquella su muelle habitación, confortable y dispuesta con muebles de familia, en un desierto en el cual hubiera podido, es verdad, trepar en todas las direcciones sin el menor impedimento'. This establishes from the outset the novel's preoccupation with the opposition of interior/exterior, self/other. The metamorphosis which Elena undergoes, and the decision she takes to assume an autonomous identity, takes place in the alternating context of private/interior and public/exterior spaces: the rooms of the flat where she lives with her husband, her late mother's flat, bars, hotel bathrooms, set against the backdrop of the streets of Madrid, and, at the close of the novel, the trip to Belgium. The domestic space is transformed into the free realm of desire. Similarly, Elena's process of self-realization comes about through the jigsaw effect of the different versions of her own inner self which come to form a whole. The narrative provides her with a series of mirrors, or doubles of herself, in which she sees reflected her own image: the exercise books in which Elena's mother writes her diary, and tells a story which comes uncannily to resemble Elena's own; the antípoda, or childhood double invented by the mother and who bears Elena's name; the reports prepared by the detective who Elena hires at first to investigate her husband's extramarital dalliance, and then to shadow and report on her own movements. Throughout the novel, Elena's identity is confirmed by a series of relationships with 'others' which imply situations in time and space: by her bonds with her mother; her identification with her mother's *antípoda*; her interaction with the unseen but ever-present detective, who may be her alter ego or may be the man of her dreams; and her place in the generations of women represented in the mother, Elena herself, Elena's daughter, and the daughter's unborn, ungendered child, which ensure a continuity of identity over time. Elena becomes through these relationships, in the words of the detective in one of his first reports on her husband, the 'sujeto objeto' (p.65) of her own story, part narrated by external voices, part narrated by herself, her identity dependent on the conjunction of the language of the two narrative points of view.

In *La escala de los mapas*, the identity of the self and of others, the gap between 'La realidad y el deseo' present in the text in the volume of poetry through which Sergio tries to explain himself to Brezo (p.30), eludes both language and cartography. Sergio Prim, a specialist in urban planning and the production of maps, centres his obsession on the search for a 'hueco' beyond lived reality, beyond language, where he may take refuge from the pressures of social relationships. He tries, and ultimately fails, to capture the essence and the person of Brezo, the object of his desire, through the metaphor of mapping, and the series of motifs and metaphors which recurs throughout *La escala de los mapas* — distance, interiority, systems, street maps, mind maps, frontiers — as in *La soledad era esto*, serves to indicate the impossibility of containing or rationalizing the interior life of the self, and the distortions which arise from attempts to do just this. As Rosalyn Diprose and Robyn Ferrell observe, 'Mapping, as representation, is inextricably caught up in the natural production of what it represents'.[19] In the same way that Elena Rincón perceives that the map and what is mapped may not be one and the same thing, so Sergio Prim realizes that as he seeks Brezo and tries to understand their relationship, he invents her, and the more he invents her, the less she is a 'real' person' to whom he can relate. In many ways, Sergio Prim's interior life is obsessive and claustrophobic, yet at the same time the world which he imagines and travels through in his escapist narrative extends far beyond the confines of the streets of Madrid, and the telescoping geographical references serve to widen his otherwise wilfully limited horizons. There are abundant references to the Spanish provinces; whilst Sergio refuses to venture abroad, Brezo's connections with the cold wastes of Finland are frequently alluded to; in his mind he travels countries, continents, and even the outer reaches of the universe, the Milky Way. His ontological dilemma is made manifest in his radical sense of solitude, in the contrast between interior and exterior, and his attempts to pare existence down to its

---

19 *Cartographies. Poststructuralism and the Mapping of Bodies and Spaces*, ed. by Rosalyn Diprose and Robyn Ferrell (Sydney: Allen & Unwin, 1991), p.ix.

minimum: 'Vivo como ese pequeño país autárquico [...] En mi república se practica la autarquía de repliegue: producir para autoabastecerse y permanecer inmodificado, al abrigo de influencias extranjeras' (p.29). He attempts to control physical space by means of maps and plans and yearns to fix his own identity and that of others by means of so-called mind maps and through the text which he writes:

No hay un adentro y un afuera, no hay un hombre en su casa, una urdimbre de aceras en las calles y, entre los dos, un mapa mental o filtro que modifica el paisaje, el desnivel de las cuestas, las escalas... Con un dibujante cartógrafo a sus servicio, cada individuo podría plasmar las imágenes de su mapa mental en un papel [...] ¿Pero cómo acceder a los mapas mentales ajenos? ¿Cómo señalarlas allí? (p.85).

Just as Elena Rincón is dependent on her reflexive relationship with the individuals around her, Sergio Prim tries to achieve a relationship with Brezo which will stabilize his identity, but his contacts with her serve only to emphasize their mutual estrangement: 'Brezo: región de mi soledad' (p.61). His problems with 'la distancia que me separa de las cosas' (p.44), his 'trastornos espaciales' (p.150), and 'problemas limítrofes' (p:209) lead him to consult a psychologist, but he does not find the answer to the question which troubles him and which he formulates in a conversation with his boss: '[D]ónde está el límite entre la vida exterior y la interior? [...] ¿[C]ree usted posible que las cosas existan fuera de nuestra mente?' (p.169). For Sergio, the only refuge from a perplexing reality is in his interior life, the inner labyrinth which is threatened by Brezo's presence:

Yo soy el Minotauro y tu venida me hizo vulnerable. Yo conocía la soledad geométrica: las doscientas cincuenta y cinco calles, las seiscientas doce esquinas, los cuarenta aljibes de mi apartamento estaban solos. Y hubiera sobrevivido a las espadas fieras, a los vastos ataques de los hombres, pero no a las paredes derruidas, al exterior, la luz. Amiga, mi Ariadna, Teseo no mató al Minotauro: fuiste tu, fue tu hilo tendido hacia la muerte de su laberinto y a su muerte (p.190).

In the outside world, the idea of the maze is continued, for everything depends on invisible networks of transmission and reception: television images, phone calls, where the need to make the correct connections on the correct wavelength — '[e]s preciso conectarse, Brezo, mira qué sucesión de antenas por los tejados (p.173) — provides a parallel for the hide and seek of relationships: 'Y así también existe la red del deseo con sus líneas cruzadas, la red de los insomnes, la de los amantes de César Franck, la sutil red de puntos, rendijas e intervalos que es el hueco, ese filo de espacios parados por donde me aproximo a ti' (pp.173-174).

For Sergio Prim, the only route to salvation is through language, but this proves to be a treacherous medium: 'hay tantos cines, Brezo, y es tan raro que mis imágenes coincidan con las tuyas. ¿No te das cuenta de que si yo digo árbol me figuro un pino mediterráneo mientras tú ves abetos? Yo digo tren y escuchas Talgo rojo, mas yo en verdad decía el antiguo expreso de Lusitania' (p.224). In the pages of books, he perceives a refuge:

> di en pensar que el mismo sistema que rige para la tierra y sus mapas, rige para los hombres: escalas y signos, representación. Los mapas de los hombres son los libros. [...] Brezo, yo ando por los mapas, yo llevo conmigo el plano de Madrid, igual que un turista, porque tengo fe en los mapas. Ellos establecen una relación distinta entre nosotros y el mundo. Lo mismo hacen los libros (p.127).

Yet even in books, language cannot capture time or essence: 'El pasado no puede ser tocado y el futuro es una conjugación aguda y áspera: yo me equivocaré, tú viajarás, ella nos perseguirá, nosotros tropezaremos' (p.222). At the end of the narrative — when the reader·has been aware all along that the text is a creation, a construction designed to bear the weight of Sergio Prim's identity — the textual edifice crumbles as the narrator realizes that there is 'entre cada palabra, y al borde de cada letra, un intervalo, un hueco' (p.229). The linguistic island drowns in the ocean of endless meaning which lies outside the text.

An aspect of both narratives which challenges the construction of identity both within the text and within the reader, is the question of gender identity. *La soledad era esto* is written by a male author chiefly from the perspective of a female protagonist or narrators, *La escala de los mapas* by a female author chiefly from the point of view of the male narrator. In a literary environment attuned to issues of gender, androgyny, literary 'cross-dressing', this may seem an obvious or even clumsy device, or simply an opportunity for the author as narrator to distance her or himself from the narrative. One reviewer considers Millás's deployment of the device as demonstrating a hidden misogyny in the manner of its reinscription into a conventional female role of Elena: 'en cuya feminidad se instala Millás con una perspicacia sutilmente masculina'.[20] Another commentator, although dealing with the text as female

---

20   Echevarría, 'Otra mujer', 67.

'autobiography', draws no attention to the male author.[21] But in any case, the reaction to 'gender construction' in La soledad era esto may be quite different to the reaction to the same issue in La escala de los mapas. Millás's creation of the female persona is conventional insofar as generations of male writers have purported to depict and project the female psyche in literature; on the other hand, to embark on such an enterprise in the late twentieth century is a risky venture, since it must, in the light of feminist deconstructions of the male-authored text, be undertaken deliberately and in order to make some point about the legitimacy of such a procedure. In Gopegui's novel, she constructs a male narrator who is passive, overwhelmed by the fact that the object of his desire, strong-willed and self-sufficient, escapes him at every turn. This strategy is similarly challenging in that it defies convention, allows the movement of the female author into the area of the male psyche, creates distance, or suggests the parodying, through role reversal, of the traditionally unselfconscious literary presumption of the male author depicting or speaking for the female character. The ambiguous position of the authors in relation to the narrators they construct is further heightened by the sliding of the narratives into — or out of — voices which represent a gender other than the dominant one. La escala de los mapas starts, apparently, with the voice of the female psychologist perplexed by the visit of Sergio Prim; but quickly this female speaking subject is elided and becomes Sergio Prim: 'En aquel momento cerró la ventana y el cristal reflejó su rostro. Me tranquilicé. Sergio Prim tenía la expresión grave y no mentía. Sergio Prim no mentía porque yo soy Sergio Prim' (p.14). La soledad era esto also moves between the female narrators — the mother, Elena — and the narrative of the male detective (although the writing of his account changes constantly under the direction and orders of Elena). The effect of this shifting of the narrative is to create fluid identities within the text which are constituted by both female and male voices and which destabilize preconceptions about separate female or male identity. If the male author can construct a female narrating voice or a woman author a male narrating voice, assumptions about gender must be challenged, and gender itself seen once and for all as artifice which resides, in this case, in language.

Crucially, the conscious construction of the other-gender narrator introduces a further dimension of alienation or solitude, since these are voices which speak from somewhere where they are not, from a strange territory, another place. Sex/gender systems in social organization exist to create boundaries or territorial limits: 'their purpose is to delimit and contain the threatening absence of boundaries between human bodies and among

---

21   Ballesteros, Escritura femenina y discurso autobiográfico en la nueva novela española.

bodily acts'; the challenging of such systems can at best represent a freedom from the fixed social order: 'Ambiguities of gender and sexuality are [...] sometimes [...] celebrated as liberatory strategies for breaking with dominant ideologies'.[22] This playing with and construction of gendered identities is of particular significance in texts which deal with mapping and geography. In *La escala de los mapas*, the discipline of geography (and so, by extension, other 'professions' in both novels) is one which has until recently been male-oriented and male-directed. Gillian Rose explores the issues involved in the shift of focus as feminist subjectivity comes into play in geography and explains the threat to traditional interpretation posed by feminist subjectivity:

> Geographers believe that space can always be known and mapped: space is understood as absolutely knowable. That is what its transparency, its innocence, signifies: it is infinitely knowable [...].[23]

> Some of the founding antimonies of Western geographical thought are negated by [...] feminist subjectivity: its embodiment which overcomes the distinction between mind and body; its refusal to distinguish between real and metaphorical space, its refusal to separate experience and emotion from the interpretation of places. All these threaten the polarities which structure the dominant geographical imagination.[24]

Sergio Prim's confusion in the face of the intractability of Brezo, who refuses to be mapped, or fixed in time and space, suggests his encounter with the radical difference of the other who is also an island, an autonomous entity. This ties in with Waugh's observation that 'Women appear threatening [...] because they carry the culture's more widespread fear of loss of boundaries, of the uncontrollable',[25] with the narrator's perceptions of 'female' language in Javier Marías's *Corazón tan blanco* discussed by Ruth Christie in a later chapter of this book, and with César Miranda's complexes which centre on women and which will be investigated in the chapter on Rosa Montero's *Amado amo*.

---

22 *Body Guards. The Cultural Politics of Gender Ambiguity*, ed. by Julia Epstein and Kristina Straub (London: Routledge, 1991), pp.2 & 5.
23 Rose, p.38.
24 Rose, p.155.
25 Waugh, p.203.

Part Three
Postmodern Personae

CHAPTER SEVEN
Modernity and postmodernity: personal and textual identities in Juan Goytisolo's *Makbara.*

JOHN MACKLIN

Makbara[1] is not a text that has been located within the so-called *nueva narrativa española*, but is nonetheless exactly contemporaneous with it. By the time of its publication, Juan Goytisolo, approaching fifty years of age, had established himself as the most significant novelist of contemporary Spain with a reputation as the possessor of an outstanding, and iconoclastic, literary talent and as the unequalled scourge of Spanish orthodoxy. If his inclusion in this book needs to be justified, it is because his work raises precisely those questions of writing and identity which are its central concerns and offers points of contrast and contact with other writers whose works are analysed here. For the critic attempting to chart a typography of modern narrative, there are essentially only three points of reference: realism, modernism and postmodernism. This may seem unnecessarily reductive, but as a broad framework it is entirely defensible so long as there is a willingness to accept that these tendencies encompass many subcategories and, more importantly, that while they can be mapped on to the concept of literary periods (and would correspond to the nineteenth, early twentieth and mid-to-late twentieth centuries, respectively), they can and do coexist and coalesce within specific periods and within specific works. *Makbara* is interesting because it openly problematises the questions of generic and period classification.

There is nothing controversial in stating that there are multiple narratives of modernism and postmodernism. To take only two, somewhat antagonistic, versions, postmodernism has sometimes been seen as an intensification of the antireferential features of modernism, taking them to an unprecedented degree of radicality, or alternatively, as a break with modernism's aesthetic and integrating tendency and a return to mimesis, albeit ironised and problematised. It is within this problematical framework that *Makbara* is considered in this chapter in relation to textual and other identities. The very

---

1   Juan Goytisolo, *Makbara* (Barcelona: Seix Barral, 1980). All references are to this edition and are incorporated in the text.

questions which arise with regard to the identity of the subject arise equally in the case of the literary text, and can be construed in terms of essence and construct. Is the text's identity conferred by those inner structures which, as New Criticism and later structuralists imply, make it a self-sustaining artefact? If the author as sole authenticating source of the text's identity has been discredited by the New Critics and subsequent deconstructionists, what roles do writer and reader have in the construction of the text's identity? To what extent are the writer's and reader's own identities implicated in the processes of textual engagement? The circularities implied here suggest that the boundaries between textual identity and readerly strategies are blurred and that the difference between them is difficult to define and disentangle. A commonsense approach might be to suggest that the identity of the text is partly created by the interpretative and classificatory strategies of a reader, immersed in this case in the discourses of realism, modernism and postmodernism, and also from where it is positioned in relation to other texts which are in turn defined by interpretative strategies applied to and derived from other discourses. This is to accept that any approach to the textual identity of *Makbara*, and to the identity of the subject, will perforce be limited and provisional. Moreover, identity will be not be equated with coherence and any approach to *Makbara* must seek not only to establish an identity of difference from other texts but also of difference within it which will account for its multiplicities and contradictions and thus free it from the dangers of fixity. The text's identity, like that of the subject, is a dynamic process.

Juan Goytisolo, in an interview with José Escudero, published in 1993, stated that 'los textos literarios que he escrito, para mí, es una manera de introducir la modernidad en la literatura española.'[2] This is undoubtedly an accurate comment on Goytisolo's work since the publication of *Señas de identidad* in 1966, in which he is concerned with questions of identity, the nature of writing, and politics, ideology and society, and the relationship between them. The Mendiola trilogy, with its autobiographical basis, stands as a repudiation of the realist concept of fiction and, in its espousal of structuralist principles, it appears to conform to a version of modernism which asserts the self-sufficient nature of the literary artefact or, as Goytisolo put it in *Juan sin tierra*, the 'autonomía del objeto literario'.[3] *Makbara* is usually considered to be a text whose identity is founded upon the aesthetics of modernity, that is, through its self-realisation as a verbal artefact, but one whose radical textuality and challenge to the interpretative abilities of the reader are also a rejection of the project of modernity in its sociopolitical

---

2   José Escudero, 'Muerte, erotismo y espiritualidad. Entrevista con Juan Goytisolo', *Revista de Estudios Hispánicos*, 23 (1993), 139.

3   Juan Goytisolo, *Juan sin Tierra* (Barcelona: Seix Barral, 1975), p.312.

manifestations. This is one reason why, presumably, Stanley Black' comments that *Makbara* marks 'a change from a basically structuralist mentality to one more characteristic of post-structuralism or post-modernism'.[4] It is instructive, before looking at the text in some detail, to recall some of Goytisolo's own pronouncements on the work, in which he is at pains to stress the role of literary tradition in its genesis.

It is well known that the composition of *Makbara* is due in part to Goytisolo's reading of Juan Ruiz's *Libro de Buen Amor* in the market place of Xemaá-el-Fná in Marrakesh. The novelist insists that the formal features of the novel, which could indeed be deemed to be postmodernist, already existed in the work of the Arcipreste: 'La realidad textual que nos brinda no es bidimensional ni uniforme: presenta quiebras, desniveles, rupturas, tensiones centrífugas, transmutación de voces; en una palabra, polifonía'.[5] This juxtaposition of the modern and the medieval forms part of a more general scheme proposed by Goytisolo which postulates the influence of Arab literature on Juan Ruiz and *mudejarismo* as a characteristic, overt or hidden, of a large part of Spanish literature since the twelfth century. What is significant, however, is that what is in question is not just the possible presence of Juan Ruiz in Goytisolo, but, more importantly, our (and Goytisolo's) modern and postmodern readings of Juan Ruiz. Each epoch rejects, in order to surpass, the literature of the past, but almost always ends up by appropriating it, by colonising it. This could be seen as the essence of synchronicity, the overcoming of temporality through the synthesis of texts separated in time, which is characteristic of modernism. In particular, Goytisolo links the *Libro de Buen Amor* with 'la aventura literaria, posjoyceana, su diferente concepción del personaje, argumento, lenguaje novelescos'.[6] The complex interaction of the traditional, the modern and the postmodern, and the coherences and incoherences this entails, constitutes the peculiar textual identity of *Makbara*. This identity is, as we shall see, bound up with other questions of identity in the text in which not only epochal and generic boundaries are blurred.

If *Makbara* can be related, on a formal level, to certain literary antecedents, its main political, social and ideological impact is due to its fierce attack on the values of the whole of Western society, an attack anticipated towards the end of the preceding trilogy. The attack encompasses capitalism which has invaded everything, creating a society dominated by consumerism,

---

4   Stanley Black, 'Orality in *Makbara*: a postmodern paradox', *Neophilologus*, 78 (1994), 586. This article appeared after a first draft of this chapter was read at a symposium on '*nueva narrativa española*' in Leeds in May 1994.

5   *Crónicas sarracinas* (Barcelona: Seix Barral, 1989), p. 54.

6   Juan Goytisolo, *Contracorrientes* (Barcelona: Seix Barral, 1985), p.20

advertising, the creation of false needs, political propaganda, the mass media, all manifestations of the processes of production, reproduction and consumption, which, in Goytisolo's eyes, lead to a denaturalisation of life and a repression of instinct. This thesis, as widespread as it is unoriginal, is clearly set out in the section entitled 'Radio Liberty', an extended parody of the language of the mass media, where reference is made to 'los sabios imperativos de la producción', 'una sólida mentalidad consumista', 'invención incesante de nuevas necesidades', 'adaptar la tecnología al hombre, e inversamente, el hombre a la tecnología', 'preservar el nivel de consumo del pueblo' (p.25). We can recognise here the basic postulates of postmodern society as set out by commentators such as Jean Baudrillard and Frederic Jameson.[7] Consumption defines the spirit of postmodernity and, in its alliance with advertising and marketing (there are several pastiches of the language of advertising in the text), has created a unidimensional world from which it is impossible to escape, denying the individual (a concept it extols) the opportunity to occupy an oppositional space. Against this homogenised uniformity is set the ideal of cultural diversity. The illusory site of opposition is sought outside, not inside, the system and in *Makbara* is occupied by two marginalised creatures, the Moroccan immigrant/pariah and the transvestite Angel, whose multiple transformations across the various sequences of the book challenge and undermine the certainties, stabilities and coherences of this postindustrial world, the reader's world. It is a double challenge, one based on the values of a preindustrial order and another on the use and abuse of the images and objects of modern society.

Makbara begins by establishing a series of dualities or binary oppositions, and though these are largely kept on a thematic level, they do function on a structural level as well. In the first section, 'Monstruo del más acá venido' the pariah wanders through Paris, represented metonymically by concrete allusions to Goytisolo's own district, which embodies, in its commercial premises, its commodified sex, and its citizens and families, all the paraphernalia of modern society. His presence in Paris is an example of the exploitation of the Third World by the First, but it is also a threatening occupation by the Other, a cultural infusion which Goytisolo undoubtedly welcomes. The pariah is the immigrant who works down the mines in France, and is thus an image of exploitation, but the presence of large numbers of such immigrants breaks down the cultural homogeneity of

---

7   In works such as Jean Baudrillard, *La Société de Consommation* (Paris: Denoël, 1970), *Le Miroir de la Production* (Tournai: Casterman, 1973), *L'Echange Symbolique et la Mort* (Paris: Gallimard, 1976), *Simulacres et Simulation* (Paris: Galilée, 1981), and Frederic Jameson, 'Postmodernism, or the Cultural Logic of Late Capitalism', *New Left Review*, 146 (1984), 53-92.

Western society, opening it up to cultural diversity. More interestingly, the presence of the Arab, the product of colonialism, displaced now from the periphery to the centre, throws into question the Western conception of its self. The implications of this become clearer as the text develops, but initially at least the East is opposed to the West, Islam to Christianity, since Goytisolo portrays the Muslim world as the antithesis of the West and also as an antidote to its reifying practices and dehumanising ideologies. 'Cementerio marino', for example, presents the Muslim world in contrast to the Paris of the opening sequence. In a further inversion, there is a chiaroscuro effect to the narrative as a whole, in which black and white, light and dark, are set in opposition, though the traditional positive and negative associations are reversed. In an interesting article, Paul Julian Smith, drawing on the work of Jean Baudrillard, especially his ideas of symbolic exchange in preindustrial societies and simulacra in modern ones, focuses on the dangers of Goytisolo's technique of inversion in setting up these marginal figures as the epitome of rebellion, and categorises his attempt as a failure. He nevertheless argues that there is a 'productive' dimension to his failure, since the 'very compulsion to repeat (to simulate) is at once an effect of the system and a form of resistance to that system'.[8] This is one reading of the text, but it is also possible to read the 'failure', the reversal of inversion, as simply a refusal of fixity, in which persons, things, places and positions metamorphosise and interpenetrate through the force of fantasy and desire. Multiplicity replaces unicity.

From the Western perspective, and perhaps more specifically for the Spaniard, the Arab represents the dark other,[9] against which one's own identity is defined, and in *Makbara* the Moroccan is constantly associated with darkness, which he deliberately seeks, as in the cinema and in the sewers, which in his case are given positive value. The pariah is alienated, but in the darkness of the cinema finds refuge, and his imagination can take him 'camino del mercado' and home to his own country. This is the initiation of a search which leads to the sewers, the cemetery and finally to the market of Xemaá-el-Fná, and parallels the text's other journey which embraces Paris and Pittsburgh, the surface world of Western capitalism. It is true that what appears to be emerging is indeed a simple inversion of hierarchies, for in the words of the reporters from PB News later, darkness is preferred to light, filth to cleanliness, chaos to order (p.34). The search for a more authentic

---

8   Paul Julian Smith, 'Juan Goytisolo and Jean Baudrillard: The Mirror of Production and the Death of Symbolic Exchange', *Revista de Estudios Hispánicos*, 23 (1989), 37-61.

9   Goytisolo comments on this specifically in a number of essays collected in *Crónicas sarracinas*.

identity appears to be invested in the Arab's freedom from the categories of the Occident. Against the logical, controlled, ordered world of the West is set the free, chaotic, sensual world of the Arabs, described in many passages of the book in highly idealised terms: 'suspensión temporal de las jerarquías', 'pasear lentamente [...] sin la esclavitud del horario [...] viajero en un mundo inmóvil y errático [...] espacio neutral [...] colectividad fraterna [...] territorio común' (pp.204-05). In addition to this process of inversion of values, Goytisolo openly uses a technique of hyperbolic parody. The advantages of euthanasia, and even suicide, are proclaimed for the non-productive old, a logical position in a society in which progress and continuous development are valued above all else. In the same sequence, capitalist concern for energy saving, for production, and for benefit in relation to costs, is extended to the realm of sexual relations and reproduction in a demonstration of the superiority of the artificial over the natural. In 'Le salon du mariage', sexual relations are inscribed within an ethic of consumerism as the universal couple, and the white clothes symbolise the lack of vitality in the Western world where everything is seen exclusively in terms of market value. The clearest example of commodity fetichisation is the image or spectacle. This is further explored in the context of tourism, which is a persistent theme in the novel. In 'Dar Debbagh', the tourists see the spectacle of the tannery, indifferent to the conditions of the workers and attentive only to the 'local color' (p.67). Armed with their cameras, they take photographs which convert reality into images as a means of possessing it, of keeping it as a personal possession. These images are added to the countless others they possess and become part of their own image, which they project to others. If tourism is the commercialisation of travel, in *Makbara*, Goytisolo opposes the traveller to the tourist, and the quest to the tour. In the novel the quest is the story of the two protagonists.

Makbara appears to assert itself as a love story in which liberation from the oppressiveness of Western civilisation is achieved through sexual love, itself a source of authenticity in a society where the needs of the body are often denied (in artificial insemination, in synthetic food, in the concealment of bodily functions). Goytisolo himself has repeatedly endorsed this interpretation of the work. In *Crónicas sarracinas*, he writes that '*Makbara* apunta a una liberación del ser humano a través del amor',[10] and in similar vein he asserts in *Disidencias* that 'Mientras el imperativo racional del trabajo tiende a convertir al hombre de hoy en un objeto más en un mundo de objetos, la llamada animalidad preserva su conciencia de existir para y por sí mismo'.[11] He makes no distinction between work in the so-called developed

---

10   *Crónicas sarracinas*, p.45.
11   Juan Goytisolo, *Disidencias* (Barcelona: Seix Barral, 1977), p.182.

world and work in the Third World. There is no idealisation of poverty, for the tannery is seen as degrading, being both production and spectacle and thus doubly commercialised, relieved only by the fantasy rape of the blonde tourist. The love between the Arab and Angel is, moreover, largely oral, that is to say, pure pleasure devoid of productive capacity. The explicit message of *Makbara* appears to be that liberation is achieved through sexual love (symbolised in the enormous penis of the Arab, an object of fascination for Angel), which is a source of authenticity in an alienating society. In the extended description of the sewers in 'Aposentos de invierno', the pariah is protected by the darkness, accompanied by the rats which run over his body and masturbate him, feeding themselves on his semen. If the intention is to portray the repulsive as something natural and even attractive and to make it contrast with the sanitised orderliness of the capitalist world, which flees before animality, the reader's reaction must still be one of shock. A more acceptable example occurs outside the cinema, in the first sequence, when the pariah comes face to face with the oversize teddy bear, an image like him of the domestication of instinct, and also of the substitution of image for reality, whereas he is assimilated to the world of advertising. The horror produced by the presence of the Moroccan leads to his assimilation within the symbolic system of capitalism, to the hypothesis that he is an advertisement for a horror film. The way in which modern societies have been conditioned to read the world is obvious here and the Arab is subject to a number of imposed identities. This identity nonetheless seems to be born also from the fear of the dark side of humanity which is repressed and which the horror film in its commercialism exploits. There is an enemy within (the monster is, after all, 'del más acá venido') and order is always threatened. For his part, the Arab seeks obscurity which liberates him from the enslaving perspective of Western onlookers, and the Parisian cinema where it is found anticipates such similar sites of darkness in the text. If the Moor represents for Western man his dark side, his other, the pariah accepts willingly (and also with a fatalism which Goytisolo portrays as being characteristic of the Arab) this association and confers on it a positive value. As in the cinema, the underground passages are a refuge from the alienating gaze of the so-called civilised world, a uterine space, but they are equally spaces of creativity and imagination, as will be the Arab market-place later in the work, the space from which and to which all paths lead. On the level of ideology, then, East and West are constructed as opposing identities.

In his treatment of the Arab, Goytisolo draws extensively on the stereotypes created by Western colonialism, political and literary, and he has acknowledged his affinities with, if not debt to, Edward Said's *Orientalism*. The lasciviousness of the Arab (his twenty-six centimetre penis), his lack of logic, inability to comprehend European rationalism (lack of ears), disregard for hygiene, are curiously features which appear as part of the author's exaltation of the Arab way of life, and are not simply parodied. They reinforce the stereotype, even though Goytisolo converts them into weapons of resistance, the marginal which threatens the centre. The uneasy coupling of parody and exaltation does little to sustain unreservedly the Arab as the site of revolt, suggesting as it does the appropriation of the stereotypes of the imaginary Other. And yet, in a very brief but interesting article, 'Lectura marroquí de *Makbara*', Malika Jdidi Embarec speaks warmly of Goytisolo's knowledge of Morocco, and his vision born of 'una sensibilidad, un conocimiento intelectual y una intuición creadora'.[12] It would appear that the stereotype and reality merge, or, to put it differently, signs are seen to be slippery and mutable. In this sense, it is appropriate to talk of the ambivalent identity of the text, founded on paradox and contradiction, and generating other ambiguities and unresolved conflicts which transcend the binaries suggested hitherto. If the text appeared to court the danger, frequently commented on by critics of Goytisolo's previous trilogy, of falling into a series of binaries in which the established code, value, or whatever, is simply inverted, this straightforward, and largely positive, message is complicated by the metamorphoses of the text itself in which elusiveness and fluidity run counter to the obvious oppositions it contains. For one thing, the site of this resistance is located in two figures of doubtful definition, the immigrant Arab and the transvestite (and indeed in a third, the Christian storyteller in a Moslem world), whose identities are often difficult to disentangle, forming part of an elusive pattern of transformations, displacements and confusions.

The confusions begin with Angel, who appears in the third sequence. The sudden and unexpected use of the feminine adjective disorients the reader, perhaps confused and hypnotised by the language of the first two sequences, but its essential effect is to highlight identity as a central concern of the book. Angel is expelled from a communist society for his/her failure to conform and for being critical of Marxist ideology, with its brainwashing, blind obedience, its new hierarchies, with gods and saints. This society is described in the text in a vocabulary of churches, dogmas, and theologies, with the Father, the interceding Mother and the Holy Spirit, whom Linda Gould Levine has identified, respectively, with Santiago Carrillo, Dolores Ibarruri, and Tierno Galván.[13] Marxism shares with Christianity a mistrust of the body, a public disdain for sexual activity, considered to be unimportant and possibly even counterrevolutionary, and the intolerant homophobia of Marxism-Leninism-

---

12   Malika Jdidi Embarec, 'Lectura marroquí de *Makbara*', *Voces: Juan Goytisolo* (Barcelona: Montesinos, 1981), p.84.

13   Linda Gould Levine, '*Makbara*: entre la espada y la pared - ¿política marxista o política sexual? *Revista Iberoamericana*, 47 (1981), 97-106.

Stalinism is of course well known. It is no surprise that Angel leaves the communist paradise deprived of a physical body, as her name indeed indicates, and that her liberation is achieved through a series of sexual experiences and in her occupation as a prostitute. Her life history, told to her clients in a parody of the sentimental autobiography, runs from infantile trauma, the impossibility of finding a solution in the capitalist world, or in psychiatry, the manufacture of her artificial vagina, a sex-choice rather than a sex-change, to her search for the Moor and her obsession with his gigantic member. Angel thus also reinforces the stereotype of the Arab and, despite her marginalised and dissident position, embodies the typical Western perspective. The Arab's penis is of course the instrument of his alienation, but it is also the instrument of his challenge to the West. Nevertheless, to enthrone the penis as a site of rebellion, together with the exaltation of sexual love, implies a sustained phallocentrism on Goytisolo's part. It is a posture which appears to replace the tyranny of reason with a new tyranny of desire. Moreover, it appears to institute a hierarchy which exalts the male, undermines equality between the sexes and subordinates and indeed humiliates Angel, who often appears as the submissive female. There are obvious analogies between *fellatio* and oral discourse, but in this context the observation of Linda Gould Levine is telling in that she argues that the act of swallowing semen is equivalent to swallowing male discourse.[14] This is a common metaphor for patriarchal domination (both linguistic and physical) in several of the texts discussed in this book. Goytisolo refutes such an interpretation, arguing that far from being 'un himno a la potencia genésica del sexo viril',[15] the Arab is a reflection of the European construction of the Arab Other, 'un "moro" esperpéntico, deformado por la imaginación "blanca" '.[16] Be that as it may, it would appear from the evidence of the text that the glorification of carnal love as a response to the oppression of capitalism is a chimera, unable to offer a sure route to authenticity. It is merely another reduction of the self to a specific impulse. The uncertainties which surround the characterisation of the Arab, including those in Goytisolo's own mind, are the uncertainties of identification, interesting in relation to questions of identity, but ineffective as instruments of attack and polemic.

If sexual liberation does not appear to hold the key to potential liberation but to a new enslavement, it might appear that language itself is emancipatory, or that radical artistic activity is a way of contesting conventional systems of representation. Goytisolo observes of language: 'No se puede fingir inocencia frente al lenguaje, porque el lenguaje no es jamás

---

14 Levine, p.99.
15 *Crónicas sarracinas*, p.43.
16 *Crónicas sarracinas*, p.45.

inocente'.[17] The idea is well-known. We perceive reality through mental structures which are cultural in origin. Art can contribute to the creation of new structures enabling reality to be perceived in new and different ways. *Makbara* is markedly experimental in form and highly inventive in linguistic terms. Its language is rich, suggestive, alluring, and is undoubtedly one of the great successes of the work. In its self-presentation as a linguistic artefact, the text concedes diminished importance to character, plot and narrative space, the hallmarks of realist fiction. It is distinguished, moreover, from classic modernism in that it reacts against the modernist exaltation of subjectivity. On one level, modernist novels delighted in the exploration of individual consciousness and in consequence required the creation of a highly individual style. Modernist aesthetics imply the existence of a unique subject, a private identity, and breaks with the public perspective of realist practice. *Makbara* rejects this position, and in its repudiation of modernism asserts itself as a text mediated through a plurality of texts, a convergence and divergence of voices, in which personality is dissolved. While the dissolution of personality would appear to be totally incompatible with a philosophy which proclaims personal authenticity, what is at issue here is even a refusal of this notion as being a classifiable and verifiable quality, defined by some standard, in favour of authenticity as eluding categorisation and determination. This idea is to be found in an earlier form in Nietzsche whose rejection of fixity and certainty is expressed in the image of a self as internally split into 'a multiplicity of subjects, whose interaction and struggle is the basis of our thought and our consciousness in general'.[18] This has implications for the writer's identity too, for writing is an activity involving combination, the rearrangement of old styles and dead voices, and is a site of conflict and contradiction. In *Makbara*, linguistic fragmentation, the plurality of discourses, indetermination, narrative self-reflexivity, the denial of teleology, create a text which interrogates the conventional ways in which the reader organises his knowledge of reality and by which individual identity is constituted. The interrogative mode extends also to the presuppositions of the text which is being constructed, so that the text is both self-confirming and self-contesting, its identity inevitably unstable.

One obvious tension in *Makbara* is the sustained dialectic between oral literature (itself a contradiction in terms) and chirographic literature. The text's oral character is adumbrated at the outset, in its proclamation of what Bakhtin so memorably called 'the culture of the loud word'[19]: 'al principio fue

---

17   *Disidencias*, p.296

18   Friedrich Nietzsche, *The Will to Power* (New York: Random House, 1965), p.490.

19   Mikail Bakhtin, *Rabelais and his World* (Cambridge: Massachussetts Institute of Technology Press, 1968).

el grito' (p.13). But this phrase also undermines the Biblical enthronement of the power of the word and denies the word as the origin of all things. Language in this text is subject to elisions, voids, multiplicities and evasions. The text that we are reading asserts itself as a production which resists attempts at consumption, which denies its status as a consumer product. One aspect of this in *Makbara* is the way in which sense is often subordinated to sound. It has been claimed that Goytisolo makes his Spanish take on some of the qualities of the more melodic Arabic language and he himself has argued that the text should be read aloud.[20] The language of the text has a tremendous power, almost self-generating, which carries the reader along at times without any reference to meaning, so that its hypnotic effect draws him into a web of incomprehension. This hypnotic effect of the words, the overload of textual excess, at times removes any need for coherence. It is pure creation, production without purpose. Indeed, some of the embedded language is incomprehensible, either because it is foreign (the use of multiple languages is a feature of the book), or because it is impenetrable. Each of the section titles is in a different language, but they are not all of the same order of cultural significance. The attempt to free the text from monologism is apparent, but whereas Latin, French and English are the patrimony of the educated Spaniard, or Westerner, Arabic is an alien language, and its incomprehensibility does reinforce the polarity between East and West drawn in the novel. Moreover, Arabic is used by the pariah in moments of intense emotion, as when he strikes the Salvation Army member distributing leaflets, or in moments of sexual arousal. But Spanish too is used in a variety of registers creating a rich linguistic tapestry. Some of this is for comic effect, as in the phonetic script of the letter written from the prison, or in the extended sports commentary on the sperm reaching the egg in a kind of crosscountry fertilisation race. There are comical variations on well-known Spanish phrases, such as 'Eché por los cerros del Rif', or 'Se me fue la paganía al cielo'. The novel draws on and parodies the systems of representation of consumer society (advertising, public relations, political propaganda, lonely hearts columns), indicating the heavily conventionalised nature of language and of our inscriptions within it, and perhaps reinforcing the notion of 'linguistic islands' discussed by Judith Drinkwater elsewhere. Equally, it draws on a whole series of literary representations, the *Libro de Buen Amor*, *A Thousand and One Arabian Nights*, Abelard and Heloise, Beatrice and Dante, or cinematic ones, horror movies and sentimental romances in particular. Like the rats, which feed off the semen of the Arab,

---

20 '*Makbara* como otras novelas mías y algunos escritores afines, entronca, modestamente, con dicha tradición (oral). Una de sus mejores lecturas sería una lectura en voz alta'. *Contracorrientes*, p.20.

Makbara asserts its own parasitism as it feeds upon and devours other texts. In a modern society, cultural, literary and linguistic parasitism is inevitable. There is no unmediated perception. The degree of defamiliarisation employed in the text to overcome this means that it is possible to speak of the generic instability of *Makbara*, which is intensified due to the abandonment of the traditional rules of grammar, the absence of normal punctuation, interchanges between pronouns, and the persistent use of the infinitive as the preferred verbal form, transforming sequentiality into synchronicity, thus inhibiting the chronological progression of the narrative, leaving it open to endless permutations, a recombination of signs freed from their referents. Signs migrate freely from one sphere to the other, as the random nature of the texts asserts the need for freedom from the conventional constraints of literary practice. The transformation of sequence into synchronicity is consonant with the aesthetics of modernism in which spatial arrangements take precedence over temporal ones. Repetitions, echoes and juxtapositions contribute to the effect of a synchronic whole in which the fusion of different perspectives destroys the limitations of a single viewpoint, but creates an integrated work through the reader's reconstructions. The totalising vision thus created operates at the level of the processes of the text, but not on the basis of a logic of representation. The stability of the omniscient vision of the nineteenth-century realist novel is destroyed. The reader is faced with a technique of incoherence, which is resolved only at the end when it is revealed that the story has been narrated by a 'halaiquí nesraní', a Christian in Moslem lands and hence another figure of doubtful identity. Goytisolo ends by satisfying the reader's desire for coherence, enabling him to order, up to a point, the disparate elements of the narrative. It is the text's concession to, or mockery of, the conventional demand for closure, but also a recognition that fragmentation is itself an invitation to impose an order. However, just as the encounter between the Arab and the Angel is constantly deferred, so the search for meaning on the part of the reader is prolonged throughout the text. If *Makbara* thus goes beyond modernism, inscribing itself within a postmodernist discourse, offering the reader a fragmented text which leaps without logic from one thread of the narrative to another, weaving and unweaving simultaneously, combining and recombining the elements in a process of constant self-renewal, it contains a residual modernism in its invitation to the reader to make patterns in its symmetries and asymmetries, repetitions and variations, metamorphoses and transformations. Within this fluid and undefined world, the reader can construct a storyline, he can create a series of binary oppositions, even if final meaning eludes him. The unusual use of language, its 'reencuentro con el barroco', to use Serafín Vegas González's phrase,[21] contributes to the text's elusiveness, for it is a level of the text's operation distinct from its storyline, which can be partially reconstructed through it. But if the storyline can be reconstructed, it still offers only a partial account of the experience of *Makbara*. In language and structure, the text rests on deliberately unstable foundations. *Makbara*, like the sands of the desert, or the limitless sea, which are two of the text's recurrent *leitmotifs*, refuses to offer the reader final points of reference, stability or orientation. The pronouns, as we shall see, are a very striking example of this.

Makbara, like other works by Goytisolo, is complex and perplexing in its pronominal structure. The use of first, second and third person pronouns had already been a feature of Goytisolo's writing before *Makbara*, as in the French *nouveau roman*, and also in the *Libro de Buen Amor*, as Goytisolo reminds us, but in this text it functions together with other destabilising devices to blur the boundaries between categories of character. The third person gives way to the second and then the first, altering the distance between reader and protagonist, varying from detachment, to fusion, to identification. It is a good device for creating that intimacy and fraternity which Goytisolo wishes to see established between persons and which he finds in the market of Marrakesh. More importantly, however, the switch of personal pronoun leads to slippage of identities as the play between them causes identities to dissolve and merge. The Moor, for example, is identified with the storyteller in the marketplace, where he remembers himself surrounded by listeners. Identification and differentiation are interchangeable. Taken together with other forms of character dissolution, the technique works with the dislocation of temporal sequence and indeterminate locations, to create a sense of flux and lack of definition. This process is a challenge to certainty and the clarity and categories which characterise Western thinking. Language of this sort is not essentially communicative, for communication is urged at the bodily level, and does not direct itself at the intellect. Rather it engages in its own subversion, and acts as an agent of the text's constant transformations. Thus the characters themselves are constantly transformed. The Moor has a multiplicity of names. The scene in the cemetery is repeated in the narrative, but not in reality, and each narration is different. Angel is both old and young, attractive and repulsive, a virgin and a prostitute. This is revealing about representation of the female in Western society. Angel, by assuming both stereotypes, destroys their validity as archetypes in Western iconography. At the same time, women are certainly more oppressed, and overtly so, in Moslem society. *Makbara* is

---

21 Serafín Vegas González, 'Ideología y literatura: a propósito de *Makbara* de Juan Goytisolo', *Arbor* (1983), 91.

certainly an expression of Goytisolo's admiration for Arab countries and peoples, but the simple inversions which are set up are progressively subverted. Annie Perrin perceptively relates this to the importance accorded to Angel's Hermes bag, in which she keeps the make-up of her trade.[22] Hermes is the god of exchanges and displacements, of journeys and travellers, and in mythology is found at crossroads and doors. He mediates between different spheres, but he also destroys trails, deceives, eliminates traces, and therefore is a fitting emblem of the lures and false trails of the text. The binaries and inversions which colour the surface of the text are blurred at a deeper level, where the refusal to define, to arrogate significance, is the motive force behind the text's combinatory illogicality. The text is produced and then destroyed in a refusal of the finality of production, which embraces places, stories, identities, and where the pleasures of incoherence and formlessness and flux are supreme.

Yet the tension in the text between openness and closure is never fully resolved. By giving precedence to *discours* over *histoire,* despite his claim to be eliminating Benveniste's distinction, Goytisolo demands of the reader a process of decoding. As in so many modern narratives, the chronology is totally rearranged to create an impression of atemporality. In fact, much of the storyline can be reconstructed, though with some effort. The pariah's early years, for example, are recounted in the section entitled 'Como el viento en la red', which also recounts the first encounter between him and Angel, an encounter which had been recounted earlier in 'Andrólatra', with variations. While we can reconstruct this through analysis, it is less easy on reading, where the overloading of detail, use of repetition, unusual language, and textual flow all disorient the reader making the creation of an entirely coherent pattern impossible. For example, as we have seen, Angel is in one occasion old, decrepit and ugly, on another young and attractive. In their first encounter she is described as being a virgin, after the creation of her artificial vagina, but then later as a prostitute. In a sense, the point is being made that these accidental facts do not matter, that Virgin and whore are irrelevant stereotypes. Similarly, the sequence of episodes is such that it is not possible to establish when the Arab lost his ears, though they appear to have been eaten by the rats. The name 'Orejas' is given to denote both his oversize ears and his absence of ears. Language is seen to be reversible. In another sense, these discrepancies are a consequence of oral storytelling, for if the text is not held in print, it can be endlessly varied. There is no official version, and the technique of dual or multiple possibilities finds its most obvious expression in the storyteller's doubts about how the tale ended,

---

22   Annie Perrin, '*Makbara.* The Space of Phantasm', *Review of Contemporary Fiction* (1984), 157-75.

and in his freedom to choose a happy outcome to please his audience. Literature is shown to be arbitrary and any teleology fictional. The other two denouements, Angel working as a prostitute in the cemetery and Angel living in the town and wandering around the tannery in search of the Moor, had already in a sense been recounted in the sections 'Cementerio marino' and 'Dar Debbagh'. All the transformations, permutations and combinations are possible in the tale of the 'halaiquí nesraní', whose presence is alluded to in the section 'Sic transit gloria mundi' and then explained in the final paragraphs of 'Noticias del más allá', where it serves as a link with the final section outside the storyline. The storyteller's words weave a net which entraps the audience 'en su sutil, invisible cárcel verbal' (p.220). The narrator's power is his 'posibilidad de contar, mentir, fabular, verter lo que se guarda en el cerebro y el vientre, el corazón, vagina, testículos [...] vomitar sueños, palabras, historias' (p.221). This word is the body, erotic, pleasurable, outside official and logical discourse, outside ordinary language, capable of endless renewal and metamorphosis. The narrator too is entwined in this process, for the narration is an obvious *mise-en-abîme*. There is a narrator (not the author), who is invisible, unknown and never characterised, who recounts the story, including the tale of the storyteller, who tells the story of his two characters, who in turn narrate their own stories, but through the voices of the 'halaiquí', who also voices the other participants such as the PB reporters, or the tourists, but also appropriates the voices of other texts, popular and learned, oral and written, literary and filmic. At the same time, the pariah often identifies with the halaiquí, and his own days in the halca. At the end, he appears to be listening to the story in which he himself is narrated. He is both the emissor and receptor. When the story is told and retold, the details are not quite the same, so that identities shift and merge, the locations differ, so that all could be the same, only told in different versions: 'lectura en palimpsesto, caligrafía que diariamente se borra y retaza en el decurso de los años: precaria combinación de signos de mensaje incierto: infinitas posibilidades de juego a partir del espacio vacío: negrura, oquedad, silencio nocturno de la página todavía en blanco' (p.222).

Reduced to a basic scheme, *Makbara* appears to be the combination of two elements: a rejection of Western, capitalist civilisation, together with its systems of representation, and a celebration of the Arab world and the primacy of oral narrative. The second element is used to deconstruct the first. Many inner contradictions remain, however, and the text does not internally cohere. The Arab world is not free from the authoritarian pressures found in the West, and this anxiety can only be increased for many readers by the emergence of new fundamentalisms. Some of the features identified with the East, especially in the realm of sex and drugs and the pursuit of unbridled freedom, are characteristics of advanced Western societies.

Goytisolo's ambiguous characterisation of the Arab is interesting here, for he is both a caricature and an ideal. The return to the medieval world, moreover, and to oral narrative, appears to be a nostalgia, but this world cannot be visited innocently. In its rejection of traditional realism, *Makbara* disdains story and history and transforms reality into shifting images. A tension remains, however, between the reader's sense-making instinct and the text's reluctance to conform, between chaos and coherence, and this formal ambivalence of *Makbara* finds its equivalence in the narrative strategies and the narrator's ambiguities which create a quest for identity which never resolves the antagonism between construct and essence. The solution offered to the text's ending, from the choices available to the narrator, is an acceptance of the arbitrary, fictional nature of all endings. This is a further dimension of the ambiguous textual identity of *Makbara* whose ahistoric world, its creation of a kind of continuous present, its desire to eliminate frontiers between spaces and identities, its final undecidability, all sit uneasily, in their celebration of postmodernity, with an underlying message of affirmation. *Makbara* reworks the basic ingredients of classic realism, character, plot and place, through the intertextual and experimental prism of postmodern practice and traditional oral narrative. As the coordinates of experience, they seem to survive their transformation in a way which demonstates their durability as categories of thought. If the ideological import of *Makbara* is compromised by the confusions of its message, these confusions are significant as ciphers of identity, reminders that neither self nor text are essentially fixed nor open to infinite mutation. For all the text's and the subject's fluidity, it cannot totally resist the reader's attempts to inscribe it within the parameters of established thought and language, while at the same time seeking to deconstruct them. The identity of the self, like the text, is narrated. It is impossible not to 'vivir, literalmente, del cuento' (p.219), but this cannot mean that Goytisolo posits a destruction of identity, only a problematising of it. What *Makbara* seems to assert above all is a belief in the primacy and mutability of signs. If the Arab appears to be a parody of the Western view of the East, he also provokes a reverse view of colonisation: the feminine is not possessed by the male coloniser, rather the Western female seeks out the male stereotype. The Angel is, moreover, a figure of sexual ambivalence and the Arab becomes part of the Western imaginary, but part of it, not its defining other. He returns as a 'fantasma, espectro', from within, 'del más acá venido', an image of the male, phallic, self-image of the West. In the end it would appear that everything: protagonists, narrator, the square itself, are read as signs, for everything operates at the level of discourse; these multiple and ambivalent identities are generated purely by discourse. And it is at the level of discourse that the narratives of modernity (history, reason, gender, race) are deconstructed by a parodic probing of identities as postmodern palimpsests in which both self and writing are deprived of the certitudes of essence. In this way *Makbara* sites itself at the interface of postmodernity and modernity.

CHAPTER EIGHT
Self-writing and 'lo que pudo ser' in *Corazón tan blanco* by Javier Marías.

RUTH CHRISTIE

Not only are the techniques involved in the writing of *Makbara* and *Corazón tan blanco* strikingly different, they are also divided in the time of their publication by almost fifteen years. And yet they do share the conviction that the self is not given, but made, and that the project of remaking the self is above all one of rewriting. *Makbara* bears traces of the social concerns of earlier novels, but the sophisticated emergence of the identity of its protagonists from the confines of social stigma and stereotype is at times strikingly postmodern. Similarly, the construction of identities in *Corazón tan blanco* is dogged by moral concerns, but their scale is individual/universal rather than social/political. It is as if the personae who inhabit *Makbara* live in a tale told by others, a story which they do not understand, and in which they do not belong, and struggle to be able to tell their own story, whereas the narrator of *Corazón tan blanco*, having begun confidently to 'tell' himself, discovers that it involves paradox, uncertainty, and a great deal of compromise.

In an interview for *Cambio 16* in 1988, Javier Marías says that his novels are 'el reino de lo que pudo ser',[1] and in his book of essays, *Literatura y fantasma*, he describes the narrator of his best-selling novel *Todas las almas* as 'quien yo pude ser, pero no fui'.[2] In *Corazón tan blanco* (1992), Javier Marías's seventh novel, many of the facts of the narrator's life again correspond to those of the author, and also to those of the narrator of *Todas las almas*. But whereas in *Todas las almas* the concept of 'quien yo pude ser pero no fui' subverts the notion of autobiographical writing and its allegiance to a genre whose status is based on the particular value of the 'already lived' life, it is more productive to discuss *Corazón tan blanco*, in the context of writing the self, in relation to Marías's concept of the novel as 'el reino de lo que pudo ser'. A different approach is taken in the later novel, in which writing the self is conceived of more in terms of an imaginative or inventive

---

1   Javier Marías, 'La magia de lo que pudo ser', *Cambio 16*, 80 (1980), 31.
2   *Literatura y fantasma,* p.86.

project, rather than an autobiographical one. The problematic identity between author and narrator is no longer the focus as it was in *Todas las almas*. The first person is constructed not in relation to a 'real' past, or to a self who in some way precedes the writing, but to a self who is constructed and changes in the telling of his story, the self as a narrational project.

The similar sensation of 'perturbación' or unease, that pervades *Todas las almas*, is described in *Corazón tan blanco* as 'malestar'. This 'malestar', caused at first by the difference between the narrator's expectations and actual reactions to his married state, stir him not to action so much as to serious thought. His 'cambio de estado' from lover to husband also radically affects his sense of himself as son. The models he resists have been based on emotions and aesthetics — love, desire, envy, passion, and so on, as exemplified in his father's life. Such have been the 'authentic' marital and filial bonds, and the narrator survives by reforging them. The novel begins with a young woman, the second wife of the narrator's father, who, having just returned from their honeymoon, goes into the bathroom during a family dinner, and shoots herself through the heart. This tragic end (at the beginning of the book) works, as did the dramatic suicide of Clare's mother in *Todas las almas*, as a contrast to the narrator's own more mundane affairs. But the effect is not one of a lost sense of weight, or nostalgia for a more meaningful world, but just the opposite. In the last pages of the novel the narrator imagines an analogous situation, in which his wife Luisa has an affair, and her lover obliges her to choose between him and the narrator, as happened with his father and Teresa. 'Pero en ese caso me contentaría con que ella saliera al menos del cuarto de baño, en vez de quedar tirada en el suelo frío con el pecho y el corazón tan blancos'. He is able to say this, so convincingly and tenderly at the end of the book, because he has managed to redefine his marriage, not in terms of his love for his wife, or hers for him, but in other, and often contradictory ways, disturbing and unresolved, but which look likely to ensure the survival of his marriage now that the world of his father — 'cuando el mundo [fue] más mundo' — no longer exists. In other words, by the end of the novel we find the narrator has managed to escape the path which seemed to be set before him, signposted by the ghostly repetitions and shadows of the drama of his father's past and the magnetic force of his presence, and to imaginatively reinvent himself in other terms.

At first the concept of the novel as the 'reino de lo que pudo ser' seems shallow, merely a futile attempt to imagine how things could have turned out if different actions had been taken, a rather facile synonym for 'fiction'. In its broadest sense it *does* incorporate the notion of an endless series of fictions — all those things which could feasibly have happened but did not — but it also implies what might have been *expected* to have happened but did not, the obvious path that seemed to be pre-ordained but which was not taken.

The narrator realises that he has drifted into his newly married state. In an early contemplative passage we find him remembering his thoughts of the night before his wedding. His marriage seems to him to be the inevitable result of small, chance happenings. He realises that things could easily have turned out differently :

> ¿Y si no hubiera entrado en ese bar?, [...] ¿Y si no hubiera aceptado el trabajo aquel lunes? Nos lo preguntamos ingenuamente, creyendo por un instante (pero sólo un instante) que en ese caso no habríamos conocido a Luisa [...] Pero [...] nacer depende de un movimiento azaroso, una frase pronunciada por un desconocido en el otro extremo del mundo, un interpretado gesto, una mano en el hombro y un susurro que pudo no ser susurrado. Cada paso dado y cada palabra dicha [...] tienen sus repercusiones inimaginables que afectan a quien no nos conoce [...] y se convierten literalmente en asunto de vida o muerte, tantas vidas y muertes tienen su enigmático origen en lo que nadie advierte ni nadie recuerda (p.92).

The implications and possibilities that the concept of 'lo que pudo ser' opens for the self as an identifiable entity go deep. In *Corazón tan blanco* the course that the marriage of the narrator, Juan, and his new identity as husband seemed destined to take is resisted by a championing of the concept in its 'broadest', seemingly futile, sense. The examples the narrator cites are apparently random and meaningless; the reader does not yet know, for example, that the 'frase pronunciada por un desconocido', and the 'susurro que pudo no ser susurrado' are particular 'movimientos azarosos' within the narration to come, determining factors, 'turning points', as we gradually find out. During the course of the novel we discover how some of these 'movimientos azarosos' were instrumental in determining the catastrophic events in the life of the narrator's father; in fact the narrator's own birth depended on 'un susurro que pudo no ser susurrado'. Yet any detail, we are made to feel, could have been shown, admittedly by possibly tortuous routes, to account for any other. Such 'turning points' are usually considered functions of autobiographical narrative.[3] But only in looking back on a life, in the sense of having read the book, is chance thus subsumed as fate; only in retrospect are 'turning points' created. The selection of determining causes depends only on the story we wish to tell. Speaking of his latest novel *Mañana en la batalla piensa en mí*[4] in an interview in *El País,* Javier Marías says that 'el mundo entero depende de sus relatores.

---

3   See Chapter Four, footnote 28.

4   Javier Marías, *Mañana en la batalla piensa en mí* (Barcelona: Anagrama, 1994).

Las cosas en sí mismas no son nada. [...] Depende de quién cuenta y de quién escucha'.[5] This idea is also fundamental in *Corazón tan blanco*, in which the narrator gradually realises that there is nothing inevitable about identity, that telling the story of oneself — to oneself or to others — may be a linear process, but the track it runs along is not laid down beforehand. One cannot avoid authoring one's past, but the suspicion that this authoring may be a futile attempt to impose value where none exists is something which the one-trackedness of life cannot disprove. The consequences of this are devastating for ideas of the self and personal identity, heavily based on accountability as they are, for we imagine that the important happenings in our lives are down to our ability or inability to make the right choices. The passage quoted above suggests that the really important things, the matters of life and death, are determined in the long run by tiny, valueless coincidences. The concept of self-determination, seen on this scale, is no more than an ineffective kind of meddling.

In order to indicate the kind of thought that the narrator is resisting, I would like to make what I consider to be an apt digression, by comparing Javier Marías's novelistic project of 'lo que pudo ser' with some ideas on life as a narrative expressed, again, by his father, Julián Marías, in his book *Reason and Life*. The meaninglessness of chance as a determining factor in the narrative of our lives has long been suppressed, and the work of the author's own father, heavily influenced by his mentor, José Ortega y Gasset, belongs to this tradition. It may seem that Julián Marías's concept of the narrative qualities of life are very similar to those encountered in passages such as the one quoted above. In *Reason and Life* he states, as we have seen, that: 'To live is to live one life, while not living at the same time all the other imagined ones'.[6] 'Choice', he continues, 'is not [...] the mere affirmation of one possibility [...] it is the exclusion of other possibilities. [...] I often do a thing in order not to do any of the other possible things, because I must do something'.[7] Concepts of self which suppress the chaos inherent in this realisation are manifold. They are attempts to make sense of the mystery of time by signposting the one-track journey, and they belong to the long and influential tradition which stretches from the teleological ethics of Aristotle, through to Heidegger and Ortega y Gasset. It is with the idea of 'authenticity' above all, and the faith in reason as the instrument with which we know our 'authentic' selves, that the father's concept of life as a project and the son's novelistic theory part company. The discrepancy is not new in Marías's

---

5   Javier Marías, 'El mundo es de sus relatores', *El País (Babelia)*, 9 April 1994, p.14.

6   Julián Marías, *Reason and Life*, p.330.

7   *Reason and Life* , p.329.

novels; in *El siglo*[8] the (fictional) father's concept of destiny, which he tried to impose on his son, is also rethought. And although both *Todas las almas* and *Corazón tan blanco* can be read against Heidegger's idea of the authentic 'being toward-death', they cannot be said to subscribe to the optimism of Ortega's 'yo soy yo y mi circunstancia'[9] which allowed him to view man's capacity to tell his own story as an interpretation or an unravelling rather than an actual writing of the self, with all the disagreeable moral questions this latter concept poses.[10]Although Ortega stresses that life consists in making decisions, that what we do depends on individual circumstance rather than on personal character,[11] he nevertheless insists that the decisions we make must be made according to opinions firmly held as our own:

> Se me ocurren varias ideas posibles sobre una cuestión, pero yo tengo que ponerme de acuerdo conmigo para ver cuál de ellas es la que me convence, la que es mi efectiva opinión [...] ella contiene lo que efectiva y auténticamente pienso sobre aquel asunto; por tanto, al pensar así, coincido conmigo mismo, soy yo mismo. Y la serie de actos, de conducta, de vida, que esa auténtica opinión engendre y motive, será auténtica vida mía, será mi auténtico ser.[12]

Javier Marías seems to accept what his father says — that human life takes place or is realised only as justification.[13] But without the justification of 'authentic' grounds and a sense of vocation, as expounded by Ortega, such a concept becomes highly problematical. Having to choose, as we so often have to, between equal things, between contradictions which both seem right, makes life as choosing a lottery. 'Lo que pudo ser' becomes closer and closer to *lo que fue* in moral terms, as grounds for serious justification are eroded. *Corazón tan blanco* is the story of a realisation both hopeful and painful, that the lived life, the version of 'lo que pudo ser' that comes to pass, is not necessarily either a following of the right path, nor a deviation from it, but simply a possibility, just one fiction among many. Both author and

---

8   Javier Marías, *El siglo* (Barcelona: Anagrama, 1983).

9   José Ortega y Gasset, *Obras completas*, vol. i, (Madrid: Revista de Occidente, 1946), p. 322.

10 See Antonio Regalado García, *El laberinto de la razón* (Madrid: Alianza, 1990), p.227.

11 José Ortega y Gasset, *Obras completas*, vol.v, (Madrid: Revista de Occidente, 1947), p.27.

12 *Obras completas*, vol.v, pp.72-73

13 *Reason and Life*, pp.331-334.

narrator refuse to confer special value in narrative terms on the already realised, the acted out or the physical. By revaluing the imagined, the ideal, the hoped for, the regretted, and the 'futuro abstracto' — what may be and what might have been — the identities of both author and narrator are also revalued. To revalue 'lo que pudo ser' in this way is to recognise that we have to have some concept of what we are working towards in order to act at all, but that the *telos* is often trivial, inauthentic, a question of chance, a piece of guesswork. The question is one of authorisation — if there is no pre-ordained destiny to fulfil, to what extent do we authorise our own lives, and how does this equate with writing our own selves? The concept of 'lo que pudo ser' is a summation of those narratives we explore without acting them out, which we tend to undervalue, 'relegating' them to fiction. 'Autobiografía, pero como ficción' rejects the assumption that autobiography, as the story of a *lived* life, has any intrinsic *narrative value* which *distinguishes* it from fiction. And this jeopardises the self as an authentic being. It becomes plain that the novel as 'el reino de lo que pudo ser' is by no means a facile concept. The concept of identity and self-writing behind 'lo que pudo ser' is an implicit rejection by Javier Marías of his father's central premises, yet less meaningful without them. In no way do his novels develop *out* of the work of his father; the relationship is not filial in this sense, but intertextual; there is no explicit evidence of authorial intention in this direction. But the narrator of *Corazón tan blanco*, as opposed to the narrator of *Todas las almas*, attempts to construct a living identity, a fictional, *in*authentic self which also and more explicitly resists the influence of the powerful father figure, and the temptation to accept identity as repetition and inevitability. He will not resign himself to reliving a variation of his father's life, and by extension he resists repeating conventional male roles which constantly offer themselves. Similarly, the many repetitions and coincidences in the book call for, and usually resist, interpretation. Throughout the novel what seem to be paths of destiny are crossed by the vagaries of chance.

The essential and active part the imagination plays in the identity we create for ourselves is evident in the contemplative sections of *Corazón tan blanco*, and manifest in the narrative in two particularly striking ways. We live life *a priori*, as discussed in the last chapter. We constantly review what we have done in view of what we might have done, and imagine a future of dramatic scenarios. We compare, to use the expressions used throughout by the narrator, the 'futuro abstracto' with 'lo que pudo ser'. It may be asked whether this is not just a fragmented version of following the right path. In his book *After Virtue*, Alasdair MacIntyre states that 'a crucial characteristic of all lived narratives [is] a certain teleological character [...] There is no present which is not informed by some image of the future'.[14] It is obvious that *a priori* narratives — imagining what is going to happen in advance, rehearsing dialogues, actions and behaviour — do play a vital role in 'lived' narratives. Their function is to rehearse possibilities, and it is in choosing between the possibilities that we rely — usually unconsciously — on the teleological concept of serving the authentic end. When ends are no longer treated as given, we enter into moral debate, says MacIntyre. It can be seen that life as a narrative and a moral journey are inseparable because of the obligation to choose, or make decisions. Reason is fast losing ground as a coherent project, for its coherence depends on 'quién cuenta'. And yet life can only be a moral journey; 'reasonable' choices have to be made — 'human life is, in its own substance, moral'.[15] These novels are stories of moral journeys. Compared to Julián Marías's concepts of projection and possibility, the novels under question can be read as alternative lives — what might have been, related closely to the author's 'real' life, and yet not 'semi-autobiographical' in the conventional sense of writing 'from' experience. In the chaotic coming together of the myriad sources of our individual circumstance we can only invent a path to follow. In *Corazón tan blanco*, the narrator, realising how easily we are coerced into thinking we have made the 'right' choices and renunciations, sets about redressing the balance between the two. He tries to take control of the invention of the narrative of his life rather than succumb to the illusion of choosing. Thus *Corazón tan blanco* in particular extends the concept of 'autobiografía, pero como ficción'. When criteria for choosing are lost, the difference between what did happen and what might have happened can no longer be considered essential, they both or all have only to be told: 'la idea del contar aparece como algo que [...] ayuda a que las cosas tengan existencia'.[16] And the imagination thus takes on a role very different to the expansive stretches and flights with which it is so often attributed. In moral terms, as a creative decision-taking faculty, its function must be to impose limits. Imagination or invention and authorship become one in that they must find a way to reduce the 'proliferation of meaning'.[17] In his essay 'What is an author', Michel Foucault asks 'How can one reduce the great peril, the great danger with which fiction threatens the

---

14 Alasdair Macintyre, *After Virtue: A Study in Moral Theory* (London: Duckworth, 1981), p.215.

15 Julián Marías, *Reason and Life*, p.335.

16 *Cambio 16*, 1173 (1994), 80.

17 Michel Foucault, 'What is an Author?', in *Language, Counter-memory and Practice: selected essays and interviews*, ed. by Donald F. Bouchard, trans. by D.F. Bouchard and Sherry Simon (Ithaca, New York: Cornell University Press, 1977), p.152.

world? The answer is: one can reduce it with the author'.[18] But as he states, 'It would be pure romanticism [...] to imagine a culture in which the fictive would operate in an absolutely free state'.[19] Javier Marías's concept of writing in the guise of 'quien yo pude ser pero no fui', and of his novels as 'lo que pudo ser' is a response to the question of what kind of constraining role is possible once the notion of the author as preceding the work, an 'indefinite source of significations', is no longer valid.

In 1978 Javier Marías published a short story, 'El viaje de Isaac'.[20] A curse is put on a military man in Cuba, to the effect that he and his son and his grandson will all die on journeys far from home, and never be buried. The curse comes to pass in the case of the soldier and his son, but there *is* no grandson. The son's best friend, who knows about the curse, puzzles over the enigma of its semi-fulfilment. He discovers or invents an explanation whilst reading the Bible. God, according to his reading, announces the birth of Isaac long before he is conceived. The puzzle is, where is Isaac in the meantime? He, like the unborn grandson who is cursed, is more than the potential fruit of his father's loins; he is already imagined — a story has already been told about him. He comes to the conclusion that the curse *is* truly fulfilled in the case of the unborn son of his friend, the son who might have been — whose life is announced in the curse, but who is never conceived in the flesh — in that he dies also with his 'father', when the possibility of his conception ends. In other words the power of the narrative as a realisation of what is usually dismissed as 'unrealised' or 'unfulfilled', a power which is fully explored in *Corazón tan blanco*, is intimated in this story. The theme of the son who never was[21] recurs throughout Marías's work as a

---

18   *Language, Counter-memory ...*, p.158.

19   *Language, Counter-memory ...*, p.159.

20   It is interesting to note that in the interview given by Javier Marías to *Quimera* ('La magia de lo que pudo ser', 30) he tells the same tale of a curse about his own Cuban great-grandfather and his grandfather.

21   There are several echoes of Jorge Luis Borges in relation to concepts of identity in Javier Marías's novels. Borges' poem 'Things that might have been' from *Historia de la noche* (Buenos Aires: Emecé, 1977) for example, which ends with the line 'el hijo que no tuve'; the concept of 'lo que pudo ser' brings to mind Borges' 'El jardín de los senderos que se bifurcan', *Ficciones* (Buenos Aires: Emecé, 1956). Also the idea of the indistinguishable narrator/author figure recalls a remark made by Borges in an *Arena* for BBC 2, also entitled 'Borges and I' (26 October, 1983) that he never 'invents' characters, he simply imagines himself in different situations. Most of Marías's characters in *Corazón tan blanco* speak with the same voice as the narrator, they carry on the same streams of thought, and in no way appear as 'rounded' characters. The narrator's wife forms a kind of edge or limit that the narrator comes up against, there is no attempt

metaphor for 'lo que pudo ser'. Whereas in *Todas las almas* such possibilities are tinged with nostalgia, in *Corazón tan blanco* such traces disappear, and 'what might have been' is embraced on equal narrative terms as what was, and allowed to inform the actual future; it is no longer interpreted as something lost, a missed opportunity.

The concept of 'lo que pudo ser' is employed to undermine the implicit equation of the real with the physical, and the imaginary with the fictional. The equation is strongly challenged in both these novels. The physical nature of a relationship — the physical presence of Luisa in *Corazón tan blanco* being the prime example — is felt to be *destroying* the imaginary one, and thus threatening the marriage. The girl on the station in Didcot in *Todas las almas*, although no Dulcinea for the narrator — in fact just perhaps something seized on by the mind to help pass the time (she is closer to Eugenia in Unamuno's *Niebla,* in that she is consciously his own invention) — was nevertheless important in the story, her absence from the story was as meaningful, for example, as the presence of Muriel, with whom the narrator had physically intimate, if brief, contact. Should a relationship which takes place in the flesh be considered more 'real', whereas an imaginary one is a fiction? The as yet unborn son, the whole 'futuro abstracto' which he deems so important, seems threatened by the change of state which marriage is. The delicate balance between anticipation and proximity is threatened by an enforced and permanent closeness. In *Corazón tan blanco*, Juan first becomes aware of his sensation of 'malestar' on his honeymoon, when his new wife is unwell, and lies in bed with a fever. Looking out over the street from the balcony of their hotel room, he is mistaken for her own lover by Miriam, a woman who stands waiting on the corner. He is momentarily someone else in her eyes, and the moment defines the problem of mistaken identity which he gradually realises is his own problem, and whose rectification is the story that follows. At the same time the power of the narrative imagination is launched — he feels guilty because rather than attending to the sick Luisa, he has been sidetracked by his desire to know the story of Miriam and Guillermo, her real lover, who occupies the adjoining room. Their story is, for a while, more 'real' than Luisa. By marrying Luisa, he feels, he has removed her from the world of possibilities, the 'futuro

---

made to describe her 'in herself'. They are often vehicles for, or extensions of, the narrator's thoughts - versions, perhaps, of 'quien pude ser pero no fui'. Again this ties in with Ortega, and his conviction that we can never put ourselves in the place of the 'other', whilst at the same opposing this conclusion in that for Ortega the reason would be because the self is discrete, an 'inner sanctum' available to no-one else, as discussed in relation to autobiography as fiction above.

abstracto'. Her closeness to him physically makes her more distant in his imagination.

The narrator both wants and does not want to 'know' his wife. He complains that he will have to watch her getting ready to go out with him when what he really wants is just to see the result, not the preparations. Yet he also says that he married her so that he would be able to see her asleep — a desire apparently contrary to that of seeing her dressed and made up for an evening out. Hitherto Luisa has maintained a mysterious and distanced image, and it seems that what he is afraid of is the end of this mystery, of having to confront the idea that Luisa is her own product as well as his. So we are made to think about the difference between the faces of the sleeper and of the made-up, sophisticated, wide-awake woman. They both, of course, conceal a mystery; the sleeping and waking fictions of the dream and the self-image the waker wears and hopes to present. And yet they are also contrasting images; the face of the sleeper is beyond their control, the made-up face 'artificial'. The sleeping face is both completely open and completely impenetrable. Access to the dreamer's world is impossible, to enter it would be truly to be able to identify with another. Traditionally marriage holds such an empty promise of close identification, which constantly breaks down in practice because it is based on romantic myths of the eradication of difference. The women in Ranz's life, it could be said, were victims of this myth — of Ranz's demanding too much from them in his search for fulfilment. The narrator recognises the opposite to be the case: 'cuanto más corpórea y continua, más relegada y remota' (p.33). Better to hold the other at a distance, to allow them their mystery, and thus he and Luisa survive in their respect for each other's difference.

The second way the equation of the physical with the real, and the imaginary with the fictional is confronted is in terms of language itself. The title *Corazón tan blanco* is taken from a speech delivered by Lady Macbeth, as she berates Macbeth for his cowardice. But more broadly it alludes to the instigative part played by her words in the murder of Duncan, echoed in the story of Ranz. The immense power of language to spur someone to action, as illustrated in these two stories, is due to its absolute impartiality; the difference that words can make owes no allegiance whatever to truth or reality, and because of this we are both at the mercy of the skilful rhetorician — of 'quién habla' (and Lady Macbeth is an example) — and of our own desires, as in the case of Ranz. During his first honeymoon Ranz kills his first wife in order to be able to marry the woman who becomes his second wife. This young woman, when she was still only his lover, had once casually remarked, in reference to his first wife, that 'nuestra única posibilidad es que un día muriera ella, y con eso no puede contarse' (p.279). And these lover's words, 'traducibles palabras sin dueño', (p. 268) work away at Ranz's consciousness until they finally erode a channel; released almost innocently, they are not dismissed as such, but passively allowed by Ranz to mean what he wants them to mean, finally persuading him to act and murder his wife. The 'throwaway' remark, spoken 'innocently' and 'without intent' by his lover, becomes 'la lengua que indaga y desarma, la que susurra y besa, la que casi obliga' (p.279). The subconscious is a powerful interpretative authority, promoting interpretations in which others are treated as means to an end. The narrator concludes that his father possibly kept his crime a secret for so long not out of guilt — this is too simple, typical of the emotive explanation which does not take fully into account the complexity of the imagination — but because he could not decide between 'poner en guardia o bien no dar ideas' (p.100). And it is also suggested that keeping silent is sometimes harder than speaking. This phrase encapsulates a particularly pressing contemporary dilemma as we deliberate as to whether the outpourings of our postmodern culture — and particularly problematic are those which portray violations of the kind perpetrated by Ranz — represent and reflect society, or form and create it? Should we speak now or for ever hold our peace? Neither is it a dilemma that can be avoided, as 'hablar y callar son dos maneras de intervenir en el futuro'.

The two kinds of language illustrated in the comparison between the story of the murder of Duncan and the murder of his wife by Ranz are figured throughout *Todas las almas* and *Corazón tan blanco* as male and female aspects of language. 'Male' language is a well-known concept; 'logocentric', 'phallocentric' or even 'phallogocentric': language spoken or written in the belief that it can communicate or represent unambiguously what the author or authority wants to say — a message which in some way pre-exists the words which 'carry' it, in which the meaning is felt to be 'present'.[22] Whereas 'logocentric' refers to the idea of authority in language as such, 'phallocentric' is more specific in that it indicates language which assumes, often subconsciously, that the masculine is the 'natural source of power and authority, and [...] the feminine as naturally subject to this'.[23] The narrator of *Todas las almas* struggles with his identity as founded in such a concept of male language. A reading of the explicit sexual scene with Muriel can be interpreted in apparently 'obvious' terms, phallocentric both figuratively and literally, a feminist interpretation (paradoxically) that such a piece of writing is likely to elicit, and in other more subtle ways which resist and escape such orthodoxy. When the narrator says 'tengo la polla en la boca de Muriel' the

---

22 See Jeremy Hawthorn, *Contemporary Literary Theory, A Concise Glossary of Contemporary Literary Theory* (London, New York, Melbourne, Auckland: Edward Arnold, 1992), p.95.
23 Hawthorn, p.129.

situation is ambiguous; an experience for the man of both power and pleasure, of vulnerability and danger. In the context of masculine and feminine language the act may be read both as a desire to abandon (or pass on) male authority to the female voice, and (not necessarily either/or) a desire to overcome her or silence her. In this sense it symbolises the disquiet of the narrator. Muriel has had all kinds of other things in her mouth earlier in the evening. This detail is typically Marías. The act is not only one of 'phallocentric' repetition, but also, in Muriel's terms, just one of many things she has done with her mouth that night — not necessarily the most important for her. The whole scene is full of uncertainty for the narrator, its meanings are multiple and finally undecidable — it is *not* a logocentric account. And with regard to mouths, and male language as the voice of authority, it is also interesting to compare the photographs of Marías himself on the sleeves of his novels, and those of Julián Marías in his own autobiography. Whereas the narrator, Juan's, inheritance of his father's fleshy and somewhat feminine lips does link him with Javier Marías, Marías must surely have inherited his from his mother, and not his tight-lipped father. But for Juan, they perhaps signal hope for his father, or perhaps the reference is to the fact that the father (Julián Marías) was also a writer, and the son is recognising his debt. Such complex interrelationships of father and son, not only in the realm of 'autobiografía pero como ficción', but also in the intertextual subtexts which relate to the writings of the father, and the further subtext of the inheritance of 'male' language in all its guises and figurations are richly exploited by Javier Marías in his novels and particularly as aspects of identity and self-writing.

The fecundity of language and other semiological systems as both a positive and a negative characteristic which plays such an important role in *Corazón tan blanco* is very much a postmodern concern. Like the idea of the discontinuity of the self, it seems to offer great possibilities of change. Female language is that which escapes the determining authority of the speaker (and these novels do deal to a great extent with spoken language, in which the intention of the speaker is more tenacious — the fact that spoken language in a novel has to be written adds, of course, to the complexity of the problem). But we should not embrace this fecundity too joyfully. The loss of *the* author opens the way for *many* authors, and to regard this always as healthy is too optimistic; it is to ignore the 'great danger with which fiction threatens the world'. Marías uses a very productive metaphor to illustrate what he calls the 'traducibles palabras sin dueño' (p.81) — words which have 'escaped' the speaker's intention. Such words are figured as drops of water which, once they have overflowed the channel which contained them, must either find another, or erode a new one: 'como la gota de lluvia que va cayendo desde el alero tras la tormenta, siempre en el mismo punto cuya tierra va ablandándose hasta ser penetrada y hacerse agujero y tal vez conducto' (p.79). The duct in which the water runs is not determined by the water so much as the topography and substance of the earth. In other words we must go on opposing authority and dogma, for if we do not provide new routes it will continue in or find the same courses as before.

The two concepts of language are interdependent. There is no absolutely male or female language. Perhaps this is the key — the interdependence of opposites — to the sameness and difference which make identity possible. The narrator of *Corazón tan blanco* remembers a song from his childhood that his Cuban grandmother used to sing to him, and the way this song works within the novel illustrates the phenomenon. The song tells the story of:

> una joven de gran hermosura y mayor pobreza [...] pedida en matrimonio por un extranjero muy rico y apuesto y con mucho futuro [...] La madre de la muchacha [...] concedía su mano al extraordinario extranjero [...] Pero en la noche de bodas, [...] la madre oía cantar a su hija [...] su petición de auxilio: "Mamita mamita, yen yen, yen. Serpiente me traga, yen, yen, yen." Y el yerno contesta — "Mentira mi suegra, yen, yen, yen, que estamos jugando, yen, yen, yen, al uso de mi tierra, yen, yen, yen". A la manana siguiente, [al] entrar en la habitación para llevarles el desayuno a la pareja dichosa, se encontraba con una enorme serpiente sobre la cama sanguinolenta y no había rastro de su infortunada y promisoria y preciada hija (pp.54-55).

It is not clear whether the grandmother was trying to communicate something to her grandson, and was conscious of the powerful symbolism of her song, or if she sang mindlessly and without realising how attentive her grandson was. But as a novelistic device this story of the triumph of the male voice over the female is, paradoxically, very fruitful: it works analogically with the main narrative of the novel, and its blatant and unmistakeable symbolism contrasts with the ambiguity of the sexual act between the narrator and Muriel in *Todas las almas*. It also echoes the story of Ranz. And Marías himself has a Cuban grandmother. It is a perfect example of how Marías integrates his own and his narrator's search for identity, and connects the serious, subtle and immensely productive contemplative passages so skilfully, elegantly and compellingly with the narrative.

The alter-ego narrators in *Todas las almas* and *Corazón tan blanco* branch out from Marías's own experience and follow often dark and compelling routes which seem to run beneath rather than alongside more conventional narrative tracks. They know, for example, that secrets, silences and absences can be potent ways of speaking. The narrator of *Corazón tan blanco* learns the extent to which his identity had been founded in 'male' language, and learns to speak and identify himself in terms of the 'female' also. By the end of the novel he has learned to watch his wife prepare herself to go out; he has recognised that his desire to maintain her as a mystery was also to deny her her own powers of self-invention. Identity, he has discovered, is a paradox, it is ever-changing, and if we do not take charge of who we are then we become who others think we ought to be. But as he discovers, this struggle between the 'female' and the 'male' in language — that is, between meaning as fixed and meaning as potentially free — is not an expression of gender difference; rather, male and female roles have come to figure or be founded in a simplification of such tendencies. Juan comes to recognise the possibilities in terms of his own identity of the 'female' nature of language, those words which escape the comforting but restrictive male voice seeking to control them. The 'authentic' self, the 'vocation', is the product of the 'male' voice trying to subjugate the 'female'. The world of possibilities as somehow predetermined, the desire to play god, to control destiny is inherently a male illusion, and a large part of what the father represents, from which the narrator is trying to escape. Although not optimistic, by the end of the story he has learned to 'settle down' on his own terms, to 'tomar las cosas en serio', to work out himself the meaning of his 'malestar', which he refused to allow his father to define for him in his fatalistic and dismissive question '¿y ahora qué?' (p.19).

Earlier we were told that 'la única verdad es la que no se traduce a palabras ni a imágenes' (p.201). This kind of paradox and uncertainty, echoed again in the last line, is indicative of the absence of moralising in these novels, even though they deal throughout with the moral problems which are involved in any attempt to define identity. Javier Marías passes uncertainty off as a novelistic ploy: 'La certidumbre produce desinterés en el lector. En cambio, la incertidumbre alimenta la curiosidad'.[24] However, as in his novels, the tone of Marías's extra-novelistic comments on his own work tend to be in minor keys, the significance of the subtext always underplayed. The concept of the truth as that which is never told is part of the skilful manipulation of our anticipation of Ranz's confession. Bearing this in mind, waiting for Ranz to tell his story has meant that we cannot really expect a dramatic *desenlace,* for we suspect that what Ranz may tell will be 'lies'. So we share the ambiguity of the narrator's desire *not* to know. It is even less certain if Ranz 'really' murdered his wife, and the *desenlace* device is further undermined and lost in a complex moral maze when we remember this exchange with Luisa, when she tells Ranz that:

---

24   *Quimera,* 87, 26.

La verdad es que no me extraña que se casara usted tantas veces, es una fuente inagotable de historias poco creíbles, y por tanto de entretenimiento. [...] — Hay muchos hombres que piensan que las mujeres necesitan sentirse muy queridas y halagadas, incluso mimadas, y lo que más nos importa es que nos entretengan, es decir, que nos impidan pensar demasiado en nosotras mismas (p.277).

It is quite 'possible', after all, that Ranz is telling Luisa a story to amuse and entertain her, as his self-conscious style suggests, and moreover the narrator can never be sure exactly what his status as a listener behind the curtain is, as he listens to Ranz's 'confession'. Is he simply listening, or is he eavesdropping, or overhearing? The situation is a perfect analogue of our situation as readers, in which it is impossible to know the author's (or is it the narrator's?) intent, impossible to know how far we are being deceived or not and impossible, therefore, to identify the owner of this voice whose tale has us so enthralled.

The following example of aporia is, in another sense, a major key to the way the concept of identity as a moral and narrative process works within and between the two novels under discussion. It is a striking case of repetition: of the narrator's words at the beginning of *Todas las almas*, and Ranz's words at the end of *Corazón tan blanco*. At the beginning of *Todas las almas* the narrator states quite categorically that 'El que aquí cuenta lo que vió y le ocurrió no es aquel que lo vió y al que le ocurrió, ni tampoco es su prolongación, ni su sombra, ni su heredero, ni su usurpador'.[25] This affirmation not only differentiates narrator from author, it goes further: A few lines before, the narrator/author tells us simply that 'prefiero hablar en primera persona, y no porque crea que basta con la facultad de la memoria para que alguien siga siendo el mismo en diferentes tiempos y en diferentes espacios'. The premise behind these two quotations is the discontinuity of the 'yo' or self, or, as Marías himself explains in 'Quién escribe' — 'la común idea de que ninguno somos todo el tiempo el mismo más que [...] en virtud de la memoria y el nombre'.[26] What follows in the novel is testimony to the difficulty of accepting this theory in practice. *Todas las almas* begins with an affirmation of belief in the self as a discontinuity, but carries on with the story of a search for continuity, whereas in *Corazón tan blanco* the overriding concept of identity as difference, or change, is finally undermined when, towards the end of the book, Ranz assures us in his turn, and using the same words, that 'El de entonces soy yo todavía, o si no soy él soy su prolongación, o su sombra, o su heredero, o su usurpador [...] a alguién

25 *Todas las almas*, pp. 9-10.
26 *Literatura y fantasma*, p.87.

deben pertenecer esos recuerdos' (p.287). This contradicts the thesis that the individual is a narrative construction whose identity is invented *en route*, an idea which has informed much of what the narrator has just said. The repetition underlines the facileness of the original words, which if taken to mean simply 'I've changed, I'm no longer the person I once was' completely ignore problems of responsibility and continuity which must be addressed in order to hold on to some vestige of identity, if for no other reason. Due to this repetition we are obliged to compare the two concepts of the 'yo', and to think about not only who writes, but also who is right. Ranz murdered his wife, and by repeating words from a previous novel, the question of responsibility is foregrounded. The narrator, hidden in the adjoining bedroom, listens to the story of the murder. Is the only moral commentary that he offers sufficient: 'Lo que oí aquella noche de labios de Ranz no me pareció venial ni me pareció ingenuo ni me provocó sonrisas, pero sí me pareció pasado'? (p.298) This conflicts with Luisa's belief, with which the narrator purports to be in agreement, that 'a nada se le pasa el tiempo y que todo está aquí, esperando a que se lo haga volver' (p.149). By repeating words from the beginning of *Todas las almas* at the end of *Corazón tan blanco*, Javier Marías brackets the novels together, which invites the reader to reconsider their relationship. It is a sign that Marías himself is also a reader of his own work, a double-act. It raises the question of responsibility for the actions of a 'yo' that in theory the self no longer is. Most importantly, Ranz's words recall those of the narrator earlier in the book as he ponders the situation of Macbeth and Lady Macbeth. However instrumental she was in persuading or obliging Macbeth to murder Duncan, 'ya está hecho el hecho [...] y nunca hay duda de quién es "yo" [...] Una instigación no es nada más que palabras, traducibles palabras sin dueño que se repiten de voz en voz y de lengua en lengua y de siglo en siglo' (p.81). In spite of the imagination's essential role in the reinvention or writing of the self, it is by our acts that we are judged:

> son ellos los únicos e irreversibles, mientras que hay reiteración y retractación, repetición y rectificación para las palabras [...] y aunque la ley no exculpa [...] a quien habla, éste sabe que en realidad no ha hecho nada, incluso si ha obligado con su lengua al oído, con su pecho a la espalda, con la respiración agitada, con su mano en el hombro y el incomprensible susurro que nos persuade (p.81).

Ranz's statement of responsibility is not tinged by remorse — how could it be? Remorse and guilt, when considered in the light of the concept of what might have been, become problematic. In *Literatura y fantasma* Marías quotes from Juan Benet's *Volverás a Región*: — 'La memoria es casi siempre la venganza de lo que no fue'.[27] Remorse and guilt are the painful memories of what might have been for another if we had acted differently. Would Ranz go back and do things differently, knowing that this would be to renounce his son? And for the son, the narrator, the problem is impossible, for to judge his father guilty, which is to say 'you should not have committed the murder', would be to renounce his own birth. The consequence of recognising identity as functioning as narrative is that in order that our story be meaningful we have to be accountable, we have to take responsibility for our actions. Marías's novels derive their power from the lurking presence of unasked questions and the ghostly understatement of the consequences, with no trace of a moralising tone. Such questions are inherently part of the postmodern dilemma. In *Beltenebros* the same problem arises — the girl singer and Ugarte represent identity as stasis, whereas Darman conceives of it as change. Through skilful use of repetition such philosophical and ethical points resonate through Marías's novels, and the unasked question 'whose life does not depend, at some time in the past, on the untimely death of another?' is only answerable as 'quien yo pude ser y no fui'.

In *Corazón tan blanco* the narrator does not wish to know the secret of his father's past. This is a strong indicator of the determination with which he sets about reconstructing his identity, for usually the search for family roots is an integral part of a search for identity; in this case not knowing is conceived as the best way to preserve a sense of self. As the novel progresses, it becomes increasingly clear that he is to find out. His wife is overwhelmed with curiosity, and finally his father seems glad to unburden himself of the secret. Through Ranz's confession the narrator knows his own life depended on a series of events which had nothing inevitable about them, he was the product not only of chance, but of the murder of his 'aunt'. A middle-class child, as Marías says, 'prefiere pensar en la inevitabilidad de sus padres unidos para justificar su existencia y creer por tanto en su propia inevitabilidad y justicia (me refiero a los ninos perezosos, normales)' (p.126). One's place in the world as natural or inevitable is a luxurious myth only affordable for those children who 'no van al colegio si tienen un poco de fiebre y no han de trabajar repartiendo cajas con una bicicleta por las mañanas' (p.126).

The young wife, Teresa, who commits suicide at the beginning of the book, does so — and this is the important subtext of the *desenlace* of the novel in the context under discussion — because she could not bear that fact that her happiness had been at the cost of another's life. She is young, and does not know that if she waits, the blow will be softened: 'Todo se evapora, pero eso no lo sabéis los jóvenes' (p.269). As Ranz says:

---

27 *Literatura y fantasma*, p.128.

La vida entera parece mentira, cuando se es joven. Lo que les pasa a los otros, las desdichas, las calamidades, los crímenes, todo ello nos resulta tan ajeno, como si no existiera. Incluso lo que nos pasa a nosotros nos parece ajeno una vez que ya ha pasado. Hay quien es así toda la vida, eternamente joven, una desgracia (p.266).

Corazón tan blanco yields up an extremely forceful set of ideas in relation to the concept of the written self. The self as a coherent narrative still faces problems of authorship and accountability. Even if one cannot be said to authorise, but merely to narrate the story of one's self, one has to choose the story. But the possibility always exists of telling it in other words — that is, of making a difference, of creating new meaning. Through his contemplation of the state of marriage (well chosen by Marías in that it is, as described by Macintyre, 'the paradigm of the ethical [...] a state of commitment and obligation through time',[28] an analogous state to selfhood). Juan realises the extent to which his identity has been founded in 'male' language, and learns to speak and identify himself in terms of the 'female' also. The enigmatic last line of the novel can be read as a figure for the non-essential, temporal self he has written: 'Ese canto pese a todo emitido y que no se calla ni se diluye después de dicho, cuando le sigue el silencio de la vida adulta, o quizá es masculina' (p.301).

---

28   Macintyre, p.39.

CHAPTER NINE
Postmodern identities: writing by women and Rosa Montero's *Amado amo.*

JUDITH DRINKWATER

Much has been written about directions and tendencies — or the lack of them — in contemporary Spanish writing, along with attempts to categorize and classify whole swathes of literary production under convenient headings. On the one hand, contemporary narrative seems to be firmly tied to a series of anchors, whether historical, socio-theoretical or market-directed. It is delimited (artificially) on the one hand by the phenomenon of 1975 and the process of Transition, and on the other (at least implicitly) by the millenium, with all the weight of fin-de-siècle malaise. The enterprise of new narrative has variously been seen as bound up with the freedoms of democracy, as evidenced in the social or feminist novel, or as rejecting such empiricism in the postmodern millenial turn, with the novel of introspection or crisis. Demand has shaped the market and produced detective fiction, erotic writing, genres previously unfamiliar in the Spanish tradition. In this climate, writing by women has also faced the same urge toward categorization on the part of critics, many of whose observations are valid and certainly not mutually exclusive, but the labels available to texts by women are not those generally assigned to those of their male counterparts. Furthermore, female critics try to see female-authored texts as heterogeneous, whereas male critics perceive them as disparate and incoherent. Thus the very identity of narrative by women in Spain is uncertain, and shifts with shifting points of view.

It is in this context of the crisis of identity of women's writing — which identity it either possesses in too limited a form, or does not have at all — and the need to break out of established critical paradigms, that I wish to look at the work of Rosa Montero. I shall consider the issue of the identity of women's writing in relation to Montero's narrative fiction, as well as the construction of postmodern identities as perceived in particular novels. Montero is one of the most widely read and indeed readable of contemporary Spanish women writers, and also one of those most subjected to critical scrutiny. Much of her novelistic output is dismissed by her (male) detractors as semi-autobiographical, stridently feminist, sociological exposition rather than art, although (women) critics applaud her iconoclasm and her exposing of the condition of women in Spain. Undoubtedly, her seven novels have broken new ground in Spanish literary production, thanks to the 'hardness' of their content, and also to the journalistic style of the earlier novels. *Crónica del desamor* (1980) examines the social conditions of a working single mother in a Spain lacking rights to contraception, abortion and equality of opportunity in employment; *La función Delta* (1982) analyses a woman's reconstruction in flashback of her identity; 1983 saw the appearance of *Te trataré como a una reina*, a metafictional investigation of the sleazy Madrid underworld of drugs, violence, prostitution, and the stifled lives of ordinary women.[1] *Amado amo* (1988) is a vicious denunciation of patriarchal culture as seen in the microcosm of the corporate structure; a 1990 novel, *Temblor*, breaks the mould and deals with a fantastic matriarchal distopia, and is followed in 1993 by *Bella y oscura*, a study of a mythical, private world of beauty and horror.[2]

Spanish women writers since the nineteenth century, observes Catherine Davies, tread a path 'from political strategy to personal enquiry', observing a 'pattern of writing (fiction, treatise, journalism) [which] would remain a constant feature amongst feminist writers in Spain'.[3] The '[n]ovels of female development' of the 60s, 70s and 80s analysed by Emilie Bergmann display what Elizabeth Ordóñez identifies as the archetypal motifs of 'menarche, marriage, motherhood, menopause — [...] the repetitive patterns of women's fiction [...] in Spain'.[4] Ordóñez, who sets up the central problem with women's writing as being 'the challenge of reading' what are essentially 'dissimilar texts', develops her own readings with the aid of French feminist criticism in a later article, and finds the locus of female identity and writing in the body.[5]

---

1   Rosa Montero, *Crónica del desamor* (Madrid: Debate, 1979), *La función Delta* (Madrid: Debate, 1981), *Te trataré como a una reina* (Barcelona: Seix Barral, 1983), *Amado amo* (Madrid: Debate, 1988). All page references to *Amado amo* in this chapter are from (Barcelona: Edhasa, 1992).

2   Rosa Montero, *Temblor* (Barcelona: Seix Barral, 1990), *Bella y oscura* (Barcelona: Seix Barral, 1993).

3   Catherine Davies, 'Feminist Writers in Spain since 1900: from political strategy to personal inquiry', in *Textual Liberation. European Feminist Writing in the Twentieth Century*, ed. by Helena Forsas-Scott (London & New York: Routledge, 1991), p.194.

4   Emilie Bergmann, 'Intertextuality in Spanish Novels of Female Development', *Anales de la Literatura Española Contemporánea*, 12 (1987), 141-156; in Elizabeth J. Ordóñez, 'Reading Contemporary Spanish Narrative by Women', *Anales de la Literatura Española Contemporánea*, 7 (1982), 247.

5   Ordóñez, 'Reading Contemporary Spanish Narrative...', 239.

All in all, as Ordóñez points out in this later article, reading writing by women on its own terms — if they exist — is a tricky enterprise.[6] The categories which exist, whether they be autobiography, liberatory, archetypal, or written-through-the-body, have been enlightening but may now be instrumental in re-inscribing women's writing in the periphery of literary production. This is all the more so because in a society intent on reclaiming the democratic rights which for so long had been denied, the individuality of women has been veiled in literature and other cultural production by broader concerns, namely that same-minded women are engaged in the same 'feminist' enterprises, that there is a commonality of Spanish female experience, or that the narrative fiction or other output by women of necessity reflects an identifiable historico-social experience in time and space. Furthermore, in Spain, this empirical approach to the condition of women as envisioned through fiction may be anachronistic, since, as Ordóñez states, Spanish women writers are frequently reluctant to ally themselves with the feminist cause, and anyway they speak in the main for the privileged, educated, middle-class woman with a stake in the job market who even at time of writing is not typical of Spanish womanhood.[7] For any critic of women's writing, the empirical is a line which begs all sorts of questions, most importantly the question of what purpose is served by what now appears the continued effective 'marginalisation' of women's writing which is brought about by such critical focuses, which as often as not fulfil the function of further perpetuating and reinforcing stereotypes of class, female behaviour patterns, the limitations of gender, and so forth. The result of all this is that women's writing still occupies an invidious position in Spain, too readily sited on the periphery, too infrequently invited into any canon (not that it would necessarily wish to be), and accorded precious little significance.

A recent assessment of contemporary Spanish literature sets the literary production of the 1970s and 1980s within a (more or less explicit) binary framework of value judgements. In his work, Oscar Barrero Pérez claims that contemporary fiction ('literatura light', 'literatura de consumo') is produced for a mass or popular market ('el lector o espectador de fin de semana') rather than for a cultured elite (a view articulated in the terms 'lector exigente' set against the 'lector medio' elsewhere in the analysis).[8] Thus contemporary narrative 'ha perdido la función crítica que habitualmente le ha caracterizado'

---

6   Elizabeth J. Ordóñez, 'Inscribing Difference: "L'Ecriture Féminine" and New Narrative by Women', *Anales de la Literatura Española Contemporánea*, 12 (1987), 45-58.

7   'Inscribing Difference ...', 45-58

8   Oscar Barrero Pérez, *Historia de la literatura española contemporánea, 1989-1990* (Madrid: Istmo, 1992), pp.318 & 353.

to become no more than a vehicle for the reader's 'apetencias' in a context of 'indiferencia' and 'consumo fácil'.[9] According to this interpretation, a reasoned analysis of 'problemas sociales o existenciales' (which are assumed to have existed in the Spanish narrative of preceding years) has been supplanted by the rule of hedonism and the rejection of moral boundaries. The same critic claims that the primary characteristic of 1980s narrative in Spain is 'la dispersión' (p.353), and dismisses the possible value of this phenomenon of diversity and plurality: 'o es signo de vitalidad e independencia del gran árbol novelístico o, más probablemente, síntoma de descentramiento (de los autores, de la crítica, del lector, o quizá de todos nosotros').[10] Coherence, integrity, the wholeness of literary oeuvre are (by implication) thrown into a chaotic, disordered maelstrom. Against this background, the early fictional output of Rosa Montero is quickly dismissed as one of a series of the so-called 'novela generacional que tiene su eje en el desencanto por un modelo de vida que fundamenta la existencia de un personaje y que se encuentra en trance de hundimiento'.[11] *Crónica del desamor* and *La función Delta*, he asserts, appeal to a post-Transition generation — the generation of 1968 whose ideals and literary trajectory have been exhausted — which is plagued by 'la frustración, la soledad, el vacío existencial', and, of course, by feminist issues.[12] An equally unsympathetic reading of Montero's novels is given by Fernando Valls, giving an overview of writing by women in Spain in 1989, who attempts not to patronise but fails when he describes them as 'cargadas de buenas intenciones y éticamente [...] más que convincentes, pero su afán educativo y reprochón lastra sus aspectos literarios, pues, parte de sus ideas, situaciones y personajes preconcebidos y arquetípicos'.[13] Valls goes on to try to differentiate between 'feminine' and 'feminist' writing, with a clear disdain for the Rosa Montero type of 'feminist' writing, of which he declares: 'más parece un fenómeno sociológico que literario'.[14] Rosa Montero herself in an interview admits to being dogged by the 'cartelito' which is constantly hung about her neck, whether it be that of 'testimonial, feminista, periodista', or simply 'chica'.[15] Women's writing in Spain is thus facing a crisis of identity

9   *Historia de la literatura...*, pp.318 & 319.
10   *Historia de la literatura...*, p.353.
11   *Historia de la literatura ...*, p.363.
12   *Historia de la literatura ...*, p.363.
13   Fernando Valls, 'La literatura femenina en España: 1975-1989', *Insula*, 512-513 (1989),13.
14   Valls, 13.
15   José María Plaza, 'Horror y belleza' (entrevista con Rosa Montero), *Leer*, 65 (1993), 52-54.

precisely because its identity has been circumscribed: it is too women-centred to be acceptable to the male canon, or — paradoxically — it is frequently too male-signatured to stand up to feminist scrutiny, and, characteristically in Spain since 1975, too fragmented to be a monolithic presence in a country where narrative fiction proliferates.

It has to be said that such conservative interpretations in relation to Montero's work — the labels of consumer literature, feminist propaganda, literature of disillusionment — are not found in the majority of critical appraisals of Montero, which are in the main written by female academics. The latter dwell on the feminist possibilities of Montero's novels and the agendas which they set for social reform in Spain (*Crónica del desamor*), female-male relationships (*La función Delta*, *Te trataré como a una reina*), the critique of patriarchy (*Crónica del desamor*, *Amado amo*), or a woman-centred reconstruction (and deconstruction) of distopias (*Temblor*, *Bella y oscura*). The most suggestive of these critics is Catherine Davies, who moves from an introductory overview of women's writing in Spain, in which she terms it 'polyphonic, eclectic' — which, as she points out, to the male critic may mean 'curiously unmanageable', or alternatively to the female critic 'diversity' — to her concluding assertion that Montero's work is 'a postmodern reworking of feminism'.[16] It 'inscribes diversity, engages in a critique of a patriarchal systems [sic] of thought and de-legitimizes master-narratives and cultural myths'.[17] Whereas Barrero writes of a contemporary Spanish narrative — and thus by extension the work of a writer like Montero — as one for which 'las barreras morales han dejado de existir', Davies implicitly identifies in Montero's writing an engagement with feminism as an ethics which looks beyond women-centred issues to 'all other forms of alienation and exploitation'.[18]

In both the conservative and the feminist interpretations of Montero it may be deduced that her fiction is read as a 'realist' discourse on the social conditions of the individual [woman], although the 'value' of such fiction depends on the point of view of the commentator. I should like to discuss two

---

16 Catherine Davies, *Contemporary Feminist Fiction in Spain. The Work of Montserrat Roig and Rosa Montero* (Oxford: Berg, 1994), p.5; p.178. The quotations are from Elizabeth Ordóñez, *Voices of Their Own. Contemporary Spanish Narrative by Women* (London and Toronto, 1991), p.15, and Joan L. Brown, *Women Writers of Contemporary Spain* (London and Toronto, Associated University Presses, 1991), p.23.

17 *Contemporary Feminist Fiction in Spain* , p.178.

18 Barrero Pérez, p.318; Davies, *Contemporary Feminist Fiction in Spain,* 1994, p.179, quoting Celia Amorós, *Hacia una crítica de la razón patriarcal* (Barcelona, 1985 and 1991), p.328.

issues pertinent to such an analysis, which stem from the review of critical interpretations already given. Firstly, there is the question of the status or identity of Montero's fiction, in relation to the blurring of the boundaries between so-called high and low culture which has taken place in Spain as in other contemporary cultures. Secondly, there is the question of whether Montero's work may be symptomatic, both collectively and on the level of individual novels, of wider trends in late twentieth-century Western culture, both addressing and providing a critique of the constructions of the self available in postmodern consumer capitalism.

Paraphrasing Peter Bürger's *Theory of the Avant-Garde*, Rita Felski argues for 'a sociological analysis of the function of individual texts, whether realist or avantgarde, in relation to particular audiences', as 'one which can be usefully adapted to the specific interests of a feminist cultural politics'.[19] In a modern consumer society, all art is subject to assimilation by social institutions, as even 'the works of the avant-garde themselves become exhibits in the museum'.[20] No form of cultural output, therefore, can be 'defined as inherently more radical or conservative than another', and by extension, no form can be privileged over another.[21] As Felski asserts, 'the once clear-cut theoretical distinctions between oppositional and conservative forms lose much of their authority when faced with the current diversity of cultural activity'.[22] Similarly Tony Bennett, in an analysis of Marxist approaches to the literary canon and popular fiction, asserts that the question of the 'value' of literary texts — particularly of those in 'the canon' as opposed to popular fiction — is not a valid one, since 'value is not — nor, logically, can it be — a property of the text *alone* [...] Texts do not *have* value; they can only be *valued* by valuing subjects of particular types and for particular reasons, and these are entirely the product of critical discourses of valuation, varying from criticism to criticism'.[23] Any useful distinction between high art and mass culture — literature for the elite versus 'literatura de consumo' of the type outlined by Barrero — collapses in the wake of such analyses: all

19   Rita Felski, 'Feminism, Realism and the Avant-Garde' in *Postmodern Conditions*, ed. by Andrew Milner, Philip Thomson and Chris Worth (New York, Oxford, Munich: Berg, 1990), 61-78, following Peter Bürger, *Theory of the Avant-Garde* (Manchester: Manchester University Press; Minneapolis: University of Minnesota Press,1984), p.67.
20   *Postmodern Conditions*, p.67.
21   *Postmodern Conditions*, p.68.
22   *Postmodern Conditions*, p.69.
23   Tony Bennett, 'Marxism and Popular Fiction' in *Postmodern Conditions*, ed. by Andrew Milner, Philip Thomson and Chris Worth (New York, Oxford, Munich: Berg, 1990), p.195.

texts participate in the consumer economy, whether they accept or contest it, and no text has a greater intrinsic worth than any other. Montero's narrative is written in readerly style, in realist, confessional mode, and in imitation or parody of traditional genres. It is simultaneously an artefact of popular mass culture (since it is accessible to a wide audience in terms of the colloquial language in which it is written, its availability in bookshops, the high level of education in contemporary Spain, and familiarity with the genres which it parodies) and of high culture (since its audience may be presumed to be in the main urban, middle-class and relatively affluent, and the reading of novels an elitist occupation). To assume that its reading public are passive, undiscriminating consumers of received ideologies, as Barrero does, is thus naive. Montero's narrative may indeed be assimilated into consumer culture as creative art harnessed for commercial ends, but this does not preclude it from challenging from within the tenets on which that culture is founded (patriarchal structures, traditional or popular artistic forms, the language of journalese), and its public is equipped to extract its political message. It thus participates in — cashes in on — the economy of post-capitalist Spain whilst at the same time taking issue with it, and demonstrates Felski's conclusion that the sociology of contemporary literary output leads inevitably to a need for (and establishing of) 'feminist influence in channels which can reach vast audiences', and that 'the *political* significance of such art cannot be located in any inherent formal properties, but only in relation to the social phenomenon of a feminist public sphere'.[24] What a writer like Montero has done is precisely to create such a 'feminist public sphere', a position from which women's issues can be voiced to a wide and general audience, the politics of which is embedded in the economy of consumer capitalism which is always already a condition of its existence. Thus the identity of writing by women, although it must by the very nature of its diversity remain fluid and as a consequence undecidable, has taken a significant step through Montero's work, which demonstrates new directions for women's fiction in post-1975 Spain. Her narrative occupies a unique situation by virtue of its place within the mainstream consumer economy which it occupies and contests, and the way in which it bridges the gap between 'high' and 'low' culture, and is significant because this breaking down of barriers is due in part to the dialogue between fiction and journalism — an area yet to be studied — which is implicitly established by virtue of Montero's double career as author and journalist.

In *Modernity and Self-Identity*, Anthony Giddens studies self-identity in a late twentieth-century world which demonstrates, paradoxically, a 'unitary framework of experience' (time, space, mass communications), yet 'creates

---

24 *Postmodern Conditions*, p.76.

new forms of fragmentation and dispersal'.[25] A notable feature of postmodern culture, of which a prime example is the media treatment of news items, is what he terms 'the collage effect', or the juxtaposition of the news 'stories' of the day which share nothing in common except their newsworthiness.[26] Giddens argues that this collage effect does not 'mark the disappearance of narratives' nor merely 'represent a chaotic jumble of signs', but that, significantly, whilst the elements of the collage 'do not [...] add up to a single narrative, [...] they depend on, and also in some ways express, unities of thought and consciousness'.[27] Women's narrative in Spain — and that of Rosa Montero is exemplary in this respect — illustrates the diversity typical of the collage effect, but this does not preclude the impact of women's writing in a society where women writers have been relatively few and far between.   If we move on to consider Montero's fictional work as a whole, whilst the multiple genres (pseudo-biography, detective fiction, fantastic literature) to which she has recourse may be, as Davies suggests, a deliberate ploy to evade categorizing, her use of them can be seen to be more than simply a ploy and more than mere experimentation with metafictional modes of writing. Montero's writing has matured, changed and diverged along different pathways over the fifteen years of her novelistic career, yet it still demonstrates a consistent 'unity of thought and consciousness' as regards the position of the individual in contemporary or future postmodern society. Her writings provide a critique of social microcosms: professional sub-cultures (journalism, advertising) which shape the public perception of the social order and of individual identity; underclass/marginal groups in the 'real' world of Madrid or the invented world of *Bella y oscura*; the tyranny of hierarchy in *Temblor*. Similarly, they offer a questioning of the perspectives presented by gender and sexuality. All of Montero's fictions at one level are set within the framework of familiar literary narratives of the self: Bildüngsroman, quest, ironic sagas of failure, passages from birth/youth to death, and taken together constitute the postmodern phenomenon which Giddens terms 'the reflexive project of the self, which consists in the sustaining of coherent, yet continuously revised, biographical narratives'.[28] Within individual texts, such as *La función Delta*, the self-reflexive process can be seen at work in the constitution of the self through memory, but it can be argued that it is equally visible in an overview of Montero's entire output: the shifting collages of the self in real and

---

25   Anthony Giddens, *Modernity and Self-Identity. Self and Society in the Late Modern Age* (Stanford, California: Stanford University Press, 1991), p.5.
26   *Modernity and Self-Identity*, p.26.
27   *Modernity and Self-Identity*, p.26.
28   *Modernity and Self-Identity*, p.5.

imagined contexts interlock in the production of an ongoing biographical account which includes and subsumes the diverse manifestations of the late capitalist self. Thus Montero's fiction both on the level of form (collage) and articulation of self (self-reflexivity) is characteristic of the postmodern dichotomy of fragmentation (loss of identity) and unity (hierarchy, 'corporate identity') and interrogates the interface between the two.

Montero's least studied novel to date — perhaps due to the fact it appears 'deceptively simple',[29] perhaps because it may be seen as translucently feminist in its final message, or perhaps (paradoxically) because it can also be read as not manifestly woman-centred since it focuses on a male protagonist — is *Amado amo* (1988). This novel deals with the vicissitudes and treachery of César Miranda, the one-time star of an advertising agency, 'Golden Line', as he struggles to keep his job in a changing work environment. In a recent article, Joan Lipman Brown studies the depiction of men by women in the contemporary Spanish novel, seeing them as 'stereotypical' — 'the Spanish macho male and the pathetic weakling' — or 'unique' — 'the masculine hero [...] the sensitive intellectual whose sexual prowess is based on winning over the minds (through which he reaches the bodies) of women heroes [...] this desired Other reflects women writers' ideal of a new Spanish male'.[30] Whilst there are indeed male figures in Montero's novels who fit this bill, the deployment of male characters in *Amado amo* goes beyond the analysis of Brown, or indeed Davies, who sees the novel as dealing with 'the identity crisis of a persecuted male in the age of women's liberation'.[31] The novel is written with an ample dose of black humour at the expense of César Miranda, who is never depicted as anything but a cowardly and unsympathetic character. But he, in common with the numerous male characters in the text, is a mere cipher. Insofar as the male characters in *Amado amo* are presented as stereotypes, this serves the purpose of pointing up the complex interplay of role and hierarchy within consumer capitalist society, which offers the archetypes to which the individual is expected to conform, and constructs identities which are as unsatisfactory as they are fragile.

Anthony Giddens analyses the importance in modernity of control, whereby 'the natural world has become in large part a 'created environment' consisting of humanly structured systems whose motive power and dynamics derive from socially organised knowledge-claims rather than from influences

29 Davies, *Contemporary Feminist Fiction in Spain*, p.136.
30 Joan Lipman Brown, 'Men by Women in the Contemporary Spanish Novel', *Hispanic Review*, 60 (1992), 59.
31 Davies, *Contemporary Feminist Fiction in Spain*, p.137.

exogenous to human activity'.[32] In modernity — capitalist, industrialised, urban society — the self and self-identity become enmeshed in the abstract systems which impose their order and norms upon everyday life, and this process becomes 'more and more accentuated with the radicalising and globalising of modern institutions'.[33] What results is what Giddens terms 'the sequestration of experience', the polarising of the spheres of state and civil society, the public and the private, the establishment of social norms of surveillance and control, information and knowledge systems, which site deviance (madness, illness, criminality) in locations where they are subject to correction according to moral precept. At the same time, life within the parameters of the norm is reduced to often meaningless routine: 'the ontological security which modernity has purchased, on the level of day-to-day routines, depends on an institutional exclusion of social life from fundamental existential issues which raise central moral dilemmas for human beings'.[34] In *Amado amo*, the 'sequestration of experience' has evolved even beyond the patterns explicitly articulated by Giddens. The 'socially organised knowledge claims' which Giddens sees as central to the functioning of such institutions are well-developed in Golden Line: as Cesar is demoted he begins to find that he lacks the inside knowledge to function effectively: 'El, César, ya no tenía subordinados y por ende carecía de información en un mundo en el que saber era poder y no saber era el destierro' (p.49). The abstract systems of the state have been substituted by the abstract systems of capitalist enterprise: after the demise of the Franco regime, the Spanish firm 'Rumbo' is merged with the multinational company 'Golden Line'. Thus an organisation which had retained some Spanish characteristics or traditions is colonised by an outside power which forces upon it an alien language, behaviour and ethos: any residual moral basis upon which to found working practices is eradicated and 'existential issues' are eschewed in favour of the survival of the fittest in 'un mundo homicida [...] el modelo colectivo de la colectividad depredadora' (p.195): César's ex-partner Clara offers the extended example of the Oklahoma land run of 1889 as the pattern on which United States, and by extension, all Western enterprise and social behaviour has been modelled. Ironically, then, a company which specializes in the constructing of images sets about the wholesale destruction of the identity and self-worth of its employees. The boundary between public and private is eroded as César's intimacy is invaded by the institution for which he works, signified in Morton's early, unannounced visits to César's flat — 'poseía [Morton] esa naturalidad para la invasión que proporciona el mando. Porque

---

32   *Modernity and Self-Identity*, p.144.
33   *Modernity and Self-Identity*, p.149.
34   *Modernity and Self-Identity*, p.156.

en realidad Morton invadía su casa, su territorio, sus dominios' (p.29) -, the dusty, unused study which acts as a permanent reminder to César of his failure to retain the initial momentum of his working life, and the tepid personal relationship with a work colleague, Paula, whom he ultimately betrays to the company in order to save his job. Success or failure in the company define success or failure in personal life: '¿Y [era posible que] al fracasar en la empresa fracasaras también en lo sexual, en lo afectivo, en lo sentimental; con los hijos, con los amigos, con la familia, con la amante?' (p.182). The systems of control which define the corporate identity of the 'Golden Line' employees, and the insidious erosion of the same identities forged by the company as it withdraws the signs of privilege — offices, secretaries, car-parking space — culminates in the destruction of individuals like Matías, who commits suicide by drinking a bottle of bleach. César's reaction to this environment is seen in his growing paranoia and the disintegration of his daily schedule: when we meet him at the beginning of the novel, he awakens late in the morning, only to fritter the day away in idle speculation, reading women's magazines and watching the television. The routines which might anchor his identity have lost all sense: 'César había perdido la fe en las pequeñas rutinas; y se le antojaban absurdos los gestos cotidianos que para otras personas formaban el entramado de la vida' (p.21). He fantasizes comically about a return to an idyllic rural existence — itself based on a different type of routine — of stable, unchallenged identity:

> era un hombre de ciudad, un producto de barrio, y era incapaz de distinguir un roble de una encina [...] pero ahora empezaba a considerar que el destripar terrones podía ser el único remedio para la enfermedad ejecutiva. Porque en el campo no necesitabas estar luchando constantemente para mantener tu identidad; en el campo sencillamente eras. Se era labrador o pastor o vaquero desde el nacimiento hasta la muerte; mientras el directivo tenía que conquistar su espacio y su sustancia cada día. Qué situación tan envidiable: levantarse al alba [...] dormir, en fin, el sueño sin sueños de los justos, el sueño fácil y profundo de aquellos que saben quiénes son (pp.166-167).

The 'moral dilemmas' of the individual in modernity are superseded in *Amado amo* by a moral void, in which there exist no regulatory precepts to curb the injustices wreaked by the institution on its employees, and in which, in the manner of Sisyphus, the individual is absorbed into the mindless repetition of company dictates which overwhelm the critical faculties:

El acarrear piedras durante una eternidad de una esquina a la otra y viceversa poseía su lógica, una lógica sin duda morbosa pero exacta. Porque así se disciplinaba al ser humano en la obediencia ciega, se le rompía el orgullo, se le humillaba en su capacidad crítica, se le quebrantaba la razón. (p.158)

The site of identity in the institutional order of modernity is further defined by Giddens thus:

A person's identity is not to be found in behaviour, nor — important though this is — in the reactions of others, but in the capacity *to keep a particular narrative going.* The individual's biography [...] must continually integrate events which occur in the external world, and sort them into the ongoing story about the self [...] self-identity, as a coherent phenomenon, presumes a narrative: the narrative of the self . is made explicit [...] autobiography — particularly in the broad sense of an interpretative self-history produced by the individual concerned, whether written down or not — is actually at the core of self-identity in modern social life.[35]

Amado amo is a novel in which 'stream-of-consciousness techniques blend with free indirect style narration', and Davies quotes Montero's words in an interview: 'the narration enters and leaves the head of the protagonist and his delirium. You don't know to what extent it is a delirium and to what extent it is an objective narrative in the third person'.[36] Effectively César, whilst able to single out the factors in his life which have brought him to his present state — his failed relationships with women, his underprivileged upbringing, his faded talent, the insidious pressures of the nameless presences behind 'Golden Line' — is unable to construct these into a convincing narrative, 'an 'interpretative self-history', which takes into account the external circumstances which govern his life in such a way as to overcome them. All César can do is to look into the past, to the fragments of his life, which intrude chaotically as his recollections overlap with events in the present, as the process of dissolution of his social identity relentlessly takes place. As Davies points out, the use of language and gesture in the environment which César inhabits is peculiar to Golden Line, and necessitates trained responses from the workforce, who must see through such travesties of systems of

---

35   *Modernity and Self-Identity*, pp.54 & 76.
36   Davies, *Contemporary Feminist Fiction in Spain* 136; K.M.Glenn, 'Conversación con Rosa Montero', *Anales de la Literatura Española. Contemporánea*, 16 (1990), 282.

signification 'not only the lack but also the deliberate perversion of information and truth'.[37] At the same time, the lack of dialogue in the novel reinforces César's inability to analyse his experiences or learn his lesson: he has no meaningful communication with other individuals which might permit him to engage in the construction of a 'public' account of his self-identity. César's 'autobiography' ironically is reduced to one verb, as he looks up the definition of 'dominar' in the dictionary when at a particularly low ebb, and finds in its fifty-one meanings 'un diario autobiográfico', that of the 'fino tejido de la dominación' (p.147) to which individuals must be subject or must subject others. This verb — transitive, infinitive, imperative — defines his life, without the consolation of other parts of speech which might impose different orders, descriptions, tenses, modes or possibilities on the fragments of his existence.

The ontological dilemma of César Miranda is left in dissolution but unresolved as Montero denounces the structures of late consumer capitalism and their implications for the individual. César Miranda may be obnoxious, and his siding with the male bosses against Paula an indictment of male behaviour, but it does not suffice to dismiss this as 'costumbrismo de buena ley' or quaint feminist carping on the part of the author.[38] It goes without saying that Montero's narrative takes a relevant political stance on the position of women in large organisations, but the further point that is made in *Amado amo* is that the self (however gendered) as scripted by unsympathetic regimes is a self on the verge of disintegration. A fundamental need of the individual in the constitution of self-identity is the freedom to narrate and express that identity, and the scope to reconcile, if not overcome, the disparate elements in that personal narrative. The attempt to impose some standard or 'corporate' paradigm based on immediate or short-term values so prevalent in the late twentieth century overwhelms the innate urge to narrative and the capacity of the individual to locate the self within a meaningful framework which encompasses time past and present, social relationships, and transcendent questions. Thus continuity — and hence identity — is eclipsed by Golden Line's drive for efficiency and ruthless exploitation of its workforce for commercial ends. The result is a terrifying void, an annihilation of identity, akin to that experienced by the protagonists of *La soledad era esto* and *La escala de los mapas*:

---

37 Davies, *Contemporary Feminist Fiction in Spain*, p.148.
38 Carlos Galán Lores, 'Los más jóvenes de los jóvenes', 14.

Llegó un momento en que se sentó en la cama, sabiéndose totalmente despierto pero atrapado aún en esa realidad de pesadilla, sin reconocerse, sin comprender dónde se hallaba o quién era él, convertido en la esencia misma de la soledad, la llaga de una conciencia perdida en la inmensidad de un universo ajeno. Y así permaneció, sepultado en el miedo y la noche, durante un tiempo eterno (p.201).

Conclusion

Although it cannot be claimed that the texts chosen for analysis here represent a cross-section of contemporary fiction in Spain, they are narratives which in most cases have been commercially successful, and have all received an appreciable degree of literary acclaim. The reason for grouping them together here has been their common exploration of aspects of identity and the self. In a formal sense, these are most strikingly explored in the experimentalism of *Makbara*, but the other texts, despite their wider popular appeal and greater accessibility, are far from unproblematical in their insistent probing of these themes. The appeal of much of this fiction may be due to the fact that it retains or reclaims many of the constituents of classic realism. The depiction of social and family groupings and the function of the individual within these, the engagement with a narrator figure or single protagonist and, of course, the return to a traditional narrative form are all significant aspects of the narratives discussed. In these works, as in the novels of nineteenth-century realism, personal and social identity are not distinguishable, yet the sophisticated, self-aware first-person narrator or protagonist found in the late twentieth-century Spanish novel is radically different from the citizen who moves within the constraints of his or her allotted role in the traditional realist context. This difference has much to do with the question of self-determination. Where the classic realist text is founded in a belief that identity and selfhood are ordained by physiology, society, or both, for the narrators and protagonists of the novels studied here such factors are not definitive, but only part of a vastly increased and sometimes alarming realm of possibilities. In *Makbara*, the traditional notion of character may have broken down, but in later novels, such as *Todas las almas* or Gopegui's *La escala de los mapas*, the characters depicted are also far from possessing the unity, coherence and apparent psychological roundedness of their classic realist predecessors.

What is most striking is that many of the familiar issues which have most decisively shaped identity and the sense of selfhood in Spanish literature and society — whether their role was supported or subverted in cultural production — are absent in these narratives: most notably religion in the form of traditional Catholicism, honour, and national identity. The abandonment of these central concerns as markers has left identity — both national and individual — in an uncertain and fragmented state. Spain itself is depicted as caught in the pull of conflicting cultures — North Africa, the United States, Latin America, Europe -, moving definitively from a rural to an urban consumer economy, losing its roots, inevitably participating in the upheavals and transformations of contemporary society. When the grand narratives of religion, traditional sexual categorisation, or national identities diverge or lose their coherence, the characters constructed in narrative all become, in a sense, marginalised, and identity can no longer be posited as a clear-cut opposition between dissident outsider and traditional conformist: the very concept of identity, in other words, has to be rethought. The narratives deal on the whole with undistinguished individuals — the inhabitants of apartment blocks, offices, villages and streets — who are decentred by such changes, by the pressures of modern life, by conscious choice, or simply by their own cast of mind. Together these texts form a spectrum of ways of writing the self, and their positions on this spectrum depend to a large extent on how far such breaking up of past certainties is viewed negatively or positively. It might be argued that *Makbara*, not only in its formal experimentation, but also as a novel which deals obsessively with sex and politics, is in fact the most tradition-bound, and thus its inclusion here serves as a foil for the discussion of the other texts. The outsider figure and the traditional ways of rural life still hold sway as signs of identity in the Goytisolo and Llamazares novels respectively, and in this sense the protagonists of *Makbara,* railing against the evils of contemporary consumer society, and the last survivors of a moribund order in *La lluvia amarilla* stand at each end of the spectrum along which the rest of our grouping is ranged. But the pervading atmosphere of most of these novels, albeit manifested differently in each of them, is one of impermanence, remoteness, and a sense of contingency. Marías's narrators, for example, are plagued by sensations of 'malestar' and 'perturbación', a kind of postmodern existentialism in which the depths of *angst* and the yawning void of *ennui* are replaced by the precariousness of life on the surface and the dogged remnants of old beliefs and ideologies.

It is not so much that these novelists have chosen to write about their own or another's search for self or identity but that they recognise that to write any narrative is in a sense to write the self. Moreover the selves who write or are written about, who read or are read about, are no longer clearly distinguishable from one another, and do not reflect or represent either a subjective sensibility or an objective world, but emerge from the script itself. 'Writing the self' is a contradictory concept, for to write a narrative is to authorise what happens next. If the self who authorises is also the self who is being written, that is, constructed in the act of writing, an inevitable paradox ensues. Only by working with or against established forms of identity can new selves be written, and the 'scripted self' be more than a mere figure of speech. Moreover, selfhood conceived as an ongoing narrative process will be radically temporal, and past, present and future selves will be in constant interaction. While the individual may find it ever more impossible to live in the present, as the pace of change itself increases, permanence, whether it be in terms of self or relationships with others, may be less and less an achievable goal, and indeed may no longer be a desirable one either. Whilst memory is fundamental to all of these texts, it can no longer be considered the only raw material from which identity can be constructed, and thus notions of writing the self as unproblematically grounded in the past will be subverted. This interpretation of temporality finds expression in a number of ways, for example the frequent occurrence of coincidence and repetition in *Beltenebros* or in Marías's novels, the apparent lack of resistance to digression and meandering in *Todas las almas*, and the openness to the concept of what might have been, and to the power of the imagination in overcoming the tyranny of time in *Corazón tan blanco* and in Merino's *La orilla oscura*. And because past certainties and hopes for the future have also lost their pull, the tension which held in place such unremarkable characters as some of those who people these novels has been released, leaving them, as it were, temporarily suspended. But whether or not they go on improvising with old scripts, or consciously weave new narrative selves from old threads, they are all involved to some extent in what seems to be an ever more urgent process.

Three strands of questioning were suggested as basic in the Introduction to this book — literary-historical questions, socio-political concerns, and theoretical aspects such as the influence of poststructuralism and the philosophy of language. These three issues overlap considerably; it has been found impossible, for example, to talk about the reworking of the autobiographical genre without also addressing the role of the individual in society and the politics of authority, or the place and function of the subject in language and the relationship between language and memory in the recollection or evocation of the past. Likewise, it has been noted that the novels discussed, at least in so far as scripting the self is concerned, in no way belong to, or participate in, the formation of any new generic categorisation. Instead they borrow to various extents from old ones — autobiography, the detective novel, the experimental novel, the psychological novel. The postmodernism which has been ascribed to the texts does not always manifest itself in formal or generic terms, but rather abandons or breaks down the divisions between such categories, ironising the very concept of genre. The idea of the postmodern is as dangerous as it is useful, yet even in the few books discussed here, and particularly in relation to self and identity, a strong indication of its disturbingly fragmentary and provisional nature can be intuited.

Similarly, some of the conclusions reached here should be considered to be merely provisional. In its own way this book represents the imposition of a pattern of some kind upon the diversity of Spanish narrative writing of the last twenty years, but it also attempts to suggest that such an imposition should be resisted. Far from wishing to fix a picture of contemporary fiction, the authors have aspired to follow in the spirit of the novelists themselves, to recognise the fluid nature of literary creation and to provide a basis for further research. In concentrating on the themes of identity and selfhood, the authors' aim has been to offer one approach to a significant aspect of current cultural production in Spain, in the hope that this book will promote further interest in, and complementary readings of, the contemporary Spanish novel. It is the authors' conviction that any such critical interest would not be misplaced.

Bibliography

Principal Novels Studied
Gopegui, Belén, *La escala de los mapas* (Barcelona: Anagrama, 1993)
Goytisolo, Juan, *Makbara* (Barcelona: Seix Barral, 1980)
Llamazares, Julio, *Luna de lobos* (Barcelona: Seix Barral, 1985)
------- *La lluvia amarilla* (Barcelona: Seix Barral, 1988)
------- *Escenas de cine mudo* (Barcelona: Seix Barral, 1994)
Marías, Javier, *Todas las almas* (Barcelona: Anagrama, 1989)
------- *Corazón tan blanco* (Barcelona: Anagrama, 1992)
Merino, José María, *El caldero de oro* (Madrid: Alfaguara, 1981)
------- *Cuentos del Barrio del Refugio* (Madrid: Alfaguara, 1994)
Millás, Juan José, *La soledad era esto* (Barcelona: Destino, 1990)
Montero, Rosa, *Amado amo* (Barcelona: Edhasa, 1992)
Muñoz Molina, Antonio, *Beltenebros* (Barcelona: Seix Barral, 1989)

Critical and Other Sources
Acín, Ramón, *Narrativa o consumo literario (1975-1987)* (Zaragoza: Univ. de Zaragoza, 1990)
Alonso, Santos, 'Un renovado compromiso con el realismo y con el hombre', *Insula*, 464-465 (1985), 9-11
------- 'La transición: hacia una nueva novela', *Insula,* 512-513 (1989), 11-12
------- 'La renovación del realismo', *Insula,* 572-573 (1994), 12-14
Amell, Samuel, 'Conversación con Juan Marsé', *España Contemporánea*, 1 (1988), 88-101
------- (ed.) *España frente al siglo XXI. Cultura y literatura* (Madrid: Cátedra/Ministerio de Cultura, 1992)
Amorós, Andrés [et al], 'Novela española 1989-1990', *Insula,* 525 (1990), 9-23
Aparicio, Juan Pedro and Merino, José María, *Los caminos del Esla* (León: Everest, 1980)
------- 'Encuentro de narradores leoneses', *Insula*, 572-3 (1994), 3-7
Arribas, Inés, 'Poder y femenismo en *Amado amo* de Rosa Montero', *Romance Languages Annual*, 3 (1991), 348-53
Ayuso, César Augusto, 'La crisis de identidad como ficción: El último Juan José Millás', *El Norte de Castilla*, 19 January 1991
Bakhtin, Mikail, *Rabelais and his World* (Cambridge: Massachusetts Institute of Technology Press, 1968)

Ballesteros, Isolina, *Escritura femenina y discurso autobiográfico en la nueva novela española* (New York, San Francisco, Bern, Baltimore, Frankfurt am Mein, Berlin, Wein, Paris: Peter Lang, 1994)

Barrero Pérez, Oscar, *Historia de la literatura española contemporánea, 1939-1990* (Madrid: Istmo, 1992)

Barthes, Roland, *Image — Music — Text*, selected and trans. by Stephen Heath (Glasgow: Fontana Collins, 1977)

Basanta, A., *La novela española de nuestra época* (Madrid: Anaya, 1990)

Baudrillard, Jean, *La Société de Consommation* (Paris: Denoël, 1970)

------- *Le Miroir de la Production* (Tournai: Casterman, 1973)

------- *L'Echange Symbolique et la Mort* (Paris: Gallimard, 1976)

------- *Simulacres et Simulation* (Paris: Galilée, 1981)

Belsey, Catherine, *Critical Practice* (London and New York: Methuen, 1980)

Bennett, Tony, 'Marxism and Popular Fiction', in *Postmodern Conditions*, ed. by Andrew Milner [et al] (New York, Oxford, Munich: Berg, 1990), pp.188-210

Benveniste, Emile, *Problems of General Linguistics*, trans. by Mary Elizabeth Meek (Coral Gables, Florida: University of Miami Press, 1971)

Bergmann, Emilie, 'Intertextuality in Spanish Novels of Female Development', *Anales de la Literatura Española Contemporánea*, 12 (1987), 141-156

Black, Stanley, 'Orality in *Makbara*: a postmodern paradox', *Neophilologus*, 78 (1994), 585-98

Borges, Jorge Luis, 'Borges and I', for *Arena*, BBC 2, first broadcast 26 October, 1983

------- *Ficciones* (Buenos Aires: Emecé, 1956)

------- *Historia de la noche* (Buenos Aires: Emecé, 1977)

Brody, Baruch A., *Identity and Essence* (Princeton: Princeton University Press, 1980)

Brooks, Peter, *Reading for the Plot* (New York: Random House, 1984)

Brown, Joan L., ed., *Women Writers of Contemporary Spain: Exiles in the Homeland* (Newark, Delaware; London; Toronto: University of Delaware Press; Association of University Presses, 1990)

Burgin, Victor, *The End of Art Theory: Criticism and Postmodernity* (Atlantic Highlands, New Jersey: Humanities Press International, 1986)

Candau, Antonio, *La obra narrativa de José María Merino* (León: Diputación Provincial de León, 1992)

Cantavella, Juan, 'Antonio Muñoz Molina. El que no entra en la literatura por amor a ella se equivoca', *Diario de Cádiz*, 12 March 1989, p.15

Caramello, Charles, *Silverless Mirrors: Book, Self, and Postmodern American Fiction* (Florida: Florida State University Press, 1983)

Carr, David, *Time, Narrative and History* (Bloomington, Indianapolis: Indiana University Press, 1986)

Carrero Eras, Pedro, *Españoles y extranjeros: última narrativa* (Salamanca: University of Salamanca, 1991)

Carroll, David, *The Subject in Question: The Languages of Theory and the Strategies of Fiction* (Chicago: University of Illinois Press, 1982)

Castellanos, Luis H., 'La magia de lo que pudo ser' (Interview with Javier Marías), *Quimera*, 87 (1988), 24-31

Castro García, María Isabel de, and Montejo Gurruchaga, Lucía, *Tendencias y procedimientos de la novela española actual (1975-88)* (Madrid: UNED, 1990)

Ciplijauskaité, Biruté, *La novela femenina contemporánea (1970-1985)* (Barcelona: Anthropos, 1988)

Connor, Steven, *Postmodernist Culture. An Introduction to Theories of the Contemporary* (Oxford: Blackwell, 1989)

Conrad, Joseph, *Heart of Darkness* (Harmondsworth: Penguin, 1973)

Crimp, Douglas, 'On the Museum's Ruins', in *The Anti-Aesthetic: Essays on Postmodern Culture*, ed. by Hal Foster (Port Townsend, Wash: Bay Press, 1983), pp.111-125

Davies, Catherine, 'Feminist Writers in Spain since 1900: from political strategy to personal inquiry', in *Textual Liberation. European Feminist Writing in the Twentieth Century*, ed. by Helena Forsas-Scott (London and New York: Routledge, 1991), pp.192-226

------- *Contemporary Feminist Fiction in Spain. The Work of Montserrat Roig and Rosa Montero* (Oxford: Berg, 1994)

de Man, Paul, 'Autobiography as Defacement' in *The Rhetoric of Romanticism* (Columbia: Columbia University Press, 1984), p.67

Dennett, Daniel C., 'Why everyone is a novelist', *Times Literary Supplement*, 16-22 September, 1988, pp.1016 & 1028-9

Derrida, Jacques, *Of Grammatology,* trans. by Gayatri Chakravorty (Baltimore: John Hopkins University Press, 1976)

Diprose, Rosalyn and Ferrell, Robyn, eds., *Cartographies. Poststructuralism and the Mapping of Bodies and Spaces* (Sydney: Allen and Unwin, 1991)

Eakin, Paul John, *Fictions in Autobiography* (Princeton: Princeton University Press, 1985)

Echevarría, Ignacio, 'Otra mujer' (Review of *La soledad era esto*), *Quimera*, 98 (1990), 67

Embarec, Malika Jdidi, 'Lectura marroquí de *Makbara*', in *Voces: Juan Goytisolo,* coordinated by Pere Gimferrer (Barcelona: Montesinos, 1981), pp.83-86

Encinar, Ángeles, *La novela española actual: La desaparición del héroe* (Madrid: Pliegos, 1990)

Epstein, Julia and Straub, Kristina, eds., *Body Guards. The Cultural Politics of Gender Ambiguity* (London: Routledge, 1991)

Escudero, José, 'Muerte, erotismo y espiritualidad. Entrevista con Juan Goytisolo', *Revista de Estudios Hispánicos,* 23 (1993), 123-139

Fajardo, José Manuel, 'Antonio Muñoz Molina. En España nos gusta ser genios', *Cambio16,* 902, October 1989, 122

Federman, Raymond, *Surfiction* (Chicago: Swallow Press, 1975)

Felski, Rita, 'Feminism, Realism and the Avant-Garde' in *Postmodern Conditions,* ed. by Andrew Milner [et al] (New York, Oxford, Munich: Berg, 1990), pp.61-78

Fernández, James, *Apology to Apostrophy* (London: Duke University Press, 1992)

Flanagan, Owen and Oksenberg Rorty, Amélie, eds., *Identity, Character and Morality* (Cambridge, Massachusetts, London: Massachusetts Institute of Technology Press, 1990)

Fontes, José Antonio, *Novelas para la transición política* (Madrid: Libertarias, 1987)

Foucault, Michel, 'What is an Author?', in *Language, Counter-memory and Practice: selected essays and interviews,* ed. by Donald F. Bouchard, trans. by D. F. Bouchard and Sherry Simon (Ithaca, New York: Cornell University Press, 1977), pp.152-159

Frosh, Stephen, *Identity Crisis: Modernity, Psychoanalysis and the Self* (London: Macmillan, 1991)

Galán Lores, Carlos, 'Los más jóvenes de los jóvenes', *Insula,* 512-3 (1989), 14-15

Gallego,Vicente, '*Beltenebros* de Antonio Muñoz Molina', *Insula,* 514 (1989), 19

García, Ángeles, 'El mundo es de sus relatores', *El País,* 9 April, 1994, pp.14-15

García-Moreno Barco, Francisco, *La narrativa española a la luz de la crítica posmodernista: El caso de Antonio Muñoz Molina.* PhD dissertation, Michigan State University (1992)

Gawsworth, John, *Above the River* (London: Ulysses Bookshop, 1931)

Giddens, Anthony, *Modernity and Self-Identity. Self and Society in the Late Modern Age* (Stanford, California: Stanford University Press, 1991)

Gil Casado, Pablo, ' *Makbara* es un cementerio', *Cuadernos Americanos,* 40 (1981), 217-26

------- *La novela deshumanizada española (1958-1988)* (Barcelona: Anthropos, 1990)

Glenn, K.M., 'Conversación con Rosa Montero', *Anales de la Literatura Española Contemporánea,* 16 (1990), 275-283

Goytisolo, Juan, *Juan sin tierra* (Barcelona: Seix Barral, 1977)

------- *Contracorrientes* (Barcelona: Seix Barral, 1985)

------- *Crónicas sarracinas* (Barcelona: Seix Barral, 1989)

------- *Disidencias* (Barcelona: Seix Barral, 1977)

Graff, Gerald, 'Babbitt at the Abyss: The Social Context of Postmodern American Fiction', *TriQuarterly*, 33 (1975), 305-307

Grande González, Concepción, *La guerra civil en la novela de la democracia: en busca de una identidad perdida.* PhD dissertation, University of Massachusetts (1993)

Gray, Rockwell, *The Imperative of Modernity: An Intellectual Biography of José Ortega y Gasset* (Berkeley, London, Los Angeles: University of California Press, 1989)

Gullón, Germán, 'La perezosa modernidad', *Insula*, 464-5 (1985), 8

Haraway, D., *Simians, Cyborgs and Women: The Reinvention of Nature* (London: Free Association Books, 1991)

Harges, Mary Claire, *Synergy and Subversion in the Later Novels of Rosa Montero.* PhD dissertation, University of Oregon (1993)

Hawthorn, Jeremy, *A Concise Glossary of Contemporary Literary Theory* (London, New York, Melbourne, Auckland: Edward Arnold, 1992)

Herzberger, David K., 'Split Referentiality and the Making of Character in Spanish Metafiction', *Modern Language Notes*, 103 (1988), 419-435

Howells, Christina, ed., *The Cambridge Companion to Sartre* (Cambridge University Press: Cambridge, 1992)

Iglesias, Amalia, 'Antonio Muñoz Molina. Todas las buenas novelas son tratados morales', *Diario 16*, 7 March 1989, 30

Izenberg, Gerald N., *Impossible Individuality* (Princeton: Princeton University Press, 1992)

Jameson, Frederic, 'Postmodernism and Consumer Society' in *Postmodern Culture*, ed. by Hal Foster (London and Sydney: Pluto Press, 1985), pp.111-125

------- 'Postmodernism, or the Cultural Logic of Late Capitalism', *New Left Review*, 146 (1984), 53-92

Juristo, Juan Ángel, 'Antonio Muñoz Molina. Para hacer la literatura hay que huir de la vida literaria', *El Independiente*, 7 July 1989, 30

Kerrigan, Michael, Review of *All Souls* (*Todas las almas*), in *Times Literary Supplement*, 4675 (1992), 21

Landeira, R., and González-del-Valle, L.T., eds., *Nuevos y novísimos: Algunas perspectivas críticas sobre la narrativa española desde le década de los 60* (Boulder: Society of Spanish and Spanish American Studies, 1987)

Larequi García, Eduardo M., 'Sueño, imaginación, ficción. Los límites de la realidad en la narrativa de José María Merino', *Anales de la Literatura Española Contemporánea*, 13 (1988), 225-247

Lee Six, Abigail, *Juan Goytisolo: The case for chaos* (New Haven and London: Yale University Press, 1990)

Levenson, Michael, *Modernism and the Fate of Individuality* (Cambridge: Cambridge University Press, 1991)

Levine, Linda Gould, '*Makbara*: entre la espada y la pared — ¿política marxista o política sexual?', *Revista Iberoamericana*, 47 (1981), 97-106

Lipman Brown, Joan, 'Men by Women in the Contemporary Spanish Novel', *Hispanic Review*, 60 (1992), 55-70

Lissourges, Yvan (coordinateur), *La Renovation du Roman Espagnol depuis 1975* (Toulouse: Presses Universitaires du Mirail, 1991)

Llamazares, Julio, *El río del olvido* (Barcelona: Seix Barral, 1988)

------- *En Babia* (Barcelona: Seix Barral, 1991)

Macintyre, Alasdair, *After Virtue: A Study in Moral Theory* (London: Duckworth, 1981)

Mainer, José Carlos, *Historia, literatura, sociedad* (Madrid: Instituto de España/Espasa-Calpe,1988)

Marco, José María, 'Julio Llamazares sin trampas. Entrevista realizada por José María Marco', *Quimera,* 80 (1988), 22-29

Marías, Javier, 'El viaje de Isaac', *Hiperión*, 1 (1978)

------- *El siglo* (Barcelona: Anagrama, 1983)

------- 'La inspiración ocupa lugar', *El Libro Español,* 331-2 (1986), 4-5

------- *El hombre sentimental* (Madrid: Alfaguara, 1986)

------- 'The 1980s: Age of Recreation', trans. by James J. Dunlap, *Encounters*, 2 (1990), 12-15

------- *All Souls* (*Todas las almas*), trans. by Margaret Jull Costa (London: Harvill, 1992)

------- *Literatura y fantasma* (Madrid: Siruela, 1993)

------- *Mañana en la batalla piensa en mí* (Barcelona: Anagrama, 1994)

Marías, Julián, *Una vida presente: Memorias 1 (1914-1951)* (Madrid: Alianza, 1988)

------- *Reason and Life,* trans. by K. S. Reid and E. Sarmiento (London: Hollis and Carter, 1956)

------- *España inteligible: razón histórica de las Españas* (Madrid: Alianza, 1985)

Marshall, Barbara L., *Engendering Modernity. Feminism, Social Theory and Social Change* (Cambridge: Polity, 1994)

Martín Gil, Juan Francisco, 'El que habita en la oscuridad. Entrevista con Antonio Muñoz Molina', *Quimera,* 83 (1988), 27

Martínez Cachero, J.M., 'Diez años de novela en España (1976-1985) por sus pasos contados', *Insula*, 464-465 (1985), 3-4

Martin-Márquez, Susan L., 'Vision, Power and Narrative in *Luna de lobos*: Julio Llamazares' Spanish Panopticon', *Revista Canadiense de Estudios Hispánicos,* 9, 2 (1995), 379-387

Martínez Menchen, Antonio, 'La doble orilla de José María Merino', *Cuadernos Hispanoamericanos,* 439 (1987), 115-121

Masoliver, Juan Antonio, '*Todas las almas* de Javier Marías, historia de una perturbación', *Insula,* 517 (1990), 21-22

------- 'Espejismo en una galería de espejos', *Insula,* 546 (1992) 21-22

McHale, Brian, *Postmodernist Fiction* (London and New York: Methuen, 1987)

Miñambres, Nicolás, '*La lluvia amarilla,* de Julio Llamazares: el dramatismo lírico y simbólico del mundo rural', *Insula,* 502 (1988), 20

------- 'La narrativa de Julio Llamazares', *Insula,* 572-3 (1994), 26-28

Montero, Rosa, *Crónica del desamor* (Madrid: Debate, 1979)

------- *La función Delta* (Madrid: Debate, 1981)

------- *Te trataré como a una reina* (Barcelona: Seix Barral, 1983)

------- *Temblor* (Barcelona: Seix Barral, 1990)

------- *Bella y oscura* (Barcelona: Seix Barral, 1993)

Navajas, Gonzalo, 'Una estética para después del posmodernismo', *Revista de Estudios Hispánicos,* 25 (1991), 129-151

------- 'Retórica de la novela postmodernista española', *Siglo XX/ Twentieth Century,* 41 (1986), 16-26

Nietzsche, Friedrich, *The Will to Power* (New York: Random House, 1965)

------- *Ecce Homo,* trans. by R. J. Hollingdale (Harmondsworth: Penguin, 1979)

Olney, James, ed., *Autobiography: Essays Theoretical and Critical* (Princeton: Princeton University Press, 1980)

------- ed., *Studies in Autobiography* (Oxford: Oxford University Press, 1988)

Ordóñez, Elizabeth J., 'Reading Contemporary Spanish Narrative by Women', *Anales de la Literatura Española Contemporánea,* 7 (1982), 237-251

------- 'Inscribing Difference: "L'Ecriture Féminine" and New Narrative by Women', *Anales de la Literatura Española Contemporánea,* 12 (1987), 45-58

------- *Voices of Their Own. Contemporary Spanish Narrative by Women* (London and Toronto: 1991)

Ortega y Gasset, José, *Obras completas,* i, v and vii (Madrid: Revista de Occidente, 1946, 1947, 1961)

Pecora, Vincent, *Self and Form in Modern Narrative* (Baltimore: Johns Hopkins University Press, 1989)

Perrin, Annie, '*Makbara.* The Space of Phantasm', *Review of Contemporary Fiction,* 4 (1984), 157-75

Pike, Burton, *The Image of the City in Modern Literature* (Princeton: Princeton University Press, 1981)

Plaza, José María, 'Horror y belleza' (Interview with Rosa Montero), *Leer*, 65 (1993), 52-54

Pope, Randolph, 'Theories and models for the history of Spanish autobiography: General problems of autobiography', *Siglo XX/Twentieth Century*, 12 (1994), 207-218

Portoghesi, Paolo, *After Modern Architecture,* trans. by Meg Shore (New York: Rizzoli, 1982)

Reboiras, Ramón F., 'Javier Marías: "He sido el joven Marías durante demasiado tiempo" ' (Interview with Javier Marías), *Cambio 16,* 16 May 1994, 80-81

------- 'Antonio Muñoz Molina: El éxito en la literatura es durar', *Cambio 16,* 3 April 1995, 72

Regalado García, Antonio, *El laberinto de la razón* (Madrid: Alianza, 1990)

Ricoeur, Paul, *Freedom and Nature: The Voluntary and the Involuntary,* trans. by Erazim V. Kohák (Evanston: Northwestern University Press, 1966)

------- *Oneself as Another,* trans. by Kathleen Blamey (Chicago and London: University of Chicago Press, 1984)

------- *Time and Narrative,* vol. iii, trans. by K. Blamey and David Pellauer (Chicago and London: University of Chicago Press, 1985)

Rose, Gillian, *Feminism and Geography. The Limits of Geographical Knowledge* (Cambridge: Polity, 1993)

Said, Edward, *The World, the Text and the Critic* (London: Faber and Faber, 1984)

Sanz Villanueva, Santos, ed., *Historia de la literatura española. vol. vi: El siglo xx: La literatura actual* (Barcelona: Ariel, 1984)

------- 'El realismo en la nueva novela española', *Insula*, 464-5 (1985), 7-8

------- 'Una realidad en la última novela española', *Insula*, 512-3 (1989), 3-4

------- [et al], *Narrativa hispánica* (Madrid: Universidad Complutense, 1990)

Schopenhauer, Arthur, *Die Welt als Wille und Vorstellung, Sämtliche Werke* (Wiesbaden: Eberhard Brockhaus, 1949)

Sherzer, William, 'Tiempo e historia en la narrativa de Antonio Muñoz Molina', *Revista Contemporánea*, 4 (1992), 54

Smith, Paul Julian, 'Juan Goytisolo and Jean Baudrillard: The Mirror of Production and the Death of Symbolic Exchange', *Revista de Estudios Hispánicos*, 23 (1989), 37-61

Smyth, Edmund J. ed., *Postmodernism and Contemporary Fiction* (London: Batsford, 1991)

Sobejano, Gonzalo, 'La novela ensimismada (1980-1985)', *España Contemporánea,* 1 (1988), 9-36

Soldevila Durante, I. [et al], *La cultura española en el posfranquismo* (Madrid: Playor, 1986)

Sturrock, John, *The Language of Autobiography* (Cambridge: Cambridge University Press, 1993)

Suleiman, Susan R., and Crossman, Inge, eds., *The Reader in the Text: Essays on Audience and Interpretation* (Princeton: Princeton University Press, 1980)

Taylor, Charles, *Sources of the Self: The Making of Modern Identity* (Cambridge: Cambridge University Press, 1989)

Trenas, Miguel Ángel, 'Muñoz Molina: la literatura es una sociedad secreta', *La Verdad*, 7 March 1989, 15

Unamuno, Miguel de, *Ensayos* (Madrid: Aguilar, 1958)

Valls, Fernando, 'La literatura femenina en España: 1975-1989', *Insula*, 512-513 (1989), 13

Vázquez Montalbán, Manuel, 'La literatura española en la construcción de la ciudad democrática', *Revista de Occidente*, 122-123 (1991), 125-133

Vegas González, Serafín, 'Ideología y literatura: a propósito de *Makbara* de Goytisolo', *Arbor*, 114 (1983), 83-96

Velasco Marcos, Emilia, 'José María Merino, la complejidad de un proyecto literario', *Insula*, 572-573 (1994), 19-21

Vidal-Foch, Ignacio, 'Muñoz Molina: la novela ha de ser útil hasta la obscenidad', *ABC*, 15 March 1989, 18

Villanueva, Dario [et al], eds., *Historia crítica de la literatura española, vol. ix, Los nuevos nombres 1975-1990*, General ed. Francisco Rico (Barcelona: Editorial Crítica, 1992)

Waugh, Patricia, ed., *Postmodernism. A Reader* (London, New York, Melbourne, Auckland: Edward Arnold, 1992)

Zatlin, Phyllis, 'The Contemporary Spanish Metanovel', *Denver Quarterly*, 17 (1982), 63-73

Various authors, *Narrativa española actual* (Cuenca: Ediciones de la Universidad de Castilla-La Mancha, 1990)